WHAT IS YOUR CHURCH'S PERSONALITY?

WHAT IS YOUR CHURCH'S PERSONALITY?

Discovering and Developing the Ministry Style of Your Church

PHILIP D. DOUGLASS

P U B L I S H I N G
P.O. BOX 817 • PHILLIPSBURG • NEW JERSEY 08865-0817

Printed in Canada

Library of Congress Cataloging-in-Publication Data

Douglass, Philip D., 1948–
What is your church's personality? : discovering and developing the ministry style of your church / Philip D. Douglass.
    p. cm.
Includes bibliographical references.
ISBN 978-1-59638-022-6 (pbk.)
1. Parishes—Psychology. 2. Corporate culture. 3. Clergy—Appointment, call, and election. 4. Pastoral theology. I. Title.
BV640.D68 2008
250—dc22

                                    2007045233

To my wife, Rebecca, for her loving devotion to the Lord as well as to me and our four children, through all the years of our ministry in planting six churches and pastoring another two, all of which have served as the context for this book.

Contents

Preface

THIS BOOK IS ABOUT CHURCHES—specifically the million or so of them that populate our planet. This is a familiar subject to most of the two billion people who claim Jesus Christ as their Lord and Savior and interact with one another regularly on Sundays and, often, through the week as well. As much as these vast numbers of people relate to their churches, we might expect to understand these organizations better than we do. At least we might think we would have a firmer grasp of the inner workings of our local congregations. But try as we may, this mysterious organism/organization known as the church still baffles us.

The subject of how churches differ from one another in ministry style first captured my attention when I became a pastor in 1974. Soon after graduating from seminary, I was ordained as an assistant pastor in a church of three hundred people in the Washington, DC, area. I began to notice soon that my ministry style did not fit the expectations of the senior pastor, nor did it mesh well with the way he conducted ministry. I had no concepts in those days to help me understand the differences, but now I recognize that my Inspirational style (chapter 6) was attempting to serve in an Organizer church (chapter 10) which followed the style of the senior pastor. As you will see in the charts that follow, my God-given way of doing ministry was 180 degrees different from that of the pastor and church I served for those beginning five years.

Predictably, after the "honeymoon" period concluded, I found myself drifting into depression. I never got to the point that I could not get out of bed in the morning, but during my second and third years at that church, I functioned most of the time at half my capacity. It was not until I began developing and leading small groups—a primary way in which Inspirers do ministry—that I emerged from my depression and started to experience some measure of fruitfulness. I realize now that I had become the victim of what is called the "60–40 rule." The principle is that unless you are serving at least 60 percent of your time in your area of spiritual giftedness, talent, heart passion, and temperament, then you will burn out within 18 months. This is the primary reason why a third of seminary master of divinity graduates who go into the pastorate will leave ordained ministry within five years. Through the grace of God ministering to me through my mentor, Richard C. Halverson of Fourth Presbyterian Church, and my beloved classmates from seminary who also were pastoring in the Washington area, I was empowered to persevere in this difficult situation for five years.

Then in 1979, everything changed. I heard about six families, half of them from my home church, who wanted to start a church on the western growth edge of Washington. My wife, three sons (ages 6, 3, and 1), and I leaped at the opportunity, even though it meant giving up the financial security we had gained over the previous five years. In those days, I did not understand the principle that a church plant almost always takes on the ministry style of the planter. All I knew was that I immediately felt like a man set free because I was able to minister in the Inspirational church that I planted. The next six years were as fruitful as the previous five years had been lean. I felt like Joseph in the book of Genesis who endured with the people of Egypt the seven years of famine after the years of plenty, except for me the order was reversed. The difference was that Joseph understood why he and the people were experiencing such radical cycles of blessing and curse, and I did not. During those years of plenty, we planted two daughter churches and helped to plant in our region an additional nine churches. In addition, we started ministries that had impact for the gospel throughout our county: a Christian bookstore, a prayer breakfast movement for leaders, a mercy ministry for those who were struggling financially, and a youth ministry.

But all that changed when I was visited by Paul Kooistra, the new president of Covenant Theological Seminary in St. Louis, Missouri. He was looking for a new faculty member to train his students in the practical aspects of ministry, especially in church planting. On my office wall I showed him a map of the Washington area on which I had placed one hundred pins indicating where we wanted to plant new churches over the next ten years. So I said "thanks," but I was experiencing too much blessing from the Lord in doing ministry in that setting to ever think about leaving. But no sooner had the man left my office than it seemed that every ministry I touched turned to dust. So after what my wife calls our "Job year," named after the Old Testament figure who endured such intense suffering, our family—now joined by our infant daughter—moved to St. Louis.

At the time, Covenant Seminary had only 120 students (compared with 1,200 now), and the faculty was seriously divided (which is no longer the case). I began working with students to plant new churches in the St. Louis area, and the Lord gave us good fruitfulness. However, what I had not counted on—because I did not understand the concepts presented in this book—was that the seminary's ministry style meant I was once again attempting to serve with my Inspirational style in an Organizer/Classroom culture. So for the next six years, I returned to functioning at 50 percent of my capacity—at least during the part of my ministry that was on the seminary campus.

It was not until 1992, when I began PhD studies at the St. Louis University School of Education, that I began to understand the reasons for my cycle of ups and downs in ministry. Because of my concentration in educational theory, I took a course in temperament studies along with a course in educational psychology. These studies introduced me to a new world of understanding regarding the diverse ways in which people learn and serve most fruitfully—which I quickly applied to myself and my students. These studies provide the foundation for the concepts of this book.

First, in 1994, I developed a course called *Spiritual and Ministry Formation*, which is required of all first-year MDiv and MA-Educational Ministries students. In this course I have each student take seven diagnostics and then write a six-page paper in which he or she presents the results in a form that explains the student's unique ministry style. Then I spend an hour one-on-one with each student to talk about what the material indicates in regard to the types of vocational ministry that fit him best. Now, in addition, I have all final-year MDiv students in another required course, *Ministry Leadership,* in which they start with their ministry style papers from their first year at the seminary and develop individual philosophies of ministry. The students prepare papers based on what they have learned about their specific callings through their studies and the three hundred hours of ministry fieldwork that each student is required to accomplish in area churches.

In addition, through my PhD studies, I began to learn concepts of corporate culture that I discovered the business community had been developing over the previous few years. Especially helpful were Edgar Schein's *Organizational Culture and Leadership*[1] and William Bridges' *The Character of Organizations.*[2] However, to my amazement, no one had related these concepts to the church—though the application was quite obvious.

What I found especially distressing was that too many of our graduates were repeating my experience of the 1970s and serving in churches that were opposite to their ministry styles. Many of them were not making it past the five-year mark before being forced to resign or experiencing emotional and spiritual burnout. The impact on these graduates, their families, the churches they serve, and the broader kingdom of God is devastating. I am not a "weepy" sort of person, but when I tell students about the difficult experiences of our graduates in ministries that do not fit them, I break down in tears. I know the reason is that their ordeals remind me of my difficult first five years in ministry. And I am determined not to allow our students and their families to go through similar experiences.

Therefore, I began researching the eight distinctive church ministry styles—now presented in this book—that correspond to the eight unique ways that men and women do ministry. As a result, I am able to predict the level of difficulty our graduates will experience during their first five years of vocational ministry if they serve in particular churches. If a church's ministry style is within one sector of a pastor's ministry style (see the chart in chapter 3), then the probability of a fruitful ministry is high. Obviously, there are other important factors such as godliness, ministry competencies, theological convictions, and ministry experience. However, because this "degree of fit" factor is often ignored, the effectiveness of our graduates is too often diminished. I am only half joking with students when I threaten to place my body in front of the tires of their cars if they try to leave seminary to serve in churches that do not fit their God-given ministry styles. By the way, here at Covenant Theological Seminary, we have been able to lower the five-year rate of attrition of our MDiv graduates going into ordained ministry in the church from the national average of 34 percent to 6.9 percent.

Now you know that this book has been written with a personal agenda. For as many seminary graduates and churches as possible, I want to prevent a duplication of my first five years of ministry.

Acknowledgments

THIS BOOK IS THE WORK OF MANY PEOPLE. My student and teaching assistant, Ed Eubanks, spent countless hours over the course of two years brainstorming with me as this book gradually took shape. The pastors and lay leaders of eighty-three churches were essential to the process by surveying their people to provide quotes and vignettes to bring the ideas of this book to life. The people of the churches I have planted and pastored over the years have cultivated my thinking about the varieties of church personalities. Many thanks go to my faculty colleague, Robert Peterson, who was persistent in urging me to put these ideas down on paper. My editor, Rick Matt, spent much time correcting the details that help communicate these concepts with greater clarity. I am grateful to the president, Bryan Chapell, and to the board of trustees of Covenant Theological Seminary, where I have taught since 1986, for providing me the two sabbatical semesters I needed to write. Finally, I offer thanks to my faculty colleagues and many hundreds of students with whom I have interacted over the years regarding their distinctive, God-given callings. These discussions enabled me to hone the concepts so I could recognize that churches as well as ministers are unique in their callings. Finally, many thanks go to the prayer team, organized and regularly updated by my wife, who lifted this project before the Lord often over the last two years: Diane Brown, June Dare, my daughter-in-law Amy Douglass, Rhonda Frailey, Barb Gordon, Jacque Hudgens, Sue Marsh, Terry Straight, Anna Ruth Venable, and Barbie Wilkinson. My sincere gratitude goes to all of you.

PART 1

· · · · · · · · · · ·

What Is Church Personality?

1

The Value and Importance of Church Personality

· ·

CHURCHES ARE DIFFERENT. A program that earns enthusiastic praise at the church down the street could initiate heated conflict in yours. Why? While there could be many reasons, it may well be because of church personality.

There is no guarantee that spiritually mature people will work well with one another. While they usually share the same ultimate goals, there is no assurance that they will agree on the best way to achieve these goals. When people's convictions are strongly held *and* mutually exclusive (as were Paul's and Barnabas's plans for dealing with John Mark in Acts 15:36–40), conflict can emerge, which sometimes prevents progress toward the goals that everyone desires. This is why it is important for church leaders to understand their ministry styles and why it is essential to establish philosophical and relational standards of qualification for your church leaders in addition to spiritual ones.

Once you recognize the conflict created by different ministry styles, you can work proactively to lead your congregation toward necessary change. Miscommunication that hinders the gospel will give way to a fruitful and prosperous ministry. Posturing and infighting will be replaced by a spirit of teamwork and cooperation. A board once unable to agree on the most insignificant decisions can learn to deal successfully with the truly important issues of your church's ministry. Until you know and understand your church's personality, however, you cannot pinpoint what difficulties these differences present. You may not even be aware of them.

YOUR CHURCH PERSONALITY—WHAT IS IT?

Your church's personality is not the list of values published by your denomination and perhaps displayed on the wall outside your sanctuary. These are your church's ideals, and they set forth the mission of any church in your denomination—*not* how a church will carry out that mission. Your church has an identity—a set of values, beliefs, norms—that shapes its practices and behavior like a mold shapes plaster. The ideals of your denomination or church association are like the plaster: what goes into the mold is essentially the same for every church, but the shape it takes is determined by the mold itself. One mold is not inherently better than another, simply different.

IDENTIFYING YOUR CHURCH'S PERSONALITY

Assessing the personality of your church provides measurable data about the values and norms that give your church its shape. This data will, in turn, provide helpful assistance in leading the church in accordance with its specific mission. Understanding your church's personality can help you to set aside some of your impressions about what really matters in the church, and will tell you where your ideals diverge from the way things actually are. You will then be able to identify sources of conflict in the church.

Your church personality is one of the three elements that comprise your church's *philosophy of ministry* (as noted in Figure 1). Most churches are adept at expressing their theological convictions, most have established biblical standards of godly character for their leaders, and most work capably toward assessing how they can minister effectively

4

Figure 1: The three elements of church philosophy.

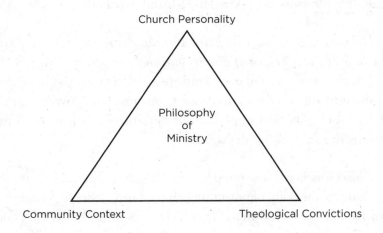

in their community contexts. But, sadly, many do not understand the nature of their church personalities—and therefore the roots of the conflicts they experience.

Think about the following contrasts regarding your church:

Achievement. How is effectiveness defined in your church? Is it measured by numbers of people, growth of the budget, or expansion of church facilities, or by the meeting of goals or the learning and maintaining of certain standards? In other words, how does your church define success?

Time Measurement. Is your church focused on the next quarter or the next five years? Is it acceptable to fail to reach goals next quarter but succeed over the long term? How much time is given for a ministry to do well before the plug is pulled? What is the church's attention span and what is its patience level regarding a new ministry effort?

Mistakes. Every church makes mistakes. How are they handled in *your* church? Are those who slip up chastised or accepted? Does your church give accolades to people who make the most mistakes because they are viewed as being on the cutting edge or stepping out in faith? Do people come together to fix a mistake, or step back and cast stones?

Does the church learn from its mistakes or tend to make the same ones repeatedly? How are mistakes defined, and by whom?

Decisions. Are most decisions made primarily by the pastor and the other leaders, or is congregational consensus a must? Are board decisions respected or second-guessed? Is reanalyzing a decision in light of new information encouraged or frowned upon? Are decisions generally explained or defended? How important is transparency in making decisions?

Risk. How is risk tolerated? Is the church more prone to attempt great things to the point of presuming on the Lord, or do the leaders tend toward small, measured steps? If you climb out on a limb, will people stand below to catch you, or wait to say "I told you so," if you fail?

Operating Principles. Does the church publicize official judgments or prefer to keep them private? Does the church consider impact on the community when making ministry decisions, or is the focus only on what is best for the members?

Trust. Do church members trust each other and you out of a sense of interdependency, or is there more of a spirit of independence and individualism? Do people tend to trust and submit to what they hear from you and the other leaders, or are they vocal in questioning authority?

Formality. Do you encourage church members to interact with you and the other leaders privately, or do you prefer a more formal process of communication? Do your meetings follow *Robert's Rules of Order*, or are they free-flowing? Do you encourage casual dress at meetings, or do you prefer that people appear in suit and tie? Does every classroom look immaculate, or does the building's appearance not matter as much as other things?

Members. Do you treat members with respect until they do something to violate your trust, or are you wary of members until they earn your respect? Do you think of members as assets with spiritual gifts that should be developed? Are you more focused on events and programs or the people who populate them?

FROM YOUR PROMINENT SYMBOLS TO YOUR MOST UNCONSCIOUS ASSUMPTIONS

Church personality can be viewed at two levels: some aspects of its personality are visible and concrete, while many characteristics are intangible and subconscious. Basic assumptions that guide a church are deeply rooted and often taken for granted. For example, avoiding conflict rather than dealing with it directly is a subconscious norm that has major influence on the way the church does things consciously. For an insider, such subconscious characteristics are difficult to see, particularly if the individual has grown up within that church's personality. New members and staff people frequently are better positioned to identify these assumptions or values because they possess a fresh, objective frame of reference by which they compare one church with another.

Some of the most powerful expressions of a church's personality are the architecture and decor, the clothing people wear, the church processes and structures, its rituals and celebrations. Other manifestations of personality are found in commonly used jargon, letterhead logos, and brochures, as well as status symbols: offices and titles, for example. Outsiders can often spot these symbols easily upon entering a church. Longtime insiders, however, no longer recognize these symbols on a conscious level, as they have become part of the church's personality.

Publicly promoted or secondary values are communicated and understood at a more conscious level; these are the standards that you discuss, endorse, and encourage people to follow consciously in their lives. All members of a church I recently pastored, for example, became familiar with the values embodied in our slogan—"Transformed Together in Christ"—because we imprinted that statement on all of our literature. However, people were not as clear about the ways we handled conflict. Everyone recognized that we treated the Bible as our "only infallible rule of faith and practice" because we often talked about this value. They were not as knowledgeable about how we budgeted funds; this process was based on the subconscious characteristics of our church's personality and therefore was conducted on a more informal basis, and was open to considerable flexibility, because that was a trait of our church personality.

PERSONALITY AS THE CHURCH'S "OPERATING SYSTEM"

Personality drives a church and its actions. We might call it the "operating system" of the church. For example, Microsoft Windows XP operates my computer, Macintosh OS X drives my son's computer, and one of the Linux systems runs the internal process of the computers of some of my high-tech friends. Although the manufacturers may not admit it, one system is just as capable as the other, even though they are quite different in the ways they are structured and run the computer's applications, or programs.

I am never conscious of the way the core of my computer operating system—something called the Windows system32 file folder—functions, even though it is essential to the machine's inner workings. When I try to examine the files in that folder, a message appears on the screen warning me that if I try to change any part of system32 then my computer will no longer work properly. In a similar manner, your church's personality is always working quietly behind the scenes, guiding how your church thinks, feels, and acts, and directing "how we do things around here." If a new pastor or staff member tries to change the operating system (i.e., the church personality) to fit his ministry style preferences, the church will malfunction in the form of conflict. Such attempts at modification are similar to installing the Linux operating system on top of Windows XP; the systems are not compatible and the computer will crash. It would be more practical to remove all the components of the computer and start afresh—which is possible although tedious in the computer world, but usually impossible to do in a church.

CHURCH PERSONALITY—YOU KNOW IT WHEN YOU SEE IT

As you can see now, church personality is one of those realities that often is difficult to define distinctly, but something you know when you see it. Newcomers identify the personality of your church (consciously or unconsciously) during the first five minutes inside your building. Not unlike what you sense about someone else's personality, some of the many things that may help others recognize your church's personality are:

- The friendliness of the people.
- The clothing of the members.
- The bulletin (or the lack of one).
- The items emphasized in the announcement time.
- The worship style.

NONVERBAL COMMUNICATION

Researchers tell us that 80 percent to 90 percent of what we convey is expressed nonverbally. Consider, for example, what you communicate when you hold your hands outstretched, palms up. Depending on the context, you may mean any of a variety of things. If you are making an appeal to your governing board with your palms up, then you may be asking, "Do you really want me to do this?" If you are in front of your Sunday school class, then you may be entreating them, "Please do this." Some gestures with lifted palms may be expressions of hopelessness, saying, "What can we do?" Others may implore, "I need your help."[1]

Consider other gestures you may use every day. A hands-on-hips stance can make you look more commanding or exude a self-assured, "take-charge" attitude. At times you may place your hand behind your head, usually a sign of frustration, uncertainty, or anger. If you fold your arms across your chest (especially if your arms are elevated and held away from the body), it is generally a sign of pride, loathing, or difference of opinion. Your hand gestures, eye movements, facial expressions, and body positions—your "body language"—tells others much more than what you say (or don't say) verbally. One expert speculates that a reason for President Ronald Reagan's remarkable popularity in the United States was his liberal use of display of his palms. In this manner he communicated geniality in a disarming, warm, and comforting way that led people to trust him.[2]

Recently, my family and I attended a church in our area for the fifth time. Within a few minutes of entering the building I could tell that the atmosphere was rather subdued. How did I come to that conclusion? The body language of the people: almost everyone was turned toward another member. Rather than being met at the entrance by greeters, as had occurred during our first four visits, we were left to ourselves as they huddled together to talk among themselves, with somber expressions on their faces. I interpreted the nonverbal communication to mean that the people were unfriendly.

There could have been any of several explanations for this behavior. To begin with, since it was a very hot day, the heat might have sapped people's energy and made them tired and unresponsive. Or it may have been that my family and I had visited often enough for people to get used to seeing us, and they therefore made no special effort to be friendly. It was not until we had been in the building for some time that we learned the 18-year-old son of one of the member families had committed suicide a few days before. Since the members were on an e-mail communication system, most of them knew about the death. They were grieving with the family and trying to make sense of the incident. The point is that the people of the church were communicating—nonverbally—and thereby creating an atmosphere that I mistakenly interpreted as unfriendliness.

2

Communicating Church Personality

MANY PERSONALITIES WITHIN a denomination, geographical region, or even ethnic culture may share certain characteristics, norms, and values while being very different from one another in other aspects. A pastor who served fruitfully in one church may not be as productive in another, regardless of whether both churches are in the same denomination, geographical area, or even ethnic group. Sometimes the choice to move from one church to another proves to be disastrous. This is because the random probability of a pastor being the best fit for a staff position at another church, apart from understanding the dynamics of church personality, is 1 in 8 as indicated by the Church Personality Wheel in Figure 2.

A friend of mine moved to a new city some years ago and proceeded to visit every church in his denomination within the area—eleven in all. He commented that this experience convinced him of the reality of the diversity of church personalities because, even though each of these churches held to the same biblical convictions and the same denominational distinctives, they were quite different from one another in how they viewed "debatable matters"—the areas in which

Figure 2: The Church Personality Wheel.

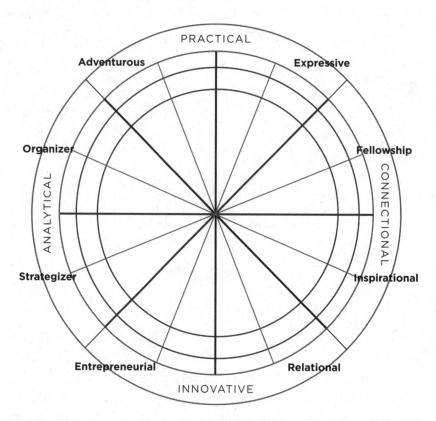

church cultural differences are most clearly expressed. To understand this disparity among churches, think of the three concentric circles (as noted in Figure 3):[1]

"Core Convictions" are the essential beliefs of the Christian faith to which a person must adhere[2] in order to be a member of any evangelical church. A short list would include belief in:

- The Trinity—God the Father, the Son, and the Holy Spirit.
- The simultaneous deity and humanity of Jesus Christ.
- The crucifixion and resurrection of Jesus Christ as the only means for salvation.
- The fact that Christians will not perish but have eternal life.

"Doctrinal Distinctives" of a denomination are those beliefs that the pastors and other officers must hold in order to be ordained and continue to serve. A short list for my denomination would include:

- The authority of the Scriptures over God's people.
- The sovereignty of God at work in our lives in special ways.
- The importance of the Sacraments as extraordinary means of grace in our lives.

"Debatable Matters" fit the apostle Paul's description in 1 Corinthians 10:25–30:

> Eat whatever is sold in the meat market without raising any question on the ground of conscience. For "the earth is the Lord's, and the fullness thereof." If one of the unbelievers invites you to dinner and you are disposed to go, eat whatever is set before you without raising any question on the ground of conscience. But if someone says to you, "This has been offered in sacrifice," then do not eat it, for the sake of the one who informed you, and for the sake of conscience—I do not mean your conscience, but his. For why should

Figure 3: The relationship among debatable matters, doctrinal distinctives, and core convictions.

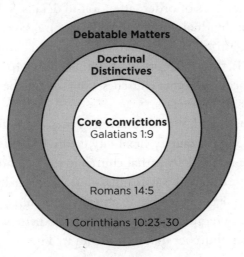

13

my liberty be determined by someone else's conscience? If I partake with thankfulness, why am I denounced because of that for which I give thanks?

The differences in the personalities of churches in my denomination are expressed through the following perspectives (plus others not on this list):

- Views on the second coming of Christ: Premillennialism, Amillennialism, or Postmillennialism.
- Preferences in children's education: Public schools, Christian schools, or homeschooling.
- Views on creation: six 24-hour days of creation or a God-centered, nonliteral approach.
- Individual expressions of Sabbath-keeping regarding recreational activities.
- Abstinence vs. moderation in the use of alcoholic beverages.

Most, but not all, members of my denomination recognize that "debatable matters" express our church personality differences rather than being matters of core conviction and theological distinctiveness, and they do not confront sister churches over these issues. However, the more a church personality focuses on issues such as responsibility; tradition; maintenance of order; attention to details; subordination to authority; and individual duty to serve, give, care, save, and share in a planned and organized church life (i.e., the more a church leans to the right in Figure 4), then the more likely is that church to be intolerant of cultural differences with other churches, even though the other churches lay within biblical parameters.

On the other hand, the more a church personality focuses on freedom of expression, spontaneity, flexibility, creativity, and quick action in a crisis, then the more likely is that church to tolerate not only cultural variations, but also differences with other churches regarding core convictions that should not be negotiable. In other words, church personality can affect the degree of temptation that one church experiences in accepting or rejecting other churches that differ from it. This is where godliness

Figure 4: Tolerance vs. intolerance of "debatable matters."

Church focused upon freedom of expression, spontaneity, flexibility, creativity, and acting quickly in a crisis.

Church focused upon responsibility, tradition, maintaining order, attention to details, and subordination to authority.

| 5 | 4 | 3 | 2 | 1 | | 1 | 2 | 3 | 4 | 5 |

Tolerance of church personality differences.

Intolerance of church personality differences.

of character is the key factor, because character trumps temperament. In other words, the fruit of the Spirit at work within a church will enable it to stand against the temptations inherent in its personality.

SHOULD YOUR CHURCH PERSONALITY BE CHANGED?

When you institute new programs and ministries in your church, how should this affect the dynamics of your church personality? Programming shifts should initiate change in your church structures, methodologies, and processes, but they should not tamper with your fundamental church personality. Though these may seem the same, they are distinct; understanding that distinction is essential for ministry.

In 1979, I planted the first of three churches in Northern Virginia on the western growth edge of the Washington, DC, region. Since no one had taught me about the distinctives of church personality, I allowed two different—though biblically acceptable—personalities to flourish within the new church. The first church ethos I call the Inspirational church (to be described in detail later), and it was a reflection of my ministry values and strengths. The second personality, the Organizer church (also to be described later), developed around the ministry values and strengths of one of our leading ruling elders—one of the core group that had called me to lead in planting the church. After six years, the Inspirational personality was the dominant ethos of the church; approximately 80 percent of the families adhered to the Inspirational personality. The Organizer personality comprised the values of the remaining 20 percent of the families.

However, because I had been educated to believe that a plurality of personalities in the local church was good, I did not resist when that elder began lobbying for an assistant pastor who fit the Organizer church personality (but not that of the dominant Inspirational church). At the time, I thought I was being gracious and open-minded; now, I realize that I was being foolish and imprudent. To make matters even more challenging, when I was called away from that pastorate to my present ministry, I led that congregation in choosing the assistant pastor who fit the Organizer church personality to be my successor. The result was anything but peaceful. The next couple years were quite difficult for the congregation as the new pastor led the church in its transformation from the personality I had developed to the personality he represented. As a consequence, the church has been altered in its ethos to that of an Organizer church, which is a 180-degree shift in the church's personality from the Inspirational pattern.

Unfortunately, there was much accusation and name-calling through those years, because many people in the church believed the differences were theologically based, while they were essentially related to church personality. Both styles of ministry are biblical and pleasing to God, but they are nevertheless quite different and therefore tend to conflict.

If I had known then what I have discovered over the ensuing years, I would have guided that church more strategically in the choice of the assistant pastor, and I would have worked to make sure that my successor not only met all of the theological and character requirements to be pastor of the church (which he did), but also that he embodied the same basic church personality characteristics with which I had planted and developed the church (which he did not). Again, I say this with the firm belief that both of our ministry styles are equally God-honoring. But both were not best for the church I had planted.

An objective church personality assessment first determines which of the eight church personalities best describes your church personality, and then enables you to search for the pastoral leadership appropriate for your personality. Your fundamental church personality should not be tampered with—so it is important that the pastoral leadership that best fits your church personality be chosen in such a manner that your church will grow and develop in its own unique way.

THE IMPORTANCE OF CROSS-MATCHING

An illustration from the medical field demonstrates the dynamics of matching pastors to specific churches. Each of us possesses two sets of three antigens (generally proteins) that produce antibodies to fight off foreign substances that enter our bodies. We receive one set from our mothers and the other set from our fathers. Because these proteins vary from person to person, you cannot receive a transplant of just any person's organ. Says Dr. Thomas Peters, "The best long-term outcomes are between persons who share all antigens, or those who are a six-antigen match. Donors and recipients who match at five antigens may not do quite as well over the long term as the six-antigen matched donor recipient pairs, but will do statistically better than donors and recipients matched at four antigens."[3]

If someone volunteers to provide an organ transplant for you, hospital technicians will draw blood from both of you for a cross-match. If this testing indicates the compatibility of at least four of the six antigens, both of you go to surgery for the transplant operation. These compatibility tests have been carefully developed to ensure that your antibodies do not reject the donated organ—which would make you even more ill. In similar ways, consider the cross-matching tests in this book to be of major importance in determining whether a prospective pastor would be a good match as a transplant into your particular church body.

TWO CONTRASTING CHURCH PERSONALITIES: AN EXAMPLE

Consider two churches: First Church has existed downtown in the same location for two hundred years. City Church has been in existence only ten years and is located in a deteriorating section of the urban area. Both conduct the same basic ministry—the proclamation of the Word of God.

First Church's bulletin might present the church to visitors in the following way: "For more than two centuries our witness has been uniquely interwoven with the life of this city. As you learn of our history and share in our memories, you will find that our past is witness to God's fidelity, the present attests to his goodness, and the future contains his promise. We hope you will visit the church, carry away happy memories, and come again in God's good time."

On the church's Web site you might find stories from the church's past and references to famous city, regional, and national leaders who were members of the church over the course of its history. You might also find stories about notable pastors from the past and even excerpts from their sermons. The glory days of the church—sometimes a hundred years ago or more—will be highlighted. The worship service will tend to be more formal or "high church," and liturgically oriented, using primarily historic responsive readings and traditional music. Finally, much will be written about the impact of the church over the last two hundred years on the city, its leaders, and its institutions. First Church will tend to quote 1 Corinthians 14:40: "But all things should be done decently and in order."

In contrast, City Church serves with a mindset that exhorts the people to minister as social activists among the impoverished and downtrodden. The desired result of this church is greater opportunity for the disadvantaged and handicapped. There is great compassion for the oppressed and much involvement in social programs for the sake of the community. City Church's Web site might emphasize interaction with people across all racial, social, and economic divisions through multicultural worship and community relationships. This church is determined to be a place where fellowship, love, and a commitment to take care of people's basic human needs are practiced through mobilizing each member to be part of extending God's justice and mercy to all people.

City Church will tend to quote Isaiah 58:6–7: "Is not this the fast that I choose: to loose the bonds of wickedness, to undo the straps of the yoke, to let the oppressed go free, and to break every yoke? Is it not to share your bread with the hungry and bring the homeless poor into your house; when you see the naked, to cover him, and not to hide yourself from your own flesh?" City Church likes hymns and Scripture songs, uses a flexible order of worship, dresses informally, and fosters a loose, relational environment.

Imagine the conflict that would develop if these two church personalities attempted to merge institutionally. They may be able to work alongside one another as part of a regional network of churches, but even then there will be sparks. Nevertheless, these two churches are different parts of the body of Christ and therefore, "The eye cannot say to the hand, 'I have no need of you,' nor again the head to the feet, 'I have no need of you'" (1 Cor. 12:21).

PERSONALITY DIFFERENCES WITHIN A LARGE CHURCH

Similar distinctions can exist within a single church—especially in larger churches and mega-churches—just as between one church and another. It can be almost as if two distinct churches exist in one body, because the functions that a church undertakes—and the people who fulfill those functions—are so different. For instance, in even tightly organized churches, outreach and bookkeeping have different personalities. Outreach, by definition, is concentrated "out there" on visitors and the unchurched community. When an outreach ministry wants to develop a strategy, it turns outward toward those people. Bookkeeping, on the other hand, looks to its own accounting processes and to the internal structure of the church. Those committed to outreach tend to be more "big picture" and inspirational, while those with a passion for keeping finances in order tend to be more systematic and step-by-step in their approach.

Conflicts take place most commonly between departments of larger churches: either between one subdivision and another, or between one subdivision and the overall leadership of the church. Because of this, the ministry departments are where the overall mission of the church is determined. At this level of ministry, church personality is both most

19

practical in its workings and most easily shaped on a day-to-day basis. Therefore, leaders in larger churches who use the diagnostic tools in this book to determine the personalities of their churches should not stop with assessing personality for the church as a whole. It is important to conduct the assessment for each specific subdivision of the church as well. When all is said and done, you will see much more clearly why the ministry departments of your church may often have difficulty working and communicating with one another.

WHERE DOES PERSONALITY COME FROM?

As the examples of First Church and City Church indicate, a church's personality is greatly influenced by its traditions and origins. Some churches have a long history, while others are new church plants. Some churches reflect the personality of their denominational affiliation and others are independent churches with very little involvement in associations of churches. The personalities of some churches are profoundly shaped by the theological seminaries or Bible colleges from which they recruit their pastors. Others are more eclectic because they draw their leadership from a number of seminaries or educational institutions.

No two churches follow the same path. The bottom line is this: at any given time, a church will have a particular personality, which will shape its present and future to a large extent. That being the case, let us turn to the question of how to recognize a church's personality.

3

Building Blocks of
Church Personality

PERSONALITY VARIES SIGNIFICANTLY from church to church. At the same time, distinctions can often be subtle. In one sense, there are as many personalities as there are churches. But those endless, varied distinctions can be clustered into eight basic categories. These categories are identified by recognizing the factors that make up each distinctive personality and discerning which ones describe a church. I have created a diagnostic tool to help with the process of pinpointing these factors.

This diagnostic, presented fully in reproducible form in the appendix, is based on the assumption that the personality of a church is determined by the true leadership of the church: the thirty individuals who exercise the greatest official and unofficial influence on the church. These may be pastors or lay leaders, or they may be people who do not hold a formal leadership office.

Each question in the diagnostic contains two opposite ideas that relate to the types of behaviors or traits of these leaders. The questions should be answered according to the church leaders' *preference* of interaction and leadership, rather than how the church leaders

21

think they should behave as they relate to one another and others in the church.

INFORMATION-GATHERING

1. Do the church leaders depend on their personal observations in order to gather data about what's happening, or do they rely more on their intuition and hunches in order to form impressions about what's going on?
2. Do the church leaders prefer straightforward ways of communicating—the more specific and concrete the better—or do they prefer to use imagery and symbolism to engage the imagination of the people of the church?
3. Are the leaders of the church observers of tradition who do not easily break with custom, or are they able to break with tradition and lay aside customs that seem too cumbersome for a new situation?

DECISION-MAKING

1. Are the church leaders secure in basing their decisions on objective analysis—weighing the pros and cons of a situation—or, regardless of the pros and cons, are they more confident when they feel their conclusions are based on what is important and valuable?
2. Can the church leaders usually get on with their work and ministry, regardless of relational harmony, or do they find that harmonious relationships are essential for them to function effectively in a situation?
3. Does making a critical evaluation come more naturally for the church leaders than speaking an appreciative word, or are they more spontaneous with an appreciative word than with a critical evaluation?

LIFESTYLE

1. Do the church leaders prefer to plan their work first and then work their plan, or do they tend to be more casual and informal in developing their plans?

2. Do the basic contributions by the leaders often stem from being systematic, orderly, proactive, and decisive, or do they bring to church leadership such characteristics as spontaneity, open-mindedness, tolerance, and adaptability?

3. Do the church leaders prefer bringing programs and projects to completion—finishing one task at a time—or do they like the feeling of getting new things started and having many things going at the same time?

When we apply these distinctions to churches, we see that they can be either Practical or Innovative according to the ways in which they prefer gathering information; Analytical or Connectional according to whether they are more focused on tasks or people; Structured or Flexible depending on the method by which they process information.

INFORMATION-GATHERING: PRACTICAL VS. INNOVATIVE CHURCHES

Practical-oriented churches are more likely to pay attention to facts, details, and current reality. Innovation is the preference for working with information on the basis of its meaningfulness, originality, and future possibilities. The most common distinctives between Practical churches and Innovative churches are described in Table 1.

DECISION-MAKING: ANALYTICAL VS. CONNECTIONAL CHURCHES

Analytical churches are more likely to deal with information on the basis of its structure and function. Connectional churches interact with information on the basis of its dynamism and potential for enhancing relationships. The most common distinctives between Analytical and Connectional churches are found in Table 2. See also Figure 5 for how Practical, Innovative, Analytical, and Connectional churches fit into the Church Personality Wheel.

23

Table 1: Practical churches vs. Innovative churches.

Practical churches are influenced by leaders who:	Innovative churches are influenced by leaders who:
• live in the "here and now" • work well with facts and details • like realistic challenges and problem solving • are experience and action-oriented • are realistic and matter-of-fact	• prefer to live in the past and future • are interested in new and unusual experiences • do not like routine • are attracted to theory rather than practice

Table 2: Analytical churches vs. Connectional churches.

Analytical churches are influenced by leaders who:	Connectional churches are influenced by leaders who:
• are interested in systems, structures, patterns • like to expose issues to logical analysis • can be aloof and unemotional • are likely to evaluate issues through their intellect and decide on the basis of right and wrong • may have difficulty talking about emotions • may not work as diligently at clearing up arguments or quarrels	• are interested in people and their feelings • easily communicate their moods to others • pay attention to relationships • tend to evaluate issues through their ethical system and decide on the basis of good and bad • can be sensitive to rebuke • may tend to give compliments to please people

LIFESTYLE: STRUCTURED VS. FLEXIBLE CHURCHES

Structured churches are motivated into action proactively on the basis of planning. Flexible churches are easily motivated into action through responding to changes in events. The most common distinctives between Structured and Flexible churches are found in Table 3. See also Figure 6 for how Structured and Flexible churches fit into the Church Personality Wheel.

THE CHURCH PERSONALITY'S EFFECT ON ITS MEMBERS

Fundamentally, your church's personality is a set of shared values among its most influential members. A personality conveys a com-

Figure 5: How practical, innovative, analytical, and connectional churches fit into the church personality wheel.

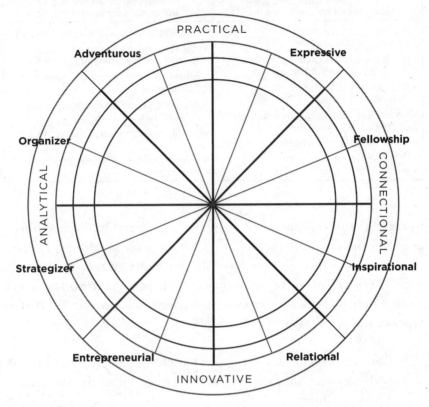

mon identity to the individuals and thereby generates commitment on the part of the members and strengthens social, emotional, and spiritual solidity. Overall, it provides a common sense of meaning and purpose for all members and thereby helps the church move in the same direction.

Not every aspect of the church ethos is positive because each personality has its challenges—forms of temptation to which it is more susceptible. For instance, some church personalities may be tempted to set up barriers to change, thereby hampering the adaptability of its outreach methods if the surrounding community changes. Other church personalities may be easily persuaded

Table 3: Structured churches vs. Connectional churches.

Structured Churches are influenced by leaders who:	Flexible Churches are influenced by leaders who:
• do not like to leave many unanswered questions • are likely to plan their work ahead and finish it in a timely fashion • make an effort to be exact in what they do • do not like to change their decisions once they are made • are likely to demonstrate stable work habits • easily follow rules and discipline	• may act impulsively in their ministry • can do more things at once without feeling compelled to finish them • prefer to be free from long-term obligations • are curious and like taking a fresh look at things • are likely to work according to their mood • often act without as much preparation

to resist the development of a diverse membership. Some church personalities are more inclined to resist ministering alongside sister churches, even though they have similar belief systems.

There are no right or wrong church personalities. But every church personality experiences temptations to engage in particular types of sinful behavior. For example:

- *Practical* churches are sometimes tempted to do something simply because it is the next feasible thing to do, rather than because it honors Christ.
- *Innovative* churches are occasionally tempted to become so enthralled by future possibilities that they do not pay attention to necessary aspects of everyday ministry.
- *Analytical* churches are tempted, from time to time, to study situations and people logically, while remaining aloof and personally uninvolved.
- *Connectional* churches are now and then tempted to use emotional manipulation to bring about results.
- *Structured* churches are tempted, on occasion, to be rigid in their direction once they have made decisions, and may try to control people who do not submit.
- *Flexible* churches are sometimes tempted to be impulsive in their ministry and unwilling to make long-term commitments.

Figure 6: How structured and flexible churches fit into the church personality wheel.

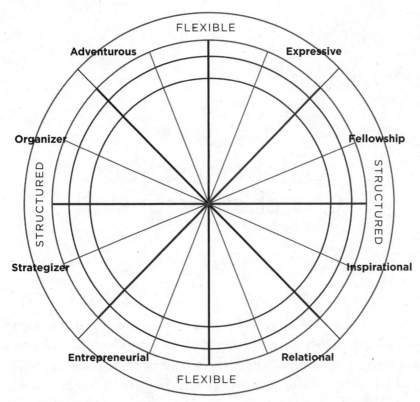

These temptations can lead to miscommunication, conflict, and mistrust of leadership. However, understanding them and how they combine to form distinctive church personalities can alleviate all of these problems and safeguard against the temptations themselves. In the next chapter we will discuss how these six factors combine to form a church's personality, and what this means for the life of the church.

4

Determining Your
Church's Personality

NOW THAT WE KNOW the building blocks, or categories, we can see how they work together. Each category should be understood as a component of several church personalities. Every category contributes a quality to the various personalities to make each one unique.

The categories can be combined so that we can identify eight prominent church personalities. You likely will be able to see aspects of your church in more than one of the descriptions that follow. However, research demonstrates that one of these eight profiles will be most descriptive of your church. This one core profile will more completely define your church's personality characteristics.

CHURCH PERSONALITY COMBINATIONS

Fellowship churches are conscientious, hard-working, orderly, and sensitive to the needs of people in general, but especially those who are members of their church. These churches bring out the best in people by helping them work toward personally meaningful goals in an organized manner. Therefore, they usually have many people who are eager and willing to serve. Usually, they are especially strong in children's programs, shut-in visitation of relatives, neighbors, and longtime members of the church, as well as programs that train their laypeople in practical care ministries. However, these churches may tend to resist disturbances to their routine even when the disruption is good for the health of the church.

Inspirational churches are encouraging and supportive to their people and conscientious about putting personal relationships ahead of ministry tasks. Since they focus on the ways individuals feel, they closely monitor how people interact with one another as well as the ways their ministry efforts impact people positively and negatively. These churches are careful to accommodate people, and usually put needs of individuals ahead of what is best for the institution as a whole. They carefully study and evaluate circumstances by applying biblical and relational values to them. These churches usually have strong counseling programs as an essential aspect of their ministry.

Relational churches focus on personal connections, values, opinions, and people interactions. They actively strive to bond with one another, create harmony, and cooperate—making sure that everyone is involved and positive about the church. Because they place a high priority on meeting the needs of everyone in the church, they focus on organizing and coordinating events, projects, and activities that genuinely help people grow, develop, and be all that God intended them to be. They naturally care about people in the community and want to be appreciated for their unique effort to make the community a better place in which to live.

Entrepreneurial churches are drawn to opportunities that require them to anticipate the future and create new approaches, because they see every need as an opportunity for trying something different. They regularly scan the community to find connections with people and ministries that already exist so they can become involved. Since they envision what could be rather than what is, they are motivated to link creative ideas together in practical but original ways. Because they like to imagine and then develop new ministries, they see a multitude of ways in which they can bring transformation to the community. Since they are motivated to create change, they enthusiastically focus their attention on the future.

Strategizer churches develop creative ideas and insights to initiate innovative transformation in the surrounding community through encouraging their people to develop their giftedness and give themselves sacrificially to ministry. These churches are willing to take time to consider the facts and new ideas in the context of past experiences to better enable them to discern the Lord's direction for the future. Because they want to understand and interpret the meaning and purpose of life, they are willing to create theological models that help them expand their perspective. Since they are visionary, they like to look at new possibilities and are willing to formulate multifaceted plans to change their organizational structure in order to improve their methodologies.

Organizer churches like to solve complex problems in a methodical manner by using logical analysis to critique their ministry programs, spot flaws, and make necessary changes that complete their ministry tasks efficiently. They are organized and competent, priding themselves in getting the most accomplished in the least time. Before they mobilize people to engage in a new ministry, they systematically analyze all the opportunities and then painstakingly undertake their plans. Because their Christian education programs are so important to them, they take satisfaction in developing them to a high level.

Adventurous churches respond quickly to issues in their midst and in the community around them by being action oriented. Because they are at their best in emergency situations, they see problems as an adventure and an opportunity for ministry. As they approach difficulties and crises of the present, they will reflect on their previous ministry experiences and use strategies that worked well for them in the past. Since they value spontaneity, they do not function well when forced to work within traditional structures that impose tight schedules on them. These churches improvise, adjust, and maneuver to make sure things get fixed so they can accomplish their mission.

Expressive churches are friendly and outgoing in communicating their love for people as a means of motivating them to join in the fellowship. These churches like to be at the center of the action because they are comprised of easygoing, optimistic, and considerate people who enjoy talking, laughing, and sharing their lives with newcomers. They build relational bridges by becoming loyal friends and great companions with those new to the church as they express their generosity and eagerness to please through formal and informal entertainment.

UNDERSTAND YOUR CHURCH PERSONALITY BEFORE DEALING WITH THE CONFLICT

In one of the eight chapters that follow, you will find a number of stories, examples, and statements that describe churches like yours. These can be used to develop a description to help everyone understand the personality of your church. Specifically, this process is designed to help you develop a ten- to twenty-page ministry style description of your church so everyone can become familiar with:

- Your church's distinctive personality
- Your church's philosophy of ministry
- The qualifications and expectations for your staff and lay leaders
- Your church's mission values
- Your leadership's budgeting priorities

These statements provide a seedbed of ideas from which you can begin to describe your church. (You can make the descriptions even more particularized to your unique ministry by refining them or adding your own qualifications.)

This process will move program development and conflict resolution along in a focused manner, because you will begin with a framework of descriptions from which to work rather than try to create each statement afresh. Such a presentation would take outside church consultants several months to develop through the normal means of observing your church, but you and other church leaders can complete the description in a few hours because you know your church best.

In addition, by discerning the key themes of your church personality you can:

Create a questionnaire based on a "degree of fit" scale to determine more accurately how closely new staff and lay leaders would mesh with your church personality.

Communicate to your new staff and lay leaders aspects of your church's personality that would take them a year or more to discover by normal means.

Provide specific ministry development goals that are in accordance with God's unique mission for your church.

Craft annual pastoral and lay leader review standards that are in accordance with agreed-upon benchmarks reflecting your church personality.

Develop brochures that describe your church for first-time visitors, so they will have a better sense of whether they would fit in with your church personality.

More easily cross racial, socioeconomic, generational, and cultural lines.

Make distinctions between matters of ministry style vs. sinful behavior in regard to worship, preaching/teaching, outreach, etc.

CONCLUSION

For most of us, an airline flight begins when we line up at the gate and then slowly make our way on board so that we can store our carry-on items, take our seats, and adjust as the passengers entering after us fill the seats around us.

But for the pilots, the flight begins long before that. They physically inspect the plane, check the fuel and instruments, review the weather report, and go over hundreds of other detailed items to ensure the safety of the flight. This happens because the pilots have responsibility for our well-being, and before takeoff they must have a thorough understanding of the aircraft.

Although you do not have to fly a 747 safely from Los Angeles to Atlanta, you still need to follow the example of these pilots before you set your strategy for dealing with conflict in your church. Get a clear sense of the church personality in which you are ministering, the resources you possess, and the rules you need to communicate accordingly. Then determine your expectations for people involved in conflict. If you do not take the time to resolve these matters first, you can expect turbulence (and you won't be able to blame your difficulties on the weather!).

Your next step is to choose the thirty most influential staff and lay leaders in your church and ask them to respond to the questionnaire in the appendix. When you collate the results, you will discover which of the eight church personalities fits your church best. Then you can begin working through the specific chapter that describes your church's personality to form the ministry style description for your church. May the Lord guide and bless you in this very important endeavor.

PART 2

· · · · · · · · · · · · ·

The Eight Church Personalities

5

The Fellowship Church
. . . .

*Orderly, Conservative, Relationally Oriented in
Ministry to People through Gifts of Helps and Service*

SUMMARY STATEMENT

Because Fellowship churches are gifted at helping and serving
people, they develop well-organized ministries that are coordinated
in working toward a better life spiritually, socially, and physically for
themselves and the community. Conscientious and hard working in their
ministries, they are eager and willing to be involved in one another's
lives as well as to be useful to the community through their gifts of helps
and service. Out of a sense of duty and responsibility, members will
step into leadership roles when firmly asked, even though at first they
may be reluctant. Transitions can be difficult for Fellowship churches,
and rapid changes can lead to distress. Consequently, they tend to resist
disturbances to their routine even when the unsettling is good for the
church. See Table 4 for a summary of these characteristics.

MISSION STATEMENT

Fellowship churches are called of God to form ministry teams that
demonstrate the love of Christ through prayer and practical, generous,

Table 4: Characteristics of the Fellowship church.

Strong Points	• Listening to People and Understanding their Feelings • Valuing Teamwork and Harmony with Others in the Church • Following-through on Projects
Challenges	• Can be Oversensitive to Criticism • May Take on Too Many Projects • May Struggle to Respond to Changing Needs and Opportunities
Primary Ministries	• Ministries of Mercy, Helps and Compassion • Children's Ministries
Ministry Tempo	• Deliberate and Relaxed
What Inspires Them	• Involvement in Ministries that Genuinely Help People in Practical Ways
What De-motivates Them	• Insensitivity and Impatience with People • Disrespect for Tradition and Authority • Disharmony
Under Stress	• Can Feel Overwhelmed • Become More Submissive to Authoritative People
Decision-making	• Through Consensus Building
Desire	• Acceptance and Approval from People Important to Them • Peace and Agreement in the Church
Priority	• Organize Ministries to Do What Is Best for People
Church Ethos	• Personal • Relational • Loyal
Outward Appearance	• More Formal and Traditional
Gain Confidence Through	• Friendships • Cooperation • Serving
Fear	• Sudden Changes

no-strings-attached acts of service to individuals, families, and organizations in the community through their gifts of helps and shepherding as a means of serving people in pain and distress. These ministries then bring some in the community to the point at which they become open to their greatest need—being drawn into a relationship with Christ and his church where they can serve others as an expression of their love for the Lord, even as they have been served by him and his church.

Theme verse: "In the same way, let your light shine before men, that they may see your good deeds and praise your Father in heaven" (Matt. 5:16).

FELLOWSHIP CHURCH CHARACTERISTICS

Friendship-Oriented

Members of Fellowship churches value one another for their warmth, dependability, depth of emotional awareness, and understanding. These friends are blessed by these thoughtful, conscientious, and devoted people. For Fellowship members, the definition of *church* includes the people *they* most like to be with, the ones who are their friends and remain with them through thick and thin. (Note: The quotes in this chapter are from Fellowship churches that have been promised anonymity.)

We are a friendly and relational church with a strong connection among the members.

Although Fellowship church members are likely to place their families above their church friends in their priorities, they genuinely enjoy spending time with fellow church members. They typically select a few special friends and nurture these friendships over long periods of time.

We have a strong sense of family that includes a concern for others within the small groups and ministries that make up our fellowship.

Fellowship church members want to serve within a positive, supportive, and harmonious ministry environment in which hard work

39

and responsibility are appreciated. They "wear well" with each other and people in the community. With their moderate, controlled stance and modest demeanor, they are able to serve a wide range of people. They are considerate, patient, and always willing to help those they consider friends.

> *We provide meals and take care of people who are sick. Even my co-workers are impressed when they hear of my involvement in that because they don't have that kind of community.*

They tend to build close relationships with a relatively small group of people in the community, but genuinely desire to widen that circle of relationships. Sometimes they want more relationships but don't know whether they can handle more. Small groups work well in these churches because they allow the people not to become overwhelmed with relationships and the needs of other people.

> *The church's strengths are "a core of good solid relationships and friendliness."*

They are quite loyal to one another in the church, and are ready to provide emotional and practical support at a moment's notice. However, people in these churches dislike confrontation, so they tend to stay on the sidelines if a conflict develops. The older the friendship, the more they will value it.

> *One of the church's strengths is "a ministry to our senior members with an attempt to share love and concern."*

Sensitive and sympathetic, Fellowship church members are good listeners and eager to help people in practical ways. They do this by using their wealth of experience and perceptive observational skills to guide their efforts toward the needs of others. Because of their warm and selfless nature, Fellowship churches quietly see to it that caretaking is scheduled for the health and welfare of those in need.

> *We have good children's programs and a fine nursery.*

Because of their commitment to people, they empathize with those around them. As some Fellowship churches might put it, "They feel everyone's pain." They radiate their feelings and thoughtful values outward toward the people with whom they feel comfortable. Truly warm and kindhearted, they want to believe the best of people. They value harmony and cooperation, and are likely to be very sensitive to other people's feelings. People value these churches for their consideration and awareness, and their ability to bring out the best in people by their firm desire to believe the best.

Members have been interested in all of our children, like showing up at ball games to support them and being generally interested in not only their spiritual welfare, but also the daily lives of our children. It ministers to us as parents that others in the church love our children.

The Bible on Supportiveness

Proverbs 3:3—"Let not steadfast love and faithfulness forsake you; bind them around your neck; write them on the tablet of your heart."

Proverbs 12:22—"Those who act faithfully are his delight."

Proverbs 27:9—"The sweetness of a friend comes from his earnest counsel."

Conscientious, Hard-Working Ministry Style

The no-nonsense quality to Fellowship churches communicates confidence about their competencies. These people do not chase rainbows and always balance the budget because they place a high priority on exercising financial responsibility. Their programs may not be fancy but they are productive and efficient, and these churches will stand behind them. There is a service-to-others quality about these churches.

When it comes to money my congregation members tend to be extremely frugal. They never want to spend more money than they have to. Yet, when it comes to the resources of time or

41

energy—abstract items—they often miss the high price of time or manpower that would be required and spent in order to satisfy their expectations regarding the quality of communication and level of frequency. When it comes to communication, they have 4 star restaurant tastes but insist on a McDonald's budget. They are conservative with dollars but liberal with their expectations of time and energy expenditure.

Fellowship churches relate well to people, are dependable, have a strong sense of historical continuity, responsibility, and duty, and therefore are usually conservative by nature. Bedrock loyalty and attention to detail combine to produce good-quality ministries. These churches are at their best when they conduct ministries in which hard work and responsibility count for a lot, especially if the church's expectations for membership support those values.

So many people are eager and willing to serve.

Particularly when it comes to holidays and other special events, Fellowship churches like to organize programs well in advance and pay careful attention to all the details. They will put forth tremendous amounts of time and energy in doing what they consider their duty. They are willing to serve long, long hours so that when they undertake a task, they complete it. They believe hard work is good, and they must earn their time for recreation.

An illustration of our strength in this regard is Vacation Bible School over the years, a bread-and-butter ministry, which has been a wonderful means of involving people of all ages in our church life and ministry. I rejoice in seeing people come together to serve in that way though it is usually a hard week.

Because of their conscientiousness, Fellowship church members like to know exactly what they are supposed to do in a ministry before they start in order to feel confident that they have the necessary skills. This is why a positive, supportive, and harmonious ministry environment is essential for them.

A lot of people have the spiritual gift of helps and service.

Fellowship church members are loyal to difficult people in their social network and will persevere with inconsiderate friends, relatives, neighbors, and work associates after others have given up on them. The people of these churches are gifted at ministering to the practical and mercy needs of people and can therefore be overworked, imposed on, and taken for granted by those who are selfish and insensitive, and do not appreciate them for what they do.

We take all our responsibilities, promises, and vows very seri-ously and love the fact that our church members bring the same degree of commitment to their ministries and relationships. Since we have strong values and a clear work ethic, we under-stand and respect each other's need to live in harmony with our heartfelt convictions. There is rarely a lot of gray area where we are concerned, and we naturally understand and accept this shared characteristic. We have high standards of personal con-duct and appreciate that we are rarely asked to compromise on what's important.

A negative tendency for these churches is a kind of credit-and-debit-sheet assessment that can develop within the church. Although new people may not understand this entitlement system, an invisible measurement compares what each person has put into the church and what the church has put into each person. People who are not used to such a balance sheet system find that they have incurred some kind of unexplained obligation in people's thinking. They seem to be indebted to the church for "service rendered," and in time that unspoken expec-tation can become burdensome.

As we live in accordance with our new nature in Christ, we experi-ence radical freedom from selfishness in greater ways and the genu-ine desire to love and serve others because we have been so loved and served by God in Jesus Christ. These motivational realities of the Gospel of grace can profoundly influence the modes and meth-ods in which we choose to communicate with others.

43

The Bible on Conscientious Service

Matthew 20:26–28—"But whoever would be great among you must be your servant, and whoever would be first among you must be your slave, even as the Son of Man came not to be served but to serve, and to give his life as a ransom for many."

Luke 6:31, 36—"And as you wish that others would do to you, do so to them. . . . Be merciful, even as your Father is merciful."

Philippians 2:3–4—"Do nothing from rivalry or conceit, but in humility count others more significant than yourselves. Let each of you look not only to his own interests, but also to the interests of others."

Orderly Planning

Planning and predictable routine are important to Fellowship churches. The people appreciate well-organized ministries that coordinate them to work toward personally meaningful goals. Fellowship church members sometimes need gentle nudging to move beyond their comfort level, because they can worry a lot about relatively small things. They function best when they can set goals ranging from daily objectives to long-range ones.

We tend not to be drawn to flashy type ministries.

They are super-dependable, but never happy serving in situations where the plans are constantly changing; instead, they operate most comfortably in situations where the rules are well defined. Not likely to feel comfortable with only general instructions on how to accomplish a task, they don't like being left on their own without a set of definite procedures. They function best when the plan lays out the instructions in a methodical, systematic, and orderly succession of steps.

We slip into our traditional roles both naturally and comfortably. People in our church pull their own weight and generally work well together, keeping our well-organized church running smoothly.

For instance, if a Fellowship church decides to conduct a summer mission trip, the people begin months in advance to gather accurate information on costs, save money, and make lists of what to take. This means knowing exactly who is going to be in charge of what aspects of the mission. They have a talent for executing routines that call for repeated, sequential procedures.

I have sensed a reticence to spend the money we need to do effective outreach, and I feel that this will likely be an area of disagreement as we continue to grow and more of us continue to strive to grow. Conservative financial values are important to our church.

Fellowship churches focus on providing practical help and services for others through the organizations they serve. They are often self-effacing in getting the job done and are willing to make necessary sacrifices, especially for their church family. They will go to any amount of trouble, when it makes sense to them, to help those in need.

When we re-carpeted the church and had to move all the pews out, lots of people and kids were here to help. It went more smoothly than we expected.

The Bible on Orderly Planning

Luke 16:10—"One who is faithful in a very little is also faithful in much."

1 Corinthians 14:40—"But all things should be done decently and in order."

1 Corinthians 15:58—"Therefore, my beloved brothers, be steadfast, immovable, always abounding in the work of the Lord, knowing that in the Lord your labor is not in vain."

Appreciation for History and Tradition

Fellowship churches value their sense of history and continuity with past events and relationships. Adhering to an established way of doing things and doing them well is valued and respected. They appreciate traditions and the conservation of resources. They treasure rituals, mottoes, and procedures to the point that people feel welcome only as long as they accept those traditions and practices. Their sense of personal obligation and commitment to continuing traditions and perpetuating church institutions gives Fellowship churches their characteristic of bedrock dependability.

> *We are truly blessed by many of the traditions we keep: gathering on the first day of the week to partake of the Lord's Supper, the study of God's word, regularly engaging in public and private prayer, and returning to the Lord a portion of our blessings. These God-given traditions help keep us strong in the Lord's service and prepare us for heaven.*

When no one else can be found to take on some task, they will often rise to the occasion—especially if they see the task as a way of carrying into the future what they have received from the past. Their demeanor is businesslike and they seem unflappable, regardless of the situation. They determine to finish what they start. This stable outward countenance contributes to the confidence that others feel in their abilities because of their quality of dependability.

> *In all we do we should first seek to please the Lord, and follow the traditions he has given to us. Then we should be considerate of what is good for our neighbor. And we should seek our own interests lastly, for Christ himself taught us the tradition of service.*

The Bible on Tradition

1 Corinthians 11:2—"Now I commend you because you remember me in everything and maintain the traditions even as I delivered them to you."

2 Thessalonians 2:15—"So then, brothers, stand firm and hold to the traditions that you were taught by us, either by our spoken word or by our letter."

Change

Change can be difficult for the Fellowship church, and rapid changes can lead to great distress. As a result, Fellowship churches believe in the incremental theory of improvement and are usually suspicious of large-scale renovations of the programs of the church. These churches dislike surprises and are most at ease when they are in familiar surroundings, enjoying activities they have planned. They need lots of information and support to deal effectively with change. Only when the church initiates such changes in small steps are the people comfortable with them. Churches can seem to have a built-in caution light when it comes to change.

> *We don't rush into things. We have a steadiness about us. If we see something we would like to change, we're still not going to rush. We're going to do it in a way that is not going to offend as many people as possible. It's probably good to have the steadiness and not rush into things.*

In a changing situation in which they do not have experience, Fellowship churches can feel lost and overwhelmed. Meetings may occur to discuss policies and to preserve traditional practices but not often to brainstorm or discuss new directions or ideas. As a result, they may have particular difficulties with visionaries who do not seem to appreciate "the way we've always done it before." They may view extroverted types' natural comfort with "change for the sake of change" as foolish risk-taking, and judge them as irresponsible. If trouble does occur, there will be talk about the good old days. Fellowship churches, with their hierarchy and their standard operating procedures, are not very adaptable organizationally.

> *From my perspective, and I'm an in-the-box thinker, I think we get in a set way of doing things. It's comfortable and easy. Sometimes when we step out, like a few years ago when we had the men's breakfast Bible study it was great at first and then fizzled out. It maybe wasn't comfortable or something. I think we're limited to doing in-the-box stuff.*

The typical Fellowship church does not often recognize that change is coming, so it sometimes has to run over the change before its people realize they have no choice but to respond. Perhaps this reluctance to engage change comes from a sense of continuity with the past, and appreciation for all the efforts others have made to bring the church to where it is. They treasure traditions and feel an obligation to observe and preserve them out of respect and honor for their heritage. For these reasons they tend to be careful about breaking with tradition, setting new precedents, or launching into untried ways.

> *When met with the initial prospect to change, the reaction is usually, "What? Why?" but then given some time and explanation, it is usually okay to change.*

Once engaged in a ministry, they generally try to make the most of it, since the known is preferable to the unknown. However, they can slip back into old ways and ask, "Why change?" They trust the lessons of the past so that when they look to the unfamiliar future, they can sometimes feel apprehension or even dread. Because they might find it stressful to serve effectively in rapidly changing situations, they may be more cautious and conservative than many other churches.

> *We tend to "work behind the curve" and not be ready for growth. We tend to "play catch-up" rather than plan ahead (for change).*

It is important to expend sufficient time and effort to understand the perspectives and emotions of Fellowship church members so there is a clear understanding of what they consider the disturbing aspects of changing events. Fellowship church members often communicate their emotions more subtly, so they need to be engaged through asking appropriate questions that enable them to communicate the "below the surface" issues. These church members tend to resist disturbances to their routine even when the disruption is good for the church. The problem is that the unfamiliar upsets their desire for security and solidity. Explaining how new approaches will help them and the church to be all that God intends can help them deal with their anxieties.

> *The recent board decision concerning whether or not to go forward with the purchase of the land is a good example of how we handle change constructively. There was a lot of discussion, everybody had*

the opportunity to voice their opinion, and then apparently the call was given that we don't do this without prayer. Not I, but Christ. Not my opinion, but what does the Lord really want us to do? I also felt at the congregational meeting people were given ample opportunity to voice their opinion, which you can do when it's a smaller church like ours.

The Bible on Change

Ecclesiastes 3:1—"For everything there is a season, and a time for every matter under heaven."

Matthew 6:34—"Therefore do not be anxious about tomorrow, for tomorrow will be anxious for itself. Sufficient for the day is its own trouble."

1 Corinthians 10:31—"Whatever you do, do all to the glory of God."

Conflict

Because Fellowship churches do not like confrontation and are uncomfortable when people are unhappy with them, they usually try hard to accommodate everyone. However, they struggle in conflict situations and would prefer to sweep things under the rug. Attempting to avoid disharmony and maintain cooperation at all costs, they put a lot of energy into keeping things running smoothly.

It is a tremendous challenge for people in our congregation to confront/truth-tell to one another; we like having a friendly/ harmonious atmosphere so confronting is difficult; we focus on exhortation and do not address confrontational issues hoping that contentious issues/people will just go away.

They can take it personally if others do not take their responsibilities seriously, fail to follow rules, or neglect to follow through on obligations. They are painstakingly responsible with detail and routine, and feel it is important to do the right things in the right places at the right times. They meticulously file in their memory the details from personal, hands-on experience and use that as a reference for the proper way for everyone in the church to do things in the future.

> *Because you're aware of the different perspectives it tends to make a group stronger. Because if we disagree, it should help provoke some thought about ways we could be better, maybe ways we need to change, maybe not totally accepting the other person's perspective.*

The characteristic task orientation of Fellowship churches and calm attention to responsibilities begin to disappear as they increasingly experience stress in the midst of conflict. As they experience more and more stressful conflict, they have difficulty arriving at rational conclusions. Moreover, a state of persistent stress in the Fellowship church can manifest itself in a loss of memory regarding facts and details so that impulsiveness and doomsaying may erupt among the people. At this stage, they tend to accumulate only the information they believe is relevant to their immediate situation. This tendency can be puzzling to the casual observer, who might be surprised to find what specific pieces of information they preserve or ignore. However, retention is dependent on what is important to them at the time.

> *It might be something that's been brewing for a long time. And then it just kind of popped out. A good way to view if there might be conflict would be just some of those little comments that are made or things that just slip out that could give you a clue as to what someone might be thinking. Where we might not feel comfortable sharing how we really feel with the group, we may do so one on one. So that's probably a great way to resolve the conflict. I think just realizing that the group in general is going to try to avoid it is probably a good start in dealing with it in a healthy way.*

Unfortunately, it is a common problem for Fellowship church members not to express their feelings about such issues until pushed beyond their limits. After such an incident they might explode in anger and say things that they later feel they should not have said. Such outbursts can be reduced by expressing their feelings on a more regular basis, rather than keeping them pent up inside. Spiritual and emotional growth for these churches occurs when they realize that they can face the conflict and express how they feel about it.

We don't validate the feelings of those frustrated. We say, "Oh you shouldn't be feeling that way." Or, "You're not dealing with this the right way."

The Bible on Conflict

2 Corinthians 4:8–10—"We are afflicted in every way, but not crushed; perplexed, but not driven to despair; persecuted, but not forsaken; struck down, but not destroyed; always carrying in the body the death of Jesus, so that the life of Jesus may also be manifested in our bodies."

Philippians 4:11–13—"For I have learned in whatever situation I am to be content. I know how to be brought low, and I know how to abound. In any and every circumstance, I have learned the secret of facing plenty and hunger, abundance and need. I can do all things through him who strengthens me."

Decision-Making

Structured and reliable, Fellowship churches will carefully use established methodologies in their decision-making because these churches, with their solid hierarchy and standard operating procedures, like to do things in a decent and orderly fashion. They like gathering practical data for decision-making and enjoy carefully documenting the results. As they work toward accomplishment of their goals, Fellowship churches focus on what worked in the past as the reference point for deciding the issue before them now. They are painstakingly accurate with facts, attentive to details, and methodical in applying them.

We make decisions carefully. There is nothing reactionary or impetuous about it; decisions are thoroughly discussed over a period of time. We are very willing to go to extra trouble to do research, to solicit outside information that would weigh on our decisions or the outcome.

51

Churches may have trouble appreciating the interconnectedness of things, since they naturally pay more attention to specifics than to the big picture. As a result, they continually take in facts, assimilate information, and over time develop a rich and detailed mental storehouse. Rather than trying a new approach, they generally are comfortable applying knowledge gained through experience. Decisions are pragmatic and based on a clear sense of right and wrong as well as a concern for the common welfare. Their primary focus is on using their accumulated data, especially about people, as a base of understanding and acting. When these churches receive additional facts and reassurance about precautions, they willingly amend their original resistance to a decision. Facts based on the church's experience are the evaluator of every new idea.

> *We set goals within a time frame. . . . We saved and planned for years to replace the church carpeting. Thought through it all carefully. Funds were used meticulously and were carefully watched over.*

Laypeople in Fellowship churches may be reluctant to accept the call to leadership at first, but will step in when firmly asked. They tend to support and assist rather than lead; however, they will use their personal influence behind the scenes. Expecting everyone to comply with the church's structure and hierarchy, they will follow traditional procedures and rules. They are at their best as lay leaders when they make plans, organize, set measurable goals, coordinate the work of people, manage resources, and focus on detail to reach practical results. They are especially capable at developing functional structures for the church when there is lack of organization or no measure of achievement. In carrying out the goals of the church, they use their strong follow-through skills.

> *I think of the way the men's ministry is starting. Great questions were asked at the meeting, different angles approached, and we looked from different sides of things. The way things are progressing is being handled very well.*

Because decision-making is likely to be kept relatively private in the Fellowship church, members may not actually see how problem-solving is handled. They are supposed to trust their leaders, and things usually go well when they do. However, if that trust starts to break down, the church can find itself in significant trouble. This is more the case for Fellowship churches than in church cultures where belonging, trust, and consensus are not as important.

> *We usually try to get information from key-decision makers, whether on the governing board or committees, before we actually move on decisions. Then we can look at things more directly and process them and read about something down on paper before we actually have to decide.*

At decision-making meetings, the minority of visionaries in these churches may speculate about untried procedures or uncharted possibilities they believe the church should explore. Fellowship church people, i.e., the majority, can feel overwhelmed and swamped in these brainstorming or "blue-sky" sessions. They can become frustrated easily with those who like to ask, "What if we . . ." because the Fellowship people immediately begin translating others' brainstorms into action plans and to-do lists. They do this to determine the practical consequences and concrete implications not only for the church but also for themselves personally. The Fellowship church members often shift into a defensive mode by mentally making lists of all the data they should accumulate to assess the realism of the dreams of visionaries in the church. This process entails anticipating the many possible flaws in the proposed plans and especially the costs involved.

> *I think a potential source of disagreement among us is that some members are very visionary or progressive and others are very conservative. For example, we've got extra money in the bank that is above our budget needs and the question is how to use it. Will we do more ministries with it or save it for future uncertainties?*

In working with Fellowship churches in their decision-making and problem-solving, it is important to focus on only a single topic or problem at a time in accordance with a system of orderly procedures agreed upon in advance. Remembering that a high value in these churches is the desire for steadiness, issues should be handled evenly and with a peaceful demeanor. Ask the decision-makers to offer ideas about how disagreements might be resolved in such a way that the church does the right thing and stability is restored. In addition, communicate how the decision-makers provide significant observations when they relate their thoughts, concerns, and perceptions in facilitating the plans.

> *There's wisdom behind the way we make decisions because it's not just one person trying to dictate how things should go, it's a group of Elders and it's using Scripture for guidance on how these decisions need to be made. Also, the church body is invited to know all the things that are going on in the church and are included because it's still our church.*

Since many key leaders in Fellowship churches are not inclined to make the first move in communication, it is important to initiate more of the conversation with the people of the Fellowship church on an individual basis in advance of formal decision-making times. Because people in these churches do not like being surprised, make clear beforehand any important issues to be raised with them and then move through the stated agenda bit by bit with no deviation. Also, verify that they comprehend what is being presented since the people of these churches have a tendency to misunderstand proposals. In addition, Fellowship people should not be pressured to agree quickly. Allow them time to absorb new ideas and digest them thoroughly before asking them to make a decision.

> *Our church can struggle with unhealthy communication patterns in the midst of conflict because we expect the resolution process to follow tidy guidelines or because we over-emphasize the literal meaning of words.*

The Bible on Decision-Making

Proverbs 1:7—"The fear of the LORD is the beginning of knowledge; fools despise wisdom and instruction."

Philippians 4:6–9—"Do not be anxious about anything, but in everything by prayer and supplication with thanksgiving let your requests be made known to God. And the peace of God, which surpasses all understanding, will guard your hearts and your minds in Christ Jesus. Finally, brothers, whatever is true, whatever is honorable, whatever is just, whatever is pure, whatever is lovely, whatever is commendable, if there is any excellence, if there is anything worthy of praise, think about these things. What you have learned and received and heard and seen in me—practice these things, and the God of peace will be with you."

Sermon and Teaching Style

Armed with an awareness of the Fellowship church's primary learning style, the pastor, staff, and lay leadership can adapt their sermon and teaching methods to the way the people learn and grow best. Instead of undermining the confidence of the people or frustrating them, the sermon/teaching style should fit the way they learn and lead to their spiritual growth and development.

He has a genuine love for people and people are drawn to him. Though his speaking is not dynamic, he is dynamic in his caring about people.

Fellowship churches prefer to learn in an orderly and evenly paced manner, and thus benefit from structured, well-planned sermon series. They especially appreciate the pastor preaching or teaching through books of the Bible one verse or passage at a time. Loose, unstructured preaching and teaching with unclear outcomes or with a high degree of experimentation or personal interaction does not work well for them. They do not like to explore untried ideas or methods. In summary, Fellowship churches prefer traditional forms of preaching and teaching.

He is unapologetic about what the Bible says. He's willing to offend where the Bible offends.

They respond well to sermons that exhort them to be faithful and obedient to the Scriptures in ways that allow them to avoid center stage and contribute in quiet, practical, behind-the-scenes ways. Down-to-earth illustrations and practical examples are helpful to them in understanding the message. It is important to present facts in such a way that people can link them either to their personal experience or to their values. Being presented with achievable targets in the preaching ensures that they maintain interest and provides them the benchmarks they need to assure themselves of steady progress.

> *I like messages that give me something I can use—practical advice on how to walk the Christian walk. Lately I'm working on areas of my life—time management is a big issue with me right now. Overcoming bad habits or just habits that are not necessarily bad and not that they're sinful or anything, but just not maximizing my talents most efficiently.*

Fellowship churches are most responsive to sermons that teach them how to put into practice what the Bible teaches. They respond positively to sermons and teachings that focus on responsibility, hard work, and the use of one's talents in serving. Effective sermons for Fellowship churches use the pastor or lay leader's personal experiences as examples in addition to illustrations of people in the congregation who exhibit dedicated, reliable, quality service to the Lord.

> *His sermons are real and always communicate something very human about himself in the examples that make us feel that he is just like us. He relates the biblical characters as human beings to help us understand the passage.*

Since dedication to productive, long-term relationships is among the highest values for Fellowship churches, sermons should provide biblical insight into the deepening of marriages, family ties, and friendships. They appreciate spiritual guidance regarding how best to direct the intensity of feeling that makes close relationships their first priority in life. Sermons should apply the Scriptures to real-world problems—especially those linked to the personal interests, values, and goals of the people. Clearly presented biblical expectations, standards, and goals should underline every sermon and teaching.

I like to hear a message that communicates truths I can use in practical terms.

If Fellowship church members have been loyal to their responsibilities and done their duty, they will be mystified how things can go awry in the church or their personal lives. In addition, they will be confused when someone wrongs them even though they have been a faithful friend. Therefore, sermon and teaching series on the problem of evil are important. Fellowship church members tend to be overly self-critical, so messages on the cross and the grace offered in the gospel of Christ will help them experience the warmth and love of God.

> *Our pastor preached on "the righteous suffer along with the unrighteous" and why aren't we spared suffering? He explained what the Bible says about suffering when all around us the winds cause terrible damage.*

Fellowship churches do not respond positively to sermons and teachings in which is there is extensive theological presentation or sweeping statements that are not tied directly to relevant passages of Scripture. The people will think of such sermons as vague and nebulous. These churches appreciate pastors presenting the truth in a straightforward manner without offering too many options. The people of Fellowship churches prefer knowing what the Bible says.

> *Every sermon has a strong application element. Principles are taught. While it's not elementary, it's also not impractical, it's not just simply theory or information.*

Simplicity and directness, unembellished by the preacher's personal musings, mark the best sermons and teachings for Fellowship churches. Preachers and teachers in these churches have to be painstakingly thorough in their preparation since exactness and precision in sermons and teachings are highly valued. Straightforwardness and "bare bones" factuality are characteristics that resonate with these churches. Realistic and concrete, down-to-earth touches will provide maximum impact. Outlines in the form of handouts can be helpful when presenting practical teachings in systematic fashion.

Several have said, "You know, I really needed to hear that to help me with what I'm going through right now." And I think a lot of practical things in his sermons have been helpful to everyone.

Since Fellowship church members have to process so much outside stimulation, they may experience a sensory overload if the preacher is overly energetic or excited. They need the opportunity to reflect quietly without animated distractions in the pulpit. In this way, they will be able to focus their thinking, consider how the message relates to their experiences, and sort things out.

I think of the people in our church as real people, starting with our pastor. No one is phony.

Fellowship churches have a deep gratitude for long-established traditions, customs, and things that the church has passed on from generation to generation. Therefore, sermons and teachings should present the spiritual heritage of the people of God to deepen these churches in their faith. Sermons that take the congregation on a spiritual pilgrimage by connecting them to their historical roots are valuable as a means of grace to these churches.

Thoroughness in his preparation for his sermons and teachings; regularly expounding on what the standards are and what we stand for; willing to answer any questions forthrightly.

The Bible on Communication

Ephesians 4:32—"Be kind to one another, tenderhearted, forgiving one another, as God in Christ forgave you."

Colossians 3:12–13—"Put on then, as God's chosen ones, holy and beloved, compassion, kindness, humility, meekness, and patience, bearing with one another and, if one has a complaint against another, forgiving each other; as the Lord has forgiven you, so you also must forgive."

Outreach

These churches are gifted at interacting with people because they are sensitive to the subtle social signals that communicate the needs of individuals. These perceptions focus their efforts to support those in the community in a warm and friendly manner. It is an important value for them to establish and maintain affable and genuine interpersonal relationships so they can work in tangible ways to improve the quality of life of those with whom they share the gospel.

> *We like having a friendly/harmonious atmosphere so confronting is difficult; we focus on exhortation and do not address confrontational issues.*

Outreach for these churches is conducted within a friendly environment in which the leaders express appreciation, approval, and encouragement for the efforts of those who engage new people. Face-to-face interaction allows members of the church to pursue well-planned and focused efforts that support people in need. Their outreach efforts connect with those who are new by communicating genuine interest in them as people and not as projects.

> *No matter the level of details I give to support ideas (for outreach), I always invite their suggestions about how I could have made my proposal stronger. I usually can incorporate their input and now the document becomes our creation instead of my creation. They are more open to the new idea and more open to accept it.*

Because the members of these churches are perceptive of social cues that indicate displeasure, they are motivated to create and maintain harmony with new people through expressions of empathy and sensitivity. This means they want to do outreach in a cooperative manner, free from conflict and tension with people. Otherwise, they become disheartened and immobilized when people react negatively or are upset.

> *There are multiple potential recipients for mercy ministry in the community, so deciding which families to help and how much to*

help also present their own challenges (and potential for dishar-mony in the congregation).

As these churches build relationships with the unchurched, they are patient with people's beliefs and values, within reason. They show respect for new people through promoting harmony as much as possible even when there is discontent expressed regarding the teachings of the church. It is necessary for these churches to develop plenty of opportunities to interact with unchurched people through-out their programs, because members seldom will reach out on their own initiative.

We have to encourage each other to pursue outreach to friends, relatives and neighbors and be willing to try new things to keep the outreach spark alive. This means we have to challenge one another to initiate social activities or conduct outreach events in the community.

Because they are focused on completing outreach tasks, projects, and initiatives in an organized manner, these churches maintain godly control over their programs by insisting on clear standards, rules, and procedures. They insist on good organization of each part of the pro-gram to ensure that things run as smoothly and efficiently as possible. Because they value using procedures that are sensitive to people, they involve as many members as possible in making decisions about the best ways to do outreach.

It seems each move was done quite well and the change handled well; there seemed to be very little disruption and everything was organized well. The majority was always in favor of the changes and supported each change.

These churches prefer to engage in service-oriented ministries that communicate their servant attitude toward people in the community. Through the exercise of their gift of helps, they expend considerable energy attending to the physical and social needs of people, and follow through by providing practical, hands-on assistance. However, these

60

churches are already busy being faithful to their current commitments and can feel overwhelmed by more demands on their time and energy. As a result, they want any new outreach efforts to fit within their current organizational structure and ministry system.

> *When our members positively respond to crisis, they'll often take on work to benefit the church and show practical thoughtfulness and concern for the comfort and security of others. Time and again, I have been blessed and learned from their example of how to be other-centered and serve others even when they are struggling and are tempted to serve themselves. Providing food, child care, transportation and prayer for each other are common ways for them to express love practically to one another and help take the edge off. Their reliability and determination to "be there" for each other is inspiring.*

In their presentation of the gospel, they communicate best through attention to the details of the Scriptures. Therefore, they begin presentations with the details of the gospel—and build toward the big picture. However, the level of detailed information considered necessary by these churches to communicate the gospel effectively can seem like overkill to some.

> *When it comes to information and details, most people in our congregation assume there is safety in numbers: the more the better. This need can become a huge source of energy drain for a few because they prefer much less information and details to make their decision and take action.*

They can assume so many responsibilities in meeting the physical and social needs of the members in their churches that they are not able to muster the energy to engage in outreach. The response of members when exhorted to do outreach is, "We aren't even meeting the needs of the people in the church, so how can you tell us to meet the needs of people outside the church." They become so overwhelmed by the problems of people in the church that the needs of the unchurched in the community are overlooked.

I do not get the sense that there is a universal appreciation of God's "big picture" and his grace. Most prayers, it seems, are more focused on the individual and relieving their distress than on the glory of God. The pervasiveness of man-centeredness as opposed to God-centeredness is a primary concern.

The challenge is that the percentage of people in Fellowship churches who suffer from chronic pain or other long-term physical maladies is higher than for any other type of church. Therefore, these churches can become so caught up in ministering to the physical suffering of people that the spiritual needs of people are overlooked. Instead of communicating a biblical understanding of suffering for God's glory that enhances spiritual growth, the time and energy of the people is absorbed by the focus on God healing the physical problems of people.

The routine I have seen here has been that members have a long history of complaints until they eventually see a doctor. The doctor runs a series of tests or refers them out for tests. Sometimes the tests have been inconclusive or no physiological cause has been found or another series of tests is ordered. The chronic illnesses cause the focus of prayers at the church to be for the health and safety of others. Prayer is not primarily seen as a means of grace, or a means of kingdom work, but as a means of expressing care and concern for others.

Many are attracted to these churches because of their vivaciousness, high energy, warmth, enthusiasm, and willingness to help people. They are very active, energetic people who have a desire to be around others. Fellowship churches are able to help their members become gentler, more compassionate, and more connected to the people whose paths they cross every day in their neighborhoods and places of employment. They naturally develop common interests with neighbors and enjoy spending time with others, doing things such as cooking, gardening, collecting, or enjoying nature.

About a third (over 30 percent) of our adult Sunday school members who did the spiritual gift inventory indicated that they thought they had the gift of mercy. So mercy ministry is "right up our alley" since we are people-focused and want to help in practical ways. The congregation has been blessed with a number of its members with mechanical abilities (carpentry, plumbing, electrical, construction, etc.). There are also a number of our members who have the gift of hospitality as well as others who are gifted to meet needs (cooks, nurses, willing cleaners, willing to provide rides, child care, tutoring, etc.).

The members of these churches are gregarious people who like discussing current events, their various activities, and their reactions with others. They possess good social skills because of their ability to understand other people's feelings and motivations. They need and want to talk out almost everything regarding the faith with people in their network of relationships. And since they are planners and doers, they make quick decisions and typically have several outreach projects going at once. Because they are naturally organized and productivity oriented, they gain satisfaction from drawing new people to Christ and the church.

Our biggest strengths I believe are interpersonal. We are very good at functioning as a large church family, and I think our abilities lie in being able to assist each other, meeting whatever needs come up for different individual families or members. I think the abilities and the strengths of the church really lie in assisting one another, in emotional support, and this is a key element—benevolent fund assistance.

They are good at paying close attention to present circumstances and seeing clearly what needs to be done. As a result, they are likely to lead active, busy lives and be involved in many projects at the same time. They are appreciated for their natural compassion and sensitivity to the needs and feelings of others. They bring harmony and goodwill to almost any ministry opportunity in which they find themselves, while at the same time imposing order and structure on any situation—gently, yet firmly.

The elders of the church are very good at rising to the needs of crises within families, whether it be financial, relational or on guidelines to leading a Christian life and encouraging a church member to get back on the right path. That is our biggest strength—the interpersonal connectedness and the love that's shown here. Everyone here who is a member feels like they truly belong to the larger family of God.

They desire a close and harmonious connection with people in the community, and become stressed when there is tension in their relationships. They need lots of verbal affirmation through the expression of people's loving compliments and being given credit for their high productivity. They have to develop a thicker skin so they don't take things quite so personally. In their zeal to reduce tension and maintain harmony, Fellowship church members can tend to avoid issues of contention in regard to matters of the faith or put such a diplomatic spin on things that they can create mistrust. They need encouragement to exercise courage to speak their minds about matters of the faith, even in the face of skepticism.

Relationships are so highly valued that the threat of confrontation (in evangelism) and working through differences and problems redemptively feels too overwhelming and risky. As a result, "peace-faking" is second nature.

These churches are exceptionally in tune with specific individual needs and especially sensitive to the relational nuances that open up opportunities for sharing the gospel. They are good at initiating discussions, developing intimacy, and carrying on outreach projects. They are especially capable of acting on their impulses in reaching out to new people and helping them assess their personal values. However, they can become so involved in other people's lives that they take on others' burdens, which can make them feel overloaded, unappreciated, and resentful. These experiences can contribute to stress and result in discord.

A lesson I've learned is that as I become more assured of God's approval, desire, and love for me through the righteousness of Christ, I have more motivation and confidence in revealing what I really think or feel or what my real needs are in a situation. Assured in

Christ, I'm free to accept a higher level of risk and rejection in order to speak the truth in love and move forward.

Fellowship churches want people in their communities and networks of relationships to listen, without judgment, to what they have to say about their relationship with the Lord, rather than having them simply point out why it is silly to believe as they do or immediately discount what they have experienced.

We have the opportunity to help each other grow and develop in important ways and become less prone to disappointment and hurt by learning to be a bit more objective in our decision making. By speaking our minds more assertively in the safety of our relationships, we can begin to learn how to avoid being taken advantage of by others. And together we can gently encourage each other to take some calculated risks and try new things.

Fellowship churches appreciate individualized, practical training in outreach in which the leaders begin at the first step and move methodically toward the last. By working through each part of the program in an orderly manner, participants will be more at ease with their responsibilities. During the training, Fellowship church members will need to observe others going through the steps of the outreach program. When they are ready to accomplish the assignment, then they will gradually ease into it—one step at a time. Recognizing that Fellowship church members need to go through the steps deliberately is essential to the program being fruitful. The outreach program participants need substantial acknowledgment and appreciation; therefore, events and celebrations that recognize their accomplishments are encouraging to them.

Here are some tactical steps I, as the pastor, have taken at the personal and church levels to help maintain a grace environment and good communications among us. I'm careful to show respect for the people at all times. I'm very intentional in thanking and celebrating them for all their hard and usually behind the scene work they do.

The Bible on Outreach through Fellowship

Acts 2:46–47—"And day by day, attending the temple together and breaking bread in their homes, they received their food with glad and generous hearts, praising God and having favor with all the people. And the Lord added to their number day by day those who were being saved."

Acts 20:35—"In all things I have shown you that by working hard in this way we must help the weak and remember the words of the Lord Jesus, how he himself said, 'It is more blessed to give than to receive.'"

OUTREACH MINISTRIES THAT FIT

- Sunday school programs, especially for children and teens
- Counseling ministries
- VBS/day camps
- Men's/women's special events
- A strong children's program
- A vibrant youth ministry
- Good follow-up of visitors
- Excellent nursery facilities and child care
- Stephen Ministry: a program that trains laypeople in practical care ministries
- Shut-in visitation of friends, relatives, neighbors, and colleagues of members
- Project SHARE: Support, Housing, Awareness, Resources, and Emergency
- Coffee hour refreshments before or after the worship service
- Hands-on activities that engage people's senses, such as remodeling inner-city houses, painting, and repairing
- Youth sports ministry
- Valentine's Day: teams hand out flowers to women at stores or restaurants
- Oil changes four times a year for single mothers and senior citizens
- Mother's Day: teams hand out flowers to women at stores or restaurants the day before Mother's Day

- July 4th Celebration: teams hand out free cold drinks to people waiting for fireworks
- Ornament handouts: The weekend after Thanksgiving, teams hand out Christmas ornaments at stores and invite people to Christmas services
- Gift wrapping: on weekends between Thanksgiving and Christmas, volunteers are stationed at stores to offer free gift-wrapping to busy shoppers
- Tree handout: volunteers decorate Christmas trees to donate to the handicapped

CHARACTERISTICS OF THOSE MOST RESPONSIVE TO THE GOSPEL AS PRESENTED BY FELLOWSHIP CHURCHES

- Produce services that contribute to the benefit of the community
- Appreciate meaningful relationships built on ethical standards
- Value the necessity for leaders in community organizations to have a reputation for integrity
- Like to be associated with established, reliable institutions in the community
- Want to be part of a "family" and collaborate as a team member

VOCATIONS OF THOSE TYPICALLY ATTRACTED TO FELLOWSHIP CHURCHES

Fellowship church members are inclined to be employed in the vocations listed below because the requirements, design, and style of these occupations fit them well. Therefore, it follows that the people in the community in these vocations will be more responsive to the ministry style of the Fellowship church. The following material is adapted from:

- http://www.wsc.edu/advising_services/career_planning/exploration/personality_careers
- Allan, Ross. *Connecting Personality Types with Careers and Jobs*. Washington, DC: United States Department of the Interior, 1999.[1]

Health Care

- Dentist
- Dietitian/nutritionist
- Exercise physiologist
- Family physician
- Home health aid
- Home health social worker
- Licensed practical nurse (LPN)
- Medical/dental assistant
- Medical secretary
- Optometrist
- Optometrist/optician
- Pharmacist/pharmacy technician
- Physical therapist
- Speech pathologist
- Veterinarian

Fellowship churches enjoy helping people physically as well as spiritually and mentally. Therefore, these churches attract those who focus in their vocations on health care, including prevention and instruction that helps people learn to take care of themselves. Many Fellowship churches specialize in teaching people how to make good decisions. Therefore, those in the health-related vocations will find people in these churches who have values similar to theirs.

Those in the health-care field are attracted to Fellowship church people because of their ability to work directly with other people in a helping capacity. Whether a prospective member is a physician, nurse, or other practitioner, Fellowship churches enjoy using the health-care professional's skills to help make the lives of people easier and less painful or traumatic. These churches excel in ministries that require hands-on application of practical skills and adherence to standard operating procedures, practices that are also required of those in health care.

Education

- Athletic coach
- Bilingual education teacher
- Child-care provider
- Elementary school teacher
- Home economics teacher
- Special education teacher

Fellowship churches teach by personal involvement and example. Because Fellowship churches find it rewarding to help others by teaching them basic skills, younger students and those with special needs are especially drawn to these churches. Working directly with young children appeals to the natural energy and enthusiasm for shepherding exhibited by Fellowship churches. There is often a great deal of structure and order within a school setting, an environment that many of these churches find comfortable. Fellowship churches also enjoy being physically active and teaching others physical skills and the importance of working as a team.

Social Service/Counseling

- Alcohol and drug addiction counselor
- Child welfare counselor
- Community welfare worker
- Employee assistance counselor
- Social worker (elderly and child day-care issues)

Fellowship churches are strong supporters of their communities, and often volunteer their time to establish and maintain civic services. The personal connection of helping individuals and families overcome problems and become productive members of society is rewarding for Fellowship churches. Their ease and facility in meeting people and speaking to groups makes community action ministries satisfying for them. Those involved in counseling and social services are often attracted to Fellowship churches; they share the enjoyment of helping people in very specific and profound ways. Fellowship churches tend to be conservative and traditional by nature, and enjoy working within the context of existing programs where they feel they can make their maximum contribution. It is in these community programs that they impress those in the social services and counseling vocations and draw them to their churches.

Business

- Account executive
- Credit counselor
- Human resources/training
- Insurance agent
- Management consultant
- Marketing executive: radio/TV/cable broadcast industry
- Merchandise planner
- Office manager
- Personal banker
- Public relations
- Real estate agent/broker
- Receptionist
- Retail owner/operator
- Sales representative (tangibles)

Fellowship churches appreciate the opportunity to meet people, and work hard to achieve their goals. They enjoy the contact with people along with the active, busy pace that characterizes many business environments. Those in the vocations that serve people on a more personal level, such as real estate or personal banking, are motivated to establish positive relationships with people and then work vigorously to maintain those relationships. Since these traits also characterize Fellowship churches, business people feel understood and accepted when they attend services at these churches.

Vocations in public relations and marketing require the strong interpersonal and communication skills most Fellowship church members possess. Because of the organizational skills they hold in common, both these churches and the business vocations give careful attention to details, and follow through on all project coordination. The same is true with those in the sales-oriented vocations who experience success using their interpersonal skills, their resourcefulness, and their sensitivity to the needs of others. Those who sell tangible goods, such as merchandise and real estate, especially resonate with Fellowship churches.

Sales/Service

- Caterer
- Customer service representative
- Flight attendant
- Fund-raiser
- Funeral home director
- Hairdresser/cosmetologist
- Home health-care sales
- Host/hostess
- Sports equipment/merchandise sales
- Travel sales

Fellowship church members often gravitate to the service industries primarily because of their ability to work directly with people and provide services that help make an experience more enjoyable or less stressful. Those in the sales/service fields have similar interests and skills—especially needing to be steadfast and dependable during difficult times, and rise to the occasion to help take care of details during a crisis. For instance, customer service representatives, who must show an inordinate amount of sensitivity and concern for others in their work, will often feel at home in the Fellowship church. Most Fellowship churches are warm and gracious and make excellent hosts/hostesses, which means that those in the restaurant or catering business will be appreciated.

Clerical

- Bookkeeper
- Receptionist
- Secretary
- Typist

Because Fellowship church members are often able to perform routine tasks with unerring accuracy and usually have the facility with numbers required of bookkeeping, they have empathy for those in the clerical fields. Since these kinds of workers sometimes feel isolated and unappreciated, Fellowship churches are uniquely qualified to make them feel understood and included in the church family.

THE CHURCH OF RUTH

Ruth provides an ideal example of earnest and selfless adherence to duty and affection for family. The behavior of Ruth in refusing to desert Naomi, her mother-in-law, and persevering with Naomi as she returned to her homeland of Judah, results in the affluence and joy that become hers through marriage to Boaz, and in the respect she receives as an ancestor in the royal lineage of King David and the Messiah (Matt. 1:5). Therefore, she is a model for the most significant values held by the Fellowship church.

Ruth, which means "a female friend or companion," was a native of Moab who married Mahlon, the son of Elimelech and Naomi, who were refugees from a famine in Israel during the time of the Judges, around 1100 B.C. When both Mahlon and Elimelech died, Naomi determined to return to her own family in Bethlehem of Judah, and Ruth decided to go with her, even though her mother-in-law exhorted her to stay in Moab where she could have the security of her own family and the possibility of re-marriage. Ruth responded with these magnificent, heartfelt words: "Do not urge me to leave you or to return from following you. For where you go I will go, and where you lodge I will lodge. Your people shall be my people, and your God my God. Where you die I will die, and there will I be buried. May the Lord do so to me and more also if anything but death parts me from you" (Ruth 1:16–17).

Ruth remained with Naomi, journeying with her to Bethlehem, where they arrived "at the beginning of barley harvest" (Ruth 1:22). Ruth went out into the fields to gather grain to feed herself and her mother-in-law, and while gleaning she was noticed by Boaz, a relative of Naomi. When he heard that Ruth had returned with Naomi from

Moab, Boaz spoke kindly to her and gave her permission to gather barley not only in the field but also among the sheaves already harvested by his workers. In addition, he allowed her to receive food and drink along with his reapers (2:1–16).

When Ruth asked why he was being so kind to her, Boaz responded, "All that you have done for your mother-in-law since the death of your husband has been fully told to me, and how you left your father and mother and your native land and came to a people that you did not know before. The Lord repay you for what you have done, and a full reward be given you by the Lord, the God of Israel, under whose wings you have come to take refuge!" (Ruth 2:11–12).

She was thus able to return to Naomi in the evening with over a bushel of barley (Ruth 2:17). When Ruth explained that the bountiful harvest was the result of the kindness of Boaz, Naomi counseled her to seek an opportunity to tell Boaz the claim she had on him as the nearest kinsman of Elimelech, her deceased husband. Ruth followed her advice, and Boaz promised to fulfill her request provided the nearer redeemer, who was still living, would not perform his duty (3:1–13). Since this relative was unwilling to do so, Boaz obtained from him a legal release and then took Ruth to be his wife (4:1–13).

The method that Naomi suggested and Ruth adopted to encourage Boaz to act as her redeemer (chap. 3) appears, according to our standards, to be morally objectionable. Judged, however, by the traditions of that time it was not. Boaz, who was an honorable man, praised Ruth for not looking for a husband among the younger men and was not offended at the way in which she had approached him and asked to become his wife.

Upon the birth of their son, Obed, the women of the city congratulated Naomi, who became the child's nurse, because the continuation of her family line was now assured. The women of Bethlehem also exalted Ruth as the devoted daughter-in-law who meant more to Naomi than seven sons, the ideal number (Ruth 4:15). The result for Ruth was security and blessing through the birth of Obed, King David's grandfather (Matt. 1:5).

This book of the Bible presents as an example the manner in which Ruth responded to a very human predicament with godly behavior that resulted in the Lord restoring to her the happiness of a peaceful and prosperous home. Ruth is a remarkable example of faith, perseverance, hard work, and compassion, especially in relationship to a member of her family, and therefore the godly attributes she demonstrates serve as a good model for the kind of values held in high regard by the Fellowship church.

6

The Inspirational Church

Spiritual and Relational Discernment for
Individual and Community Transformation

SUMMARY STATEMENT

Almost any people-to-people ministry where personal, sustained contact is involved capitalizes on the willingness of Inspirational churches to accept new and different people. Because they are concerned with people's relationships and are able to monitor the concerns of individuals and groups within the church, they are able to adapt their programs to meet genuine needs. In ministry situations, Inspirational churches are sensitive in their handling of people, and work hard to avoid giving unnecessary offense. If people's needs are in conflict with the schedule, then people will come first. These churches engage in ministries that require organization, clarity, and an interest in people's emotional, intellectual, and spiritual development. They focus on what the Bible teaches about how people should be treated, and then communicate these values to people working in their ministries. Outreach for Inspirational churches is a natural extension of their energetic, people-oriented, and organized style. See Table 5 for a summary of these characteristics.

Table 5: Characteristics of the Inspirational church.

Strong Points	• Take their biblical values seriously and want others to do the same • Loyalty, commitment, and responsibility are essential values
Challenges	• Take communication for granted—believing they are understood and their good intentions are accepted as genuine • Just as they are accepting, they assume others are accepting towards them
Primary Ministries	• Instruction and discipleship that relates to people, their needs, and Christ centered aspirations
Ministry Tempo	• Rapid pace, highly relational
What Inspires Them	• A ministry environment that is people oriented, supportive, and organized
What De-motivates Them	• Ministries being disorganized, indecisive and haphazard
Under Stress	• Looks for faults rather than solutions • Disconnects from people • Discontinues listening or taking into account people's needs
Decision-making	• Reflects their ideals and promotes harmonious relationships with others
Desires	• Lively and enthusiastic ministries that apply warmth and vision to help people be all that God created them to be in Christ
Priority	• Focus on individuals changing things for the betterment of others
Church Ethos	• A spirit of harmony with encouragement given for all to fulfill their calling
Outward Appearance	• Willingness to cooperate with one another
Gains Self-Assurance Through	• Caring concern and willingness to become involved in people's lives
Fears	• Being discovered as incompetent and unworthy

MISSION STATEMENT

Inspirational churches are called by God to exercise their spiritual discernment to analyze people, issues, and relationships within the body of Christ in light of biblical teaching, to develop suitable strategies to empower the healthy transformation of individuals to impact the community, nation, and world for the advancement of the kingdom of God.

Theme verse: "A new commandment I give to you, that you love one another: just as I have loved you, you also are to love one another. By this all people will know that you are my disciples, if you have love for one another" (John 13:34–35).

INSPIRATIONAL CHURCH CHARACTERISTICS

People Development

Their uncanny ability to understand people and say and do just what is needed to help them grow and develop makes Inspirational churches adept in their preaching/teaching ministries. They are talented at articulating the underlying needs of people and helping them to grow in spiritual maturity. (Note: quotes in this chapter are from Inspirational churches who have been promised anonymity.)

> *All of the pastors are willing to be vulnerable. They are willing to share how they are having to make changes and grow spiritually and in every way. Our assistant pastor was willing to share with the church as an illustration how he struggled when someone needed a band-aid (i.e., help that he felt was trivial) and in that way show his struggles, shortcomings, and weaknesses.*

Inspirational churches are valued for their warmth and consideration—when it comes to people, they will give careful thought to what is best for each individual. They develop new and interesting ways of looking at things as a means to inspire and motivate others to be the best they can be as uniquely called people of God.

Enthusiasm, entrepreneurial style, flair, zeal, idealism, and passion are some of the descriptions I think are particularly true of our church. I think that comes out a lot even in our announcement times. You see lots of different people up front taking on leadership—they are really passionate about even the little tiny announcement they give. You can tell there's a lot of excitement going on.

Relationships

Inspirational churches put a priority on gathering with friends and people new to the church in a small-group context to discuss biblical and relational values. Almost any people-to-people ministry where personal, sustained contact is involved capitalizes on their giftedness. Adept use of their biblically driven insights about the inner needs and desires of people enables them to win friends, influence people and, at the same time, avoid compromising entanglements.

Yeah, in general I think we're a very people- and relationship-oriented church. Not perfect, but I think in terms of the terminology that's used in sermons and emphases from our leadership and average people in the church. I don't know if that's something in the water . . . people are just desperate for relationships.

Inspirational churches respond to classes that present subject matter relating to people—their needs, their aspirations, and their character. This church is comprised of people who have great depth of personality; because they are themselves complicated, they can understand and interact with complex issues related to people.

We are not afraid to experiment with different people's ideas and do not mind asking for people's input.

Because it is important for them to know and be known by others, they strive to develop intimate, spiritual relationships with people in the church. Therefore, they put forth much effort to make their friendships warm, caring, healthy, and positive.

*People are a strength of the church . . . our relationships are deep
and they come easily for the most part, . . . we're bonded.*

Inspirational churches are concerned with people's relationships
and are able to monitor the concerns of individuals and groups within
the church.

*I have a friend who's very different from me and his response is
always, "Well, why isn't someone sitting us down and telling us
exactly how this is going to happen, exactly how we're going to split
groups, or exactly when the training is going to take place?"*

In ministry situations, Inspirational churches are sensitive in their
handling of people and work hard not to give unnecessary offense. They
can be hurt rather easily by others and therefore are tempted to isolate
themselves from one another.

*One area of challenge or difficulty is our being so relationally ori-
ented that we become very people pleasing, reactive, sensitive to
criticism—a little bit emotionally over-reactive sort of thing.*

Their talent for communication is directed toward applying
Scripture to people's hearts in a personalized way. In general, their
great ability with language focuses on describing and resolving
people-related issues.

*The pastor applies things from the Bible to my life on a regu-
lar basis. He speaks the truth and it is genuine and it is hard.
He doesn't skirt around it, he gets down to the tough stuff and
tells people what they need to hear, and I think that is very
valuable.*

Relating Well to All Types of People

Inspirational churches are sensitive to people. Members are careful listeners who can discern other people's needs. These churches
will attract those who place a high value on meeting the genuine
needs of people.

A lot of empathy. People are willing to enter into other people's pain wherever they are struggling relationally or physically. There is a sense of compassion and care for other people. We will pray or take a meal or send a card and in other ways there is a culture of care: people for people.

These churches are interested in all sorts of people, and are likely to be able to understand and relate to every personality type. They enjoy having access to a wide variety of information sources, and like to bring together disparate ideas to create new models and concepts to support their fundamental beliefs.

We are willing to see the points of view of others; we are tolerant of a variety of opinions.

These Inspirational churches discover that an important part of their mission is their ability to exercise spiritual discernment to analyze life, people, and relationships within the body of Christ in light of biblical teaching, and then develop strategies that engage individual and community challenges for the advancement of the kingdom of God. They can sense good and evil in people, although they seldom can tell how they came to know.

[Our leadership] does have an uncanny ability to understand people and say just what needs to be said, which makes them naturals for counseling people in the church and community.

If they find themselves in a task that does not involve talking—or does not permit some amount of socializing—these congregations may find it a painful challenge to curb relational interactions in order to get the ministry done.

We are de-motivated by routine, detailed tasks and analysis.

These churches often have a special place in their hearts for their leaders (pastors, teachers, and other leaders).

That's often the case that churches reflect the personality of the leader, especially with church plants like ours, because you're starting from scratch, so the people you're attracting are people you're jibing with.

Relational Insight and Support

In general, Inspirational churches are charming, warm, gracious, creative, and diverse, with richly developed insights about what makes people behave as they do. The pastors of Inspirational churches work hard in their study to ponder the meaning and implication of passages of Scripture, sounding the depths of each verse and exploring their richness to develop insights on human behavior. The aim of these pastors is to understand people by gaining insight about their makeup and motivation, and then to communicate with people accordingly.

I focus on the people as individuals and determine which ones appreciate change and which ones don't. Then I can make sure I am communicating with those who don't and informing those who do. I understand that knowing your people and how they relate to change is a big part of having things run smoothly.

Inspirational churches exhibit an environment that is people oriented, supportive, and organized. They excel at bringing out the best in people while warmly supporting them. Their face-to-face relationships are intense, personable, and warm.

Our pastor shares the pulpit with the staff even when he is in town as an expression of his supportiveness. He wants to support the staff in what they do because he values them for themselves. He doesn't see them as secondary.

These churches develop ministries that help people live their daily lives in accordance with biblical principles. This church value entails supporting members in their quest to give themselves to what is meaningful, and encourages personal growth toward maturity.

There is not a fear of taking risks. We like variety and a lot of new challenges. There are a lot of different kinds of Sunday school

81

classes. Recognizing there is a great variety of people and ages, there is a terrific smorgasbord of ministries and opportunities to help people take the next step.

Inspirational churches prompt support and enthusiasm for their new ministry initiatives because the people know that the staff and lay leadership have their best interests in mind.

One of the young men is so loyal to the pastors and works harder than he should because he wants things set up the way the pastors want it set up and they can count on him. He is very loyal to the pastoral staff.

The Bible on People Development

Matthew 13:52—"And Jesus said to them, 'Therefore every scribe who has been trained for the kingdom of heaven is like a master of a house, who brings out of his treasure what is new and what is old.'"

Acts 14:20–23—"[Paul] went on with Barnabas to Derbe. When they had preached the gospel to that city and had made many disciples, they returned to Lystra and to Iconium and to Antioch, strengthening the souls of the disciples, encouraging them to continue in the faith, and saying that through many tribulations we must enter the kingdom of God."

Visionary

Inspirational churches are reservoirs of creativity, imagination, resourcefulness, and vision that inspire insight and growth in their members. As a result, this type of church is more comfortable talking about its vision than many other types of churches.

We all try to have a common vision and work to create that with our community.

Change in the surrounding community stimulates Inspirational churches to develop and apply their vision of God-honoring possibilities to create positive blessing for people. This church prayerfully studies in the Bible what can occur in the lives of individuals and the community through the transforming power of the gospel, and then relates that calling to the people, working with them to bring the vision into existence.

> *I think the church has such a clear idea, a vision and sense of calling to the city. I feel it's not just something that people just talk about. I feel that it's something the church shares. And the people in the community really feel it and want to be a part of it. And I think that's exciting.*

For Inspirational church members to become fully involved in a ministry thrust, their imagination and vision have to be stimulated. Therefore, the people benefit from expository sermons, books recommended by the pastors, multisensory presentations, workshops, and small-group discussions. Stimulating the vision of these people is not difficult because they tend to find the silver lining in even the most meager signs of progress in their circle of friends, relatives, neighbors, and associates and, of course, in themselves.

> *I think people want to take ownership too, as far as serving. I just did a little study on how many of our members are serving actively—about 80 percent; and that's just amazing for any church, especially a new church that has grown rapidly to four hundred in attendance.*

Expansive Outlook

The driving force of Inspirational churches is in their global-comprehensive perspectives, which generate a constant stream of ideas and possibilities. The dynamic nature of their outlook moves this church from one project to another with the assurance that the next one will be even more significant and exciting than the one before.

> *We are always challenged with maintaining the balance between developing community among ourselves and accomplishing the church's larger vision to reach the city.*

83

It is tempting for these churches to elevate the needs of individuals above the corporate health of the church. However, they need to stay aware of their God-ordained needs as a church so they do not sacrifice themselves as a spiritual community in their drive to help a few.

> *I think our greatest challenge is to continually stress community. I think we have done a good job so far, but we always have to come back and keep checking that we are in correct balance.*

Their broad perspectives free these churches to act spontaneously and insightfully on an event-by-event basis as new opportunities arise. When other types of individuals and churches scoff at Inspirational churches because of their drivenness, they are not able to defend themselves. The problem is that they do not understand the nature of their expansive outlook and therefore cannot explain what motivates them.

> *Initiative, leadership, and vision are our strengths.*

Because they take disapproval personally when it comes from the community, they can be wounded by it and resist or, more often, they will redouble their efforts to change what was rightly criticized. Nevertheless, it is difficult for them to look at criticism objectively, which potentially limits their ability to learn from their mistakes. Even so, they usually do well in working harmoniously with those close to them through cooperation in the implementation of their goals. On the other hand, overconfidence in their expansive vision of the future can sometimes make them stubborn.

> *After one of my sermons, this college kid came up and wanted to criticize me about what I said. Not the time—right after you pour your heart out and someone comes and says it was bad.*

These churches can juggle an amazing number of responsibilities and ministry projects simultaneously with tremendous entrepreneurial ability. Their exceptional skills in working with groups arise from their willingness to see the points of view of others, be tolerant of a variety of opinions, and generate enthusiasm for a worthy task.

We have always been a group of leaders . . . people who have ideas and wherewithal and desire and motivation to create, do, start things, follow through with things.

They possess an unusual ability to relate to others with empathy, taking on themselves the concerns of others for the purpose of imparting a divine influence on the minds and souls of people.

To be doing God's work in our area—it's very powerful to feel that with the people that are sitting next to you, just so filled with what God is doing for the city.

These churches' people-communication skills and their enthusiastic creativity are communicated effectively to others during their ministry efforts.

Our pastor can feel the needs of the body very well and he's very sensitive to those. And it comes out relationally one on one but he's also very good at communicating that from the pulpit each week.

Driven by Ideals

Inspirational churches minister from the foundation of their ideals and drive themselves to conform to a high standard of excellence or even perfection. They are compelled by what they believe in, and seek to serve where their values and ideals intersect with the needs of people in the church and community.

Because people's needs are taken so seriously, we can have an undercurrent of conflict and turbulence beneath the cooperative surface.

Because of their preference for closure and completion, Inspirational churches tend to be "doers" as well as dreamers. When there is a discrepancy between their performance and their ideal, they struggle with guilt to a degree that other types of churches can't comprehend. They are highly committed to their beliefs, goals, and strategies and strive to be perfectly aligned with them.

We are idealistic and can sometimes create unrealistic expectations for ourselves and others.

When these churches take on a new ministry task, face a fresh challenge, or accept a new responsibility, their very first step is to size up the situation, look at how things can be done to include people and help them grow. The accomplishment of the task is not always the highest priority, although this church does like to have things organized.

Our enthusiasm gives us exceptional skills in working with groups because we are warm and outgoing, able to include others in our conversation and activities, facilitating interactions.

The Bible on Vision

Psalm 143:10—"Let your good Spirit lead me on level ground!"

Colossians 1:9–10—"And so, from the day we heard, we have not ceased to pray for you, asking that you may be filled with the knowledge of his will in all spiritual wisdom and understanding."

Life Transformation

Inspirational churches continue to seek transformation in every area of their individual and corporate lives as they are brought more fully under the lordship of Christ. They need to feel as if everything they do in their church and community life is in sync with their biblical value system—with what they believe to be right.

There has to be a lot of flexibility when you are working with children so people are willing to cover for one another on Sunday mornings with the nursery. We sometimes wait for the other workers to come but are willing to cover for one another.

Inspirational churches put a lot of energy into identifying the best system for getting things done, and therefore constantly define and re-define the priorities in their church life.

If people's needs are in conflict with the schedule then people will come first. The pastors are sometimes late because they get involved in intense conversations that come ahead of the schedule. They will get phone calls from people that throw off the schedule but that's okay.

These congregations are deep, intuitive, caring, peace-loving people who are equally at ease working with the personal and analytical spheres of life. These characteristics make this church valued by the community as a warm, supportive, and giving ministry.

We are a relational church that reaches out to new people at church events as well as to the people in our community. We deeply care about people and put our concern in action, especially during times of need.

Personal Growth Strategies

Inspirational church members are particularly interested in discovering how relational dynamics are supposed to work from a biblical perspective. Demonstrations and practical examples are of use to them. They need to have information presented in such a way that it connects to their personal experience and enhances their impact on people.

I think there is a good balance between the teaching of the truth from the Bible with how to apply it to our lives.

The people of these churches have high expectations of themselves and want to conduct their lives in accordance with what they know is right. They determine those standards through study of the Scriptures.

Our pastor speaks the truth and he does it with grace. He doesn't make any bones about it—he gets to the core. Those things are mentioned by people all the time.

Members of these churches learn well on their own or with others; however, they enjoy interacting with other learners and gain much by discussion, sharing information, as well as question-and-answer sessions.

We're so relational that people are wanting to be heard and addressed . . . the desire to be connecting, to have your ideas, desires, vision connected in some way personally.

Emotional Health

Inspirational churches engage in ministries that require organization, clarity, and an interest in people's emotional, intellectual, and spiritual development. As a result, the deep needs of people can overwhelm these churches to the point that they may find themselves overextended psychologically, and an undue burden falls on them and their families.

We're so relational and we want to talk and we want consensus.

Within Inspirational churches, there will be strong efforts at communication, both written and spoken, in order to keep everyone involved. However, there will be times when communication will wane because the leaders have to take time to think and renew their emotional and spiritual being.

I like the members' Web site where people can go to get updated information and it makes them feel like they are in the inner circle where there is information only members are privy to.

Inspirational churches excel at ministries that focus on the big picture, involve new perspectives, and lead to a better understanding of the spiritual and emotional needs or potential needs of people. They easily recognize the deeper issues below the surface of people's thinking and behavior. And, of course, they are genuinely concerned about the well-being, health, and psychological welfare of those people.

Even though a lot of people don't like our getting bigger and want to drag their heels, we have talked about it and had meetings where we have asked them to share how they feel about it, and asked what they are worried about, [whether] they [are] scared about losing the sense of community.

Characteristically, the people of these churches have strong empathic abilities and are aware of another's emotions or intentions even before that person is conscious of them. This empathy leads to the double-edged nature of this church's calling, because its compassion communicates deep concern for people but at the same time can cause considerable personal discomfort and pain. Under the stress that results, Inspirational church members can become rigidly narrow in their opinions as well as ill-tempered.

> *I was sort of naïve about why people are at the church—people are really just here to be with other people. Sometimes we just look like a Starbucks. It was difficult to recognize that and not become judgmental.*

The Bible on Life Transformation

2 Corinthians 3:3—"And you show that you are a letter from Christ delivered by us, written not with ink but with the Spirit of the living God, not on tablets of stone but on tablets of human hearts."

2 Corinthians 3:18—"And we all, with unveiled face, beholding the glory of the Lord, are being transformed into the same image from one degree of glory to another. For this comes from the Lord who is the Spirit."

Community Life

Inspirational churches tend to place a strong ministry emphasis on reaching into the external community, where they work with people and issues according to how their biblical values interpret them. Duty is an important motivation for these churches, because they approach life with a sense of godly responsibility.

> *We are responsive to people and their needs. A girl who worked with the youth was in need of a car and some people provided that for her.*

These churches gather impressions from their interactions with members as well as new people, and then consider how those people might be released into ministry in more fulfilling ways. This helps them translate their ideals into reality by means of the people God brings them.

> *In other churches people are just plugged in to spots rather than because that's where they are truly gifted. People get excited about what they are doing here because they feel they fit where they are ministering.*

The leaders of these churches take relational values seriously and want others to do the same. They find satisfaction in helping people find joy and contentment in their lives through spiritual understanding that centers on a relationship with Christ.

> *There was a woman in the church who was struggling financially in the midst of her divorce. But she still gave scholarship money for another woman to go to the retreat this coming weekend. She saw this as part of her calling to be loyal and supportive of others.*

A Bottom-Up Philosophy

The sovereign Lord communicates to each church community the specific calling he has uniquely ordained for it by the giftedness of the people he providentially brings to that church. When armed with an understanding of their God-given strengths, talents, and ministry passions, in addition to awareness of what aspects of ministry God has blessed in the past, Inspirational churches are able to focus on serving in ways they will find most abundantly used by the Lord.

> *From the first day I came to the church, it was apparent to me that the church was interested in helping people not only develop as persons, but also as leaders. . . . The fact that we meet with each person to help them determine their gifts and where they will fit in ministry in the church is huge.*

Personalized Worship

When Inspirational churches pray, it is natural for them to speak from the heart to the Lord, expressing their love, trust, praise, and sorrow to him. They adapt to personal use all types of prayer and worship forms, modifying each so it communicates their life experience.

> *Our worship is grace-centered in prayers and words as very tangible expressions of what grace looks like. Our pastor reminds us that being a Christian means being in need of grace and it's not about getting your act together; it's falling apart before him. Those are the things that resonate most with me.*

Members of these churches study and teach subjects in which they can focus on the meaning of the material through personalized interpretation and expression. Their ability to identify and empathize with others' feelings and difficulties enables them to enter into the Gospel accounts and apply Christ's words with special meaning to people's experiences.

> *This church has made it very safe to be an absolute mess. We've had prayer and discussion times as community group leaders where we share where we're screwing up. That's transparent teaching.*

Enthusiasm

Inspirational churches are motivated through enthusiastic zeal, building fellowship, communicating commitment, and ministries being led in accordance with the church's core values and mission. When they want to champion their ideals, they speak in a fervent and impassioned manner that fully involves people in their vision. As a result, these churches excel at generating team spirit though their characteristic energy and passion. Inspiring sermons, workshops, group discussions, and multimedia presentations are primary ways by which the church is led.

> *I think we handle change enthusiastically because there are so many things that could happen in the future of this ministry, so there's a lot of anticipation and a lot of excitement.*

Harmony

Inspirational churches value harmony. They want their ministries to run smoothly and pleasantly, with each member making every effort to contribute to that end. Encouraging individuals in their personal callings and finding ways for them to express their gifts in ministry are primary tools for promoting spiritual growth and an important means for bringing about congenial and empathetic relationships.

> *There is intense caring about people and a strong desire to bring harmony into our relationships.*

Multitasking

Inspirational churches can juggle an amazing number of responsibilities and ministry projects simultaneously. However, these otherwise accommodating individuals can become more demanding of themselves and others when pursuing a ministry goal. This is because they are gifted with common sense and recognize that things have to be organized for "people work" to be accomplished.

> *Now that the church is growing, is one maintenance/custodial person enough to handle our huge campus? What about setup for evening and weekend events? Is there a master calendar that lists daily use of all church facilities and is that conveyed to maintenance staff?*

Training-Oriented

This church focuses on what the Bible teaches about how people should be treated and then communicates these values to people working in the ministries. In order to help people improve their effectiveness in ministry, they develop good skills as presenters and trainers of individuals and groups.

> *I was here in the church only two weeks and people got me involved in things. One of our strengths is seeing people and their gifts and putting them to use.*

The Bible on Community Life

John 15:12–13—"This is my commandment, that you love one another as I have loved you. Greater love has no one than this, that someone lays down his life for his friends."

Acts 20:35—"In all things I have shown you that by working hard in this way we must help the weak and remember the words of the Lord Jesus, how he himself said, 'It is more blessed to give than to receive.'"

The Most Fruitful Ministries

When armed with an understanding of the normal strengths and weaknesses of the people, and an awareness of what they truly value, the leaders of Inspirational churches are able to choose ministry thrusts that fit the people and therefore prove fruitful. Using this model to guide the strategies of the church in practical ways is a productive means of developing ministry direction for these churches.

We have a variety of ministries that both provide for people's needs and enable others to serve—youth, children's, seniors, Bible studies, retreats, practical care, classes for the handicapped, technical services, etc.

Inspirational church members function at an optimal level in ministries that help them:

- Establish and maintain warm and supportive interpersonal relationships with leaders and other laypeople
- Develop creative solutions to problems in ministries in which they believe and see positive results of their efforts in helping people
- Conduct ministry in an environment where expectations are clear, contributions are appreciated, and personal growth is encouraged
- Be part of a ministry team of busy, productive, and creative people whom they trust
- Have time to develop creative solutions to problems and then share them with other supportive and caring people
- Serve in an active and challenging ministry environment where they are allowed to juggle several projects at once

- Use their organizational and decision-making skills to lead their own ministry projects
- Experience a variety of ministry opportunities but still work in an orderly and well-planned environment
- Work in a setting that is relatively free from interpersonal conflict and tension
- Be exposed to new ideas and ministry approaches—especially those that will improve the lives of people

The Bible on Fruitfulness

John 15:5, 8—"I am the vine; you are the branches. Whoever abides in me and I in him, he it is that bears much fruit, for apart from me you can do nothing. . . . By this my Father is glorified, that you bear much fruit and so prove to be my disciples."

Galatians 5:22–23—"But the fruit of the Spirit is love, joy, peace, patience, kindness, goodness, faithfulness, gentleness, self-control; against such things there is no law."

Learning Style

Theology is of great interest to these churches if the links can be made to their existing knowledge and skills. However, they learn the most from pastors and teachers whom they like and admire, and who are willing to give them personal attention.

The church, our leaders, and members are warm, enthusiastic, and affectionate.

A wide variety of ministry experiences enthuse these congregations, and therefore they tend to plunge in to new types of ministry—learning as they go. The most effective ways for them to learn are through study, discussion, reflection, and brainstorming. However, they need physical involvement and activity in the ministry to maintain their attention. Therefore, members learn best when given positions of leadership or responsibility such as training people, demonstrating methodologies, organizing ministry team members, etc.

To us, learning is a way of expanding our horizons and a path towards growth and spiritual development—which acts as a strong motivation.

Church members value competence in themselves and others, and work hard to achieve their goals. They prefer to learn in a relationally stimulating atmosphere in which discussion and problem-solving are encouraged. Loose, unstructured teaching that involves a lot of "fun" rather than clear results and purpose does not appeal to them.

It is good that we are made to be responsible for what we have learned. I think that is pointed out in the teaching and in the Gospel class and everything that you need to go home and think about this, that it's our responsibility, not to just sit back and watch.

These congregations are good at conceptualization and abstract reasoning, though they are less interested in facts and figures. Their members are deep, versatile people who are equally at home dealing with the personal as well as investigative spheres of life. They feel more comfortable when their learning is not rigidly structured so they are free to think for themselves.

On Sundays, you don't resolve a lot of issues in your teaching. I think that is good because it causes us to go home and wrestle with the issues ourselves.

Inspirational churches learn best in a small-group context by reading, exchanging ideas, and sharing personal illustrations for application to one another's lives. They are insightful, especially concerning people and, when the Scriptures are related to real life, they experience transformation. They are motivated to learn in order to further their own and others' spiritual development.

We talk about how the truth of Scripture impacts my life and the tension that creates.

Inspirational churches also appreciate participating in independent learning plans such as reading through the Bible in a year or a church-wide prayer project in which goals are set that can be achieved through perseverance and hard work. However, they have to be encouraged to link what they are learning to their aspirations in serving Christ.

> *We don't help people develop little sentences and catch phrases that encapsulate what we believe about certain things. Then when I say this little sentence, I feel OK about it. I know that was my experience and when I had to start picking it apart there were so many holes in it that I couldn't have debated anybody about anything.*

These churches seem to create easily, and almost continuously, positive learning experiences for the people, and interesting ministry roles for church members to play. However, the leaders have to make it clear to the people why they are to be engaged in these activities.

> *I like small groups that speak truth and challenge me to live for Christ. I enjoy a mixture of casual illustrations and basic outlines. But for me, the best studies are those that educate me in the truths of Scripture.*

Inspirational church members are good learners when the subject matter relates to their strong relationship values and people orientation and is communicated by a pastor who is warm and personal. They are stimulated by ideas and are quick to grasp possibilities, especially if the principles are presented imaginatively and in an inspiring manner.

> *I admire their openness and being real—I don't think anyone who speaks or leads worship puts on a Sunday face. They are just real and genuine.*

One of the primary goals for these churches is to aid the progress of people's development and make it possible for them to achieve their potentials as God intends uniquely for each. A second important goal is to help people appreciate God-given differences in people and to teach them how to get along with those who are unlike them because of diverse gifts, talents, temperaments, and passions for serving Christ.

These churches appreciate small-group discussions and conversations as essential sources of information for collecting, understanding, and sorting out opinions and feelings as a means of being responsive and supportive of people. They are especially capable of drawing out the potential each person possesses in his or her calling to serve the Lord.

> *That sermon was about humility and it was about really listening to God and what he has planned for you rather than sticking with what you want to do in the church that's centered on having God use you the way he wants you to be used.*

Inspirational church members learn best in structured situations— worship services, Sunday school classes, and small groups through the week—in which they are able to talk about the lesson and interact with others in the church. However, the pastors and teachers have to set a good example and be respected for their leadership abilities.

> *I think he's very good at knowing the needs of people and applying the Word accordingly.*

The pastors of these churches are abstract in their thought and speech, cooperative in their style of achieving goals, and directive and extroverted in their interpersonal relations.

> *The pastor is always honest about struggles that he has which makes it much easier for me to be honest about my struggles. His style is perfect for us because of the ways we are tempted to manipulate and use people. The ways we tend to be consumers who devour relationships.*

Pastors and leaders of these churches should value harmonious relationships, be able to handle people with charm and concern, and be admired wherever they serve. They should be leaders who are interested in the personal growth and development of the people and not in attending to their own desire for status and social rank. In the minds of these congregations, study of the Scriptures is a way of expanding their horizons and a path toward spiritual growth.

> *I like a sermon that speaks truth and challenges me to live for Christ. I enjoy a mixture of casual illustrations and basic outlines. But for me, the best sermons are those that educate me on the truths in Scripture.*

Leaders of these churches should be able to lead a group discussion or present a proposal with ease and tact. They ought to expect the very best of those in the church, and communicate their confidence in the people with enthusiastic encouragement that motivates action and the desire to live up to the high standards being presented.

> *From my perspective, the best sermons are those that allow non-Christians or those young in the faith to hear the heart of the gospel, to be challenged and encouraged as they hear that God loves them and pursues them. However, these same sermons should challenge the mature believers in their walk with the Lord.*

Pastors and leaders who value accuracy, precision, thoroughness, and adherence to rules more than they value enthusiasm, care for people, creativity, and initiative will not fit these churches very well. Routine, detailed explanations and analysis cool the enthusiasm of members of these churches. They prefer pastors to preach about human-interest issues from a biblical perspective rather than focus on technical subjects that do not connect to everyday relational issues.

> *We love the pastor's personal life stories. It shows that he is like the rest of us and that he is not afraid to share a part of himself with us.*

The Bible on Preaching and Teaching the Word

Deuteronomy 6:6–7—"And these words that I command you today shall be on your heart. You shall teach them diligently to your children, and shall talk of them when you sit in your house, and when you walk by the way, and when you lie down, and when you rise."

Acts 5:42—"And every day, in the temple and from house to house, they did not cease teaching and preaching Jesus as the Christ."

Acts 6:7—"And the word of God continued to increase, and the number of the disciples multiplied greatly in Jerusalem."

PRIMARY GIFTS AND TALENTS

Inspirational Churches Possess the Spiritual Gifts of:

Exhortation. The supernatural ability to come alongside and provide encouragement, strength, stability, and consolation through the application of biblical truth. Those with this gift easily see and communicate the big picture when studying the Scriptures.

> *I think the pastor uses a really good balance of stories with the biblical text. It keeps my attention. But it is not just stories the whole time. It helps me relate to what he is talking about.*

Faith. The gift of extraordinary confidence in God that is unshakable by negative situations, pain, apparent failure, or ridicule.

> *Sometimes things get a little messy but the pastor is willing not to be so high-strung that everything has to be neat and orderly even in the announcement times. Some people might see that as a weakness but it communicates a lot to me, indirectly, maybe more than I realize. But it's OK that he doesn't have it all perfectly ordered so he's executing everything perfectly. I think he would prefer it to be perfect, but I think it's been helpful for me that things are not always orderly.*

Teaching. The ability to understand and communicate the Christian faith so as to make the truth clear to others. This gift involves helping people fully understand a subject, topic, or idea in a worship service, classroom, seminar, workshop, or other group setting.

When the pastor uses Christian terms that maybe not all people would be familiar with, he defines them every time. That keeps the sermons at an accessible level and makes them really valuable.

Inspirational Churches Possess the Talents of:

Conversing. Talking one on one, sharing ideas and relational values, discussing current events, exchanging views, explaining things so there is a high degree of understanding.

I think he has a pretty good handle on the culture and what's going on so that he helps us understand when we are involved in working with people in the surrounding community.

Moderating. Guiding group interactions, hosting a panel presentation, or coordinating discussions between people or groups.

[I like] their openness in being real. I don't think anyone who speaks or leads puts on a religious face. They are just real and genuine.

Problem-Solving. Using biblical principles to work through practical issues that develop in ministry situations, vocational settings, personal lives, community activities, and the like.

There's a high reliance on the gospel of grace, and that's not true of every church. But it keeps us all grounded and focused.

The Bible on Gifts and Talents

1 Corinthians 12:4–7—"Now there are varieties of gifts, but the same Spirit; and there are varieties of service, but the same Lord; and there are varieties of activities, but it is the same God who empowers them all in everyone. To each is given the manifestation of the Spirit for the common good. . . . All these are empowered by one and the same Spirit, who apportions to each one individually as he wills."

1 Timothy 4:14—"Do not neglect the gift you have."

Relational Abilities

Inspirational churches possess strong relational skills under-girded by genuine consideration for what is best for the people. They are driven by genuine affection, caring concern, and a willingness to become involved in people's lives. Almost any people-to-people ministry where personal, sustained contact is involved will capitalize on the abilities of these churches.

> *Things like people being affectionate, ability to develop rapport, see potential in others. All of those types of things are definitely our strengths.*

These congregations possess a remarkable power to influence others with their exceptional interpersonal skills and persuasive abilities. They have the ability to motivate people to do what is necessary for their personal growth in spirituality and for the honor of the Lord.

> *I think we actually do use ministry to get people done. For instance, _____ and I. I didn't know her from anyone in the church and she volunteered to help with finances. And the pastor connected us and we've been great friends ever since. It's really just one of those things, where we are working together toward a common goal, but also forming deep relationships along the way.*

One of their most important skills is the ability to see the positive in people and situations as well as the possibilities for their improvement. Their orientation to people, their desire for harmony, and their relational vision often lead them to initiate ministries that use the skills of individuals in understanding and working with others.

> *You (the pastor) give the leaders the tools to develop themselves. Like with me and Divine Design (a means of discovering ministry strengths), I didn't think I could do that. You really help people to get to places they never thought they could.*

Their relational interactions are driven by an unusually strong desire to contribute to the welfare of others through helping them envision their potential.

We have also provided a place for people who could typically be on the fringe of the church, like creative people. I think it is cool that we are valuing people who are creative and giving them a place and a voice in the church community.

Outreach

Knowing the strengths and blind spots of the Inspirational church can provide a tremendous advantage in outreach efforts. In all aspects of the process, from conducting research about their community, identifying and contacting their network of relationships, developing outreach tools such as brochures, and arranging and conducting outreach visits, these churches will act true to their basic God-given ministry style. Being able to capitalize on their assets and compensate for their liabilities can make the difference between a fruitful outreach effort and one that is unproductive.

The differences among churches are sometimes subtle and other times striking. It is the subtle variation in strategies they implement that makes the real difference between accomplishment and disappointment in an outreach effort. One good example is in this church's tendency to excel at networking, or meeting with and talking to a wide range of friends, relatives, neighbors, and associates about the gospel and the church. Most Inspirational church members will naturally enjoy networking and are fruitful in doing so on a large scale, while other types of churches find it preferable to limit and target their networking to people they already know well.

Some types of churches tend to network with people in a well-defined range, while Inspirational church members can go far and wide to find people often uninterested in issues of the faith. Further, Inspirational church members take networking, like everything else, very personally, and enjoy establishing warm rapport, while other types of churches will be more objective and detached in their style. Finally, some types of churches and their members tend to ask fewer, more structured questions during their networking, while Inspirational church members could ask a wide variety of questions over long periods of time. The point is—there are many ways that different types of churches accomplish outreach effectively.

Possible Pitfalls in Outreach

Potential shortcomings for Inspirational churches in their outreach efforts may include a tendency to make evaluations of people's issues too quickly, be inattentive to the details of people's problems, and take negative responses personally. Under the stress of rejection, they may become overly critical, not only of themselves, but also of those whom they are attempting to reach. They may also begin to see their outreach challenges in an overly clear-cut manner and develop unrealistic dependence on programs that work in other types of churches. They can profit from using their intuition to provide a more expansive perspective of what will be effective in their community, and recognize that harmony with people in their network of relationships is not always necessary or possible.

Outreach Summary

Outreach for Inspirational churches is a natural extension of their energetic, people-oriented, and organized style. They are able to envision a wide array of outreach possibilities, and then develop a plan that includes working through their relational networks to gather information about people in the community, so they can effectively apply the gospel to people's lives in relevant ways.

I think we're a pretty accepting church of new people and different people.

The Bible on Outreach

Luke 19:10—"For the Son of Man came to seek and to save the lost."

Acts 2:46–47—"And day by day, attending the temple together and breaking bread in their homes, they received their food with glad and generous hearts, praising God and having favor with all the people. And the Lord added to their number day by day those who were being saved."

Acts 5:42–6:1—"And every day, in the temple and from house to house, they did not cease teaching and preaching Jesus as the Christ. Now in these days . . . the disciples were increasing in number."

CHALLENGES FOR INSPIRATIONAL CHURCHES

Exhaustion

Because people matter so much to these churches, they often find it difficult to say no to requests for help. Inspirational churches do not like to dishearten people, add to their troubles, or see them discomfited when the churches know they can do something for these people. This hypersensitivity to people clouds their ability to see their own limitations as a church. As a result, they can become exhausted and their effectiveness may be diminished.

I think that when we ignore conflict, we ignore people. But it's hard to relate to someone deeply when you know that they don't see things the way you do.

Hypersensitivity

Being closely in tune with people makes these churches susceptible to criticism, confrontation, and relational difficulties. Rather than dealing with such things objectively, they tend to deal with them personally. They may worry over comments resulting from a difference with someone or an unkind observation until it develops a polluted atmosphere. Such difficulties may make it more challenging for them to maintain a peaceful ministry environment than it is for many churches. Of course, such hypersensitivity may also make it difficult for them to use conflict as a means of spiritual growth within the church.

I was talking to some people about our conflict avoidance and the example they gave in their community group is exactly what happened in my community group. In our study of the book of Acts, when we came to where it is talking about controversial stuff, we were kind of like, 'And that happened' and then moved along because nobody wanted to have a discussion about it.

Ministry Addiction

Unfortunately, the Inspirational church ministry style can foster ministry addiction in pastors and lay leaders. Their tendency is to make an idol of ministry, because throughout their lives these people have received approval for their dedicated work habits. These churches often struggle to believe that God loves them whether they produce or not. Their temptation is to think their acceptance depends on the quantity and quality of ministry accomplished.

These churches are tempted to communicate only the value of people's accomplishments. Thus they do not learn to separate doing and being, performance from their value as a person. Instead of hearing, "The ministry they lead is very productive; they are putting in a lot of God-honoring effort," they tend to hear, "They did a great job leading that ministry; they are good people." Conditional acceptance teaches people in the Inspirational church to depend on others for approval. Many people nurtured in Inspirational churches become overly involved with ministry, usually as a way of avoiding fear of failure and rejection.

Ministry addiction develops in people whose sense of worth and value is connected to what they do rather than who they are in Christ. Ministry shifts from being conducted for the sake of other people to an endeavor that defines one's reason for being. Ministry addicts do not serve because they desire to use their God-given gifts and talents; they serve to prove they are worthy. Though they keep working harder over longer hours, they never feel they do enough to achieve genuine significance for their lives.

Not all people in Inspirational churches who work hard or long hours are ministry addicts. Indeed, many people highly involved in the ministry of these churches may display no indications of emotional and spiritual problems, and may serve in healthy ways. Such persons characteristically experience much fulfillment in their ministries, more than they find in non-ministry related work. Thus it is important to differentiate between the pastor or lay leader who experiences high ministry fulfillment and does well emotionally and spiritually, and the obsessive ministry addict, whose ministry reflects an inflexible, artificial, and often repetitive pattern of feelings and activities that are harmful to them and to others. Ministry addicts are not good workers and not a blessing to the church because they have no emotional and spiritual reserves left for their families and friends outside church.

Ministry addicts characteristically:

- Spend extremely long hours at the church or engaged in ministry for the church
- Boast much about their achievements
- Are unable to put limits on their ministry efforts
- Find it difficult to relax and recreate

Ecclesiastes 2:17–23 is pertinent to those addicted to ministry: "For all his days are full of sorrow, and his work is a vexation. Even in the night his heart does not rest" (Eccl. 2:23). On the other hand, if the unconditional love of God is reflected in the culture of these churches, then objective evaluation, impartial judgment, and positive affirmation of ministry conducted at a high level of excellence will be encouraged. A person who accepts from God the gift of worth, value, and significance will "... eat and drink and find enjoyment in his toil. This also, I saw, is from the hand of God, for apart from Him who can eat or who can have enjoyment?" (Eccl. 2:24–25).

The Bible on Temptation

1 Corinthians 10:12–14—"Therefore let anyone who thinks that he stands take heed lest he fall. No temptation has overtaken you that is not common to man. God is faithful, and he will not let you be tempted beyond your ability, but with the temptation he will also provide the way of escape, that you may be able to endure it. Therefore, my beloved, flee from idolatry."

1 Thessalonians 3:3–7—"... that no one be moved by these afflictions. For you yourselves know that we are destined for this. For when

we were with you, we kept telling you beforehand that we were to suffer affliction, just as it has come to pass, and just as you know. For this reason, when I could bear it no longer, I sent to learn about your faith, for fear that somehow the tempter had tempted you and our labor would be in vain. But now that Timothy has come to us from you, and has brought us the good news of your faith and love and reported that you always remember us kindly and long to see us, as we long to see you—for this reason, brothers, in all our distress and affliction we have been comforted about you through your faith."

Conflict

A problem area for Inspirational churches is their strong dislike of conflict in relationships. They have to discipline themselves to confront misunderstandings quickly and directly rather than allow issues to become larger or more complicated. Otherwise, the people of these churches will not engage in ministries that involve interpersonal conflict and therefore find their overall fruitfulness diminished.

We take people's needs so seriously, frequently we experience an undercurrent of conflict and turbulence beneath the cooperative surface.

The types of ministry styles that cool enthusiasm for Inspirational churches are those characterized by:

- An impersonal environment
- Only standard operating procedures being rewarded
- A serendipitous approach to planning
- Intimidating and argumentative interactions
- Resistance to originality and innovation
- Competitiveness
- Stringent task assessment
- Strong focus on facts and details rather than vision
- A highly organized, unchangeable way of doing things
- Miscommunication among the people

107

I feel like there isn't very much encouragement from people in my ministry. I do feel like I get encouragement from the church leadership, just not the people serving with me. They are always talking to me to say, "You are doing this wrong, you are doing this wrong."

The vision of these churches can also cause conflict when the "way things ought to be" is unable to deal with reality. Idealized relationships usually do not become reality, and even the most accomplished leaders experience opposition.

There was definitely this underlying tension about the discussion but people weren't really being direct about it. And then I kind of felt like the response from the leadership was dancing around a lot.

Inspirational churches are tempted to avoid conflict situations in order to guard their sense of closeness and security. These churches, however, will stifle conflict only to encounter it later in a more severe form when it erupts. It can reveal itself as explosive rage, sudden outbreaks, or disturbing outbursts.

It's almost a passive-aggressive type of criticism or conflict resolution when somebody comes up and says, "Hey, you know what would be something to consider. . . ." It hits at the heart of what you are doing and then they are like, "See you later," and you are left with their comments. Instead of coming alongside to have suggestions with action on their part.

Inspirational churches have to realize that disagreement over issues is healthy, and that working with differences quickly helps to create harmony. Disregarding conflict will not make it disappear. It only submerges it for a time and then makes it worse over the long term.

I have a lot of child care responsibilities and I have people canceling on me at the last minute all the time. Of course they usually have an emergency, and I want to be sympathetic, but it is hard. And I don't know how to really confront them about it, so I end up just breezing over the surface to create some kind of peace.

During conflict, Inspirational church members need to provide one another a lot of support, positive feedback, and reassurance that the key relationships in the church are going to weather this storm. Since they are very tuned in to the conflicts boiling beneath the surface, it is important that their insights and values be listened to and validated. They need to be allowed to voice concerns without being talked out of their perspective.

> *Somebody in our small group wasn't responding and started falling out of community—starting missing meetings and fellowships and always had excuses for not showing up. One of the other group members called him on it and said, "What's up?" He said he cared about him and that he didn't have too much going on to come. Just shared with him in grace, and I think that it has been a pivotal point in our relationship with that person.*

In the midst of conflict, Inspirational church members can become excessively anxious because they try to stifle their negative feelings about the turmoil they sense between people. To make matters worse, they are tempted to ignore the difficulties they have with people they care about. One of their strategies is to try to keep everyone under control.

> *In one of my training classes there was somebody sitting in the back of the room talking while I was presenting. I knew they were talking, but they were too far away for me to get their attention to ask them to stop. But then at the end, they said I should do the training another way. And I thought, "Who are you? You don't know me at all, you didn't ask me at all, and you were sitting back there interrupting my meeting." It just wasn't a good time.*

The leaders of Inspirational churches feel that the people of the church are as important as—or more important than—the mission toward which they are working. They find it especially upsetting when there is a lack of trust or backstabbing among the people.

Say if a person is consistently late all the time to a meeting. You understand that perhaps because of their background that it is a challenge for them that they are working on. But you also need to have a standard that says they cannot be late. How do you enforce that with a person and set up consequences when need be, but not become legalistic.

In the midst of heated conflict, Inspirational church people can become especially critical of themselves and others, even though they are normally concerned about harmony and being appreciated. They can develop a disagreeable and even bitter attitude toward specific people and toward the church in general.

One challenge with conflict resolution is how to do it out of grace, but still hold people to standards, and being very clear that things are not OK, and that they cannot do it again, but also to demonstrate grace for where they are.

The Bible on Conflict

Mark 3:24–25—"If a kingdom is divided against itself, that kingdom cannot stand. And if a house is divided against itself, that house will not be able to stand."

1 Corinthians 11:16—"If anyone is inclined to be contentious, we have no such practice, nor do the churches of God."

James 1:19–22—"Know this, my beloved brothers: let every person be quick to hear, slow to speak, slow to anger; for the anger of man does not produce the righteousness that God requires."

CHARACTERISTICS OF THOSE MOST RESPONSIVE TO THE GOSPEL AS PRESENTED BY INSPIRATIONAL CHURCHES

- Share the church's people-centered values
- Value enduring relationships
- Require innovative thinking grounded in meeting the genuine needs of people

- Energized by personal contact and the collaborative exchange of ideas
- Non-confrontational
- Like a friendly, relaxed atmosphere
- Want the certainty that programs and services are run on schedule
- Believe in and appreciate teamwork

VOCATIONS OF THOSE TYPICALLY ATTRACTED TO INSPIRATIONAL CHURCHES

Inspirational church members are inclined to be employed in the vocations listed below because the requirements, design, and style of these occupations fit them well. Therefore, it follows that the people in the community in these vocations will be more responsive to the ministry style of the Inspirational church. The following material is adapted from:

- http://www.wsc.edu/advising_services/career_planning/ exploration/personality_careers
- Allan, Ross. *Connecting Personality Types with Careers and Jobs.* Washington, DC: United States Department of the Interior, 1999.[1]

Counseling/Teaching

- Child-care worker
- Child-welfare advocate
- Counselor to runaway youth, suicide and crisis, school
- Counselor—career, alcohol and drug abuse, employee assistance
- Home economist
- Nursing consultant
- Nursing educator
- Occupational therapist
- Psychiatrist

- Psychologist
- Social scientist
- Social services worker
- Speech pathologist
- Teacher—health, art, drama, music, English, university, junior college
- Teacher—middle school, high school, language, preschool, special education, adults

Inspirational churches are attractive to those in teaching and counseling positions—including those who work with both adults and children. These people find it rewarding to see others learn and grow. If they value helping others in a group setting, or if they enjoy one-on-one counseling or teaching, they will notice when the following ministries are done well:

- Planning and organizing tasks
- Coordinating groups
- Helping people work more effectively together
- Being involved in team ministry
- Demonstrating responsibility and reliability
- Getting the ministry done with solid follow through

Health-Related Vocations

- Dental hygienist
- Dietitian
- Family physician
- Health education practitioner
- Home economist
- Nurse
- Optometrist
- Pharmacist
- Physical therapist
- Recreational director

Inspirational churches enjoy helping people physically as well as spiritually and mentally. Therefore, these churches attract those who focus in their vocations on instruction and prevention in ways that help people learn to take care of themselves. Many Inspirational churches specialize in teaching people how to make good decisions. Therefore, those in the health related vocations will find people in these churches who have values similar to theirs.

Business

- Administrator
- Human resources worker
- Manager
- Public relations specialist
- Sales associate
- Supervisor

Inspirational churches excel in developing a wide variety of administrative and supervisory ministries so they can be efficient in the way they serve. Therefore, those in the business community who have a talent for organizing people and resources to get the job done, or are involved in sales and public relations, are often attracted to Inspirational churches. These churches may appeal to them if they are especially outgoing and customer oriented in their vocations.

Arts and Design

- Actor
- Artist
- Composer
- Designer
- Entertainer
- Musician

Many Inspirational churches are attractive to those who create ideas or perform for others. If these churches have an artistic bent, they may want to consider developing their ministries in the arts and design. They will need to consider how the people already in their churches want to express themselves and find ways to draw the community into their artistry. Many people in their community choose to express their creativity as a hobby rather than as a career.

Marketing and Communications

- Advertising
- Communications director
- Interpreter
- Journalist
- Librarian
- Sales manager
- Writer

Inspirational Churches often have a flair for expressing themselves using creative language. Therefore, these churches are attractive to those in occupations that allow them to communicate words and ideas. If they are excited by marketing ideas or enhancing communications, these Inspirational Churches might be appealing to them.

THE CHURCH OF BARNABAS

The Inspirational church exhibits many of the characteristics of the apostle Barnabas. This man was an early leader of the church, according to Acts 4:36-37, and was nicknamed by the apostles "Barnabas," which in Hebrew means "Son of Encouragement." According to Acts, Barnabas introduced Saul (Paul), a new convert and fellow Greek-speaking Jewish believer, to the disciples in Jerusalem (Acts 9:27). Barnabas then became primary in discipling the apostle Paul over the next ten years.

When a new church was planted in Antioch in Syria, Barnabas was sent by the apostles to represent the Jerusalem church (Acts 11:19–26). There, he encouraged the church's outreach to the Gentiles and recruited Saul to serve with him as a leader and teacher of the church.

Acts recounts how Barnabas and Saul took the famine offering from Antioch to Jerusalem (Acts 11:27–30; 12:25).

Barnabas and Saul then served together on what is commonly referred to as the first missionary journey, to Cyprus and the Iconium region of Asia Minor, where together they planted four new churches (Acts 13:1–14:28). When they returned to Antioch, they were sent by the church to Jerusalem to work through difficult theological issues with the apostles, which they did successfully (Acts 15:1–35). Upon their return to Antioch, they disagreed between themselves and separated over the question of allowing John Mark to accompany them on a second missionary journey (Acts 15:36–41) because John Mark had deserted them at a perilous point in their first missionary journey (Acts 13:13). In summary, Acts speaks of Barnabas as "a good man, full of the Holy Spirit and of faith" (Acts 11:24) which, as well, describes the Inspirational church.

7

The Relational Church

Energetic, Innovative, and Compassionate

SUMMARY STATEMENT

Relational chursches are effective long-range planners that can easily see the potential effects of an idea, program, or service on reaching people for Christ. They always take the needs and concerns of people into consideration in their planning, and devise innovative and compassionate solutions for the problems people face. Especially through the lively and energetic ministry teams they develop, these congregations help people solve the problems that burden them in a creative manner and from a scriptural perspective. Often clever and funny, these churches find satisfaction in the fast pace and constantly changing dynamic of evangelism. Their emphasis is on the promises of God as they lead people to Christ while exhibiting an infectious, energizing style that motivates these people to make positive changes in their lives that honor the Lord. See Table 6 for a summary of these characteristics.

MISSION STATEMENT

Relational churches are called of God to meet the deepest needs of people—including those outside of Christ—by organizing and

Table 6: Characteristics of the Relational church.

Strong Points	• Energetic, creative, and warm • Stimulated by new people and new ideas • Enjoy helping people achieve their potential
Challenges	• Can be anxious during transitions • Have difficulty with people's negative feelings
Primary Ministries	• Developing a vision of the future that energizes people • Enthusiastically and articulately communicating with people in ways that are inclusive
Ministry Tempo	• Fast-paced and activity-oriented
What Inspires Them	• Cooperation, diversity, teamwork, harmony, creativity
What De-motivates Them	• Insensitivity to people
Under Stress Become	• Overwhelmed with possibilities; indecisive • Obsessed with unimportant details
Decision-making	• Tend to procrastinate because they dislike their options being limited • Have strong, people-centered values on which most decisions are based
Desire	• Openness to the moment • Minimal conflict
Priority	• Changes that make things better for people
Church Ethos	• Visionary, exciting, egalitarian
Outward Appearance	• Creative ministry that develops new ideas and programs for people • Idealism that focuses on serving, developing, and growing people so they reach their potential
Gain Confidence Through	• Connection first with what is best for people
Fear	• Being tied down

coordinating events, projects, and activities that help people come to Christ, grow, develop, and be all that God intends them to be.

Theme verse: "A new commandment I give to you, that you love one another: just as I have loved you, you also are to love one another. By this all people will know that you are my disciples, if you have love for one another" (John 13:34–35).

RELATIONAL CHURCH CHARACTERISTICS

Creative

Relational churches influence people's lives through developing relationships and sharing from the Scriptures innovative approaches to interpersonal problems. They resonate with the emotional expression of people and are comfortable with the demonstration of people's feelings. Because they are naturally inclined to help people pursue avenues of growth and development, they appreciate new ideas and ministry approaches as long as their primary values are not violated. They are motivated by opportunities to share their insights and creativity with people especially because they enjoy exploring new possibilities in ministry. (Note: Unless otherwise referenced, the quotes in this chapter are from members of Relational churches who have been promised anonymity.)

> *We like our little eight-person Communion setup rotation and . . . it is nice to have that consistency, but if we are going to be a fruitful, growing relational church, we need to be constantly adding new people to the mix and circulating new people in different areas.*

These congregations are energetic, innovative problem-solvers whose enthusiasm increases with participation in the ministries of the church. Because they are outgoing, gregarious, and activity oriented, they are driven to create innovative ways to reach new people. They are sensitive toward people, and readily identify emotions as they are communicated. As a means of avoiding conflict and promoting harmony and encouragement, they actively solicit others' points of view in problem-solving. Since they are socially at ease and proficient in building relationships, they see structures and rules as temporary boundaries and guidelines within which to reach out to people.

There has been sort of a bubbling up of new ministry activities on the horizon.

Encouraging people to meet together, for emotional support and the generation of new approaches to the difficult issues of life, is one of the primary means by which these churches deal with stress. However, they do well with uncertainty and are open to whatever emerges as long as their relational values are respected. By bringing under control any negative reactions to people and circumstances, they are resourceful when confronted with relational challenges.

We hang on to people if we can get our relational hooks into them.

These churches demonstrate a strong relational orientation that draws out the best in people and motivates them to be all God has created them to be. They build healthy and enduring relationships especially because they have exceptional communication skills that enable them to respond quickly to people's needs—they are not paralyzed by too much analysis. In addition, they are adaptable and able to shift with changing circumstances; they are willing to jump in wherever needed without being particularly concerned about "authorship" or who gets credit. Their contagious enthusiasm projects an attractive image that enables them to create a harmonious community that draws the best from people.

It is true that we strongly support people's efforts to change and do whatever the Lord's purpose is for their lives.

These churches are known for being fun-loving and energetic in their zest for helping people. They are big-picture visionaries who produce innovative, cutting-edge ministries, programs, and services that help people solve their problems, no matter how complex and confusing they may be. As enthusiastic and capable leaders with significant experience in people-oriented causes, they have exceptional insight into the needs and motivations of people. They want their ministry teams to pursue the church's primary vision of making a difference for people through communicating the gospel in word and deed. Driven by their sense of adventure, they respond to new developments and opportunities for outreach, and are eager to try new approaches and take risks.

> *Our members serving at the block party almost immediately struck up a conversation with those in the adjacent booth and the conversation continued throughout the day and through several shift changes.*

These churches prefer face-to-face interaction with people from the very beginning of any task in which they engage. Their communication is personalized, motivational, and creative as they present people with opportunities rather than directives. Their conversations may cover a variety of topics, but will always focus on the needs of people and the blessings promised through the gospel. They are expressive, enthusiastic, and often emotional as they present their big-picture goals and objectives.

> *As we see it, formation is the church taking the shape of Christ as we organize ourselves in submissive worship and intentional discipleship. Formation is about engaging and being engaged by God in any and every form possible that contributes to personal re-creation and embodiment of the Kingdom. This process of formation is a life-long journey that continually leads us to the cross for a fresh hearing of the gospel, resulting in the re-creation of our personal and corporate lives as his church. Essentially, formation is the "what" between God and man.—Missio Dei Church, Portland, Maine*

Relational churches tend to fall into two categories: the Resourceful church that develops and implements innovative curriculum and program ideas for helping people, and the Counseling church that focuses more directly on enlightening, developing, and serving people on an individual basis. The evident appeal of their innovative ministries is the opportunity to continually develop new and original approaches. Brainstorming and bouncing new ideas off similar churches are among their favorite pursuits. They are quick to seize the opportunity to expand their horizons and develop new opportunities for people. These churches are the most vibrant, optimistic, and inspirational of organizations.

> *We are not just a rubber stamp of another church. [We are full of] infectious enthusiasm, confident, good at providing compassionate and supportive counseling as well as creative and enthusiastic lay ministry development.*

These churches work well independently but need frequent, spontaneous interaction with churches that have similar ministry styles to keep their creative juices flowing and make their ministry fun. They enjoy the entrepreneurial process, especially if it offers opportunity for people to find original solutions to their problems. They specialize in being compassionate, supportive, inspirational, and enthusiastic counselors. The topics they teach reveal much about what they value: innovative problem-solving, understanding temperament differences among people, development of listening skills, and strategies for personal growth.

> *It is important for me as a natural enthusiast to remember that a leader is a first intercessor and to encourage not only creativity and hard work, but first and foremost to encourage prayer.*

They are attracted to ministries that make use of their skills in planning and devising enterprising ways for people to serve in line with the church's general goals. To communicate clearly and help people see new and more positive ways of living and serving, they use their imagination and sense of humor. A priority for them is the designing of training programs that are enlightening, fun, and relaxed while still being challenging.

> *We respond and adapt as the Lord provides rather than proactively create solutions. This ministry style will frustrate some and cause them to pressure us to change. However, to change this key operating procedure is to change our church in fundamental ways.*

Since they are particularly adept at resourceful problem-solving, Relational congregations like to help people in the midst of crises. Stimulated by new people and novel ideas, they are attuned to personal needs, and especially enjoy helping individuals achieve their God-given potential. Nevertheless, when projects become routine, they may lose interest, because what might be is more attractive to them than what is. In other words, they enjoy the process of developing an idea or a project as they go along, but are not as interested in the more monotonous follow-through.

> One way the scattering of ideas hurts us is that it drains the dutiful people in our midst as they feel the burden to implement all of our schemes. . . . [because] we will start a project and leave them holding the bag.

Their effective communication and leadership skills, added to their fun-loving personality, give them a substantial advantage in building partnerships among people in their churches. They are quick to devise new opportunities for people to serve in accordance with their gifts and talents as they pursue the expansion of their knowledge and ministry experience. Variety in day-to-day opportunities and interactions best suits their outgoing style, because they need quite a bit of freedom to undertake new and possibly risky projects.

> A contributor to conflict and stress in our church is that typically we are creative as opposed to the few who are analytical, more into what is best for people as opposed to those who are more task oriented, and are more considerate of people's feelings as opposed to those who are logical.

They pride themselves on their uniqueness and originality, and therefore want to find places where they can use their abilities to improvise and look at opportunities from an original perspective. Talented at solving problems by overcoming obstacles, they find creative ways to bend rules they consider unnecessary. They place a high priority on ingenuity, working in group settings, adventurous enterprises, and nonstructured ministry.

We have a potential conflict developing because the idea crowd tends to underestimate and is generally clueless about what it takes to bring a significant ministry into being.

These congregations consider it essential to pass their strongly held values and beliefs down to their children, and will strive fervently to create a positive, healthy environment for their growth. These concerns combine to make them especially interested in creating positive relationships with kids that provide them with all sorts of intriguing growth experiences that are fun and motivational. Because these churches are inventive in the ways they develop their youth ministries, they operate at their best in an environment that is fluid and flexible. Their rich imaginations enable them to create attractive and entertaining ministries that in turn enable them to express their genuine interest, affection, and concern for their children.

What to expect: twice a month we'll be doing a Bible study, the other two weeks will be more social. We want to try to maintain a balance between pure social time and an extended time to share what's happening in our lives on these nights. We definitely want it to be fun, but an opportunity to share our lives with each other as well. Sometimes that may just look like talking about the deep stuff while playing ping-pong!—Missio Dei, Portland, Maine

Relational churches radiate passion through their excitement about people and the spirit of fun with which they conduct their ministries. Their inspiring and imaginative manner for reaching out to people is contagious, especially as they engage in counseling, teaching, and helping ministries. Their cheerful zeal makes them among the most vivacious of all the types of churches, especially as their enthusiasm inspires people to join their cause. Their members are energetic and effective catalysts who derive great satisfaction from tapping in to their vast network of friends, relatives, neighbors, and associates to bring people together for mutual growth and blessing.

We exhibit a focus on people-oriented ministry and a warm enthusiasm driven by creative ideas.

123

These churches demonstrate characteristics that might be considered youthful, such as humor, joking, and a zestful outlook on life. When they are committed to the gospel, they are uninhibited to the point of preaching to the entire world about Christ and his life-changing impact on their lives. Their imagination and vitality empower them to be innovative in whatever ministry focus they choose as they are driven to implement new ways of conducting outreach. Their ingenuity and warmhearted people skills communicate that there is never a dull moment with them. But underneath this effervescent charm are hearts fiercely dedicated to proclaiming the meaning of life in Christ to all who will listen.

> *Mercy Hill is committed to a philosophy of community that values the development of people rather than the expansion of an organization or the promotion of an individual. We want to invite them to explore who we are and maybe they will find a home alongside us where they can experience God, develop personally, and impact our community.—Mercy Hill Church, Milwaukee, Wisconsin*

The Bible on Creative Ministry

1 Corinthians 12:4–8—"Now there are varieties of gifts, but the same Spirit; and there are varieties of service, but the same Lord; and there are varieties of activities, but it is the same God who empowers them all in everyone. To each is given the manifestation of the Spirit for the common good."

Ephesians 2:10—"For we are his workmanship, created in Christ Jesus for good works, which God prepared beforehand, that we should walk in them."

Relational

The vision of these churches molds their relational sensitivity into possibilities for people. At times, however, others may feel overwhelmed by the energy and excitement communicated regarding the wonderful plan for their lives. These churches should continually clarify their core values to help them choose which exciting possibilities they will focus on and to help them follow through on their vision for people. Otherwise, people will feel loved by these churches while they are in close proximity, but these relationships will tend to dissolve if they move away.

I think we relate pretty well because we have radars on our heads.

These churches take networking with new people, like everything else, very personally. They enjoy establishing warm rapport with visitors, while other churches may be more aloof and detached in their style. They may feel great pain if the flaws in their relationships become too obvious to them, because they put a lot of energy into developing these relationships. Because they need authenticity and depth in their close relationships, they can feel shame for being a phony, a fake, or an impostor if a relationship dissolves.

Our church's greatest strength is definitely its openness to and care for people of all shapes, sizes, colors, and odors. I say this thinking of the number of people who helped one of our regular attenders move. Let's just say that his hygiene is way below average yet people were willing to pitch in and help. Also recently a newer attendee in conversation made the comment that we are "ridiculously friendly"—a comment that I get regularly in a variety of ways.

Because they strive intensely for harmony among people, these churches can be in danger of losing touch with their own opinions, which they normally possess in wide-ranging assortment. As a result, they are vulnerable to accepting the opinions of others uncritically because they are distrustful of their own judgments. However, their feelings about people and ministry opportunities, both positive and negative, are very intense and often accurate.

One of the things I am finding is that there is always risk when they introduce people to your vision and even to parts of it. The

125

risk is that they won't like it or think it silly and then that will
reflect negatively on them.

These churches have the ability to make strangers feel like old friends. They often try to help people overcome their personal problems by encouraging them to be more positive about themselves. Highly relational types of people who are enthusiastic about life are especially drawn to these churches.

We are a church with enthusiasm and ideas. . . . Our church can be
an energizing place to be—with people brimming with enthusiasm
for the church and for the Lord.

Their understanding about the motivations of people can provide Relational congregations with a way to focus and critique their vision, but their foresight is always primary to their secondary priority of empathy. They like to be free to express themselves, and they want others to feel free to do the same. Their combination of insight and relational understanding enables them to communicate with great clarity to a wide range of people.

It was a classic case of people talking past each other. Some
were working big picture, the forest, while others were focused
on the details, the trees. It was weird coordinating this meeting
as I could see what was going on, yet I almost had to let it run
its course until each group realized what the others' concerns
were and then we came to consensus and a good plan for going
forward.

These churches need to feel they are serving and ministering in accordance with their true identity, walking in step with what they know is right. But in order to do so consistently, the members need to feel the same level of support and encouragement that they believe they give to others. When they experience conflict within the church, they withdraw and process what they are experiencing. As a result, they may get in the habit of constantly asking one another what they are feeling and how they are doing. Because chronic relational tension can devastate these churches, they have to reestablish harmony before there are long-term destructive effects.

> *During the process of the last several months, I have fallen into second guessing decisions, have gotten angry and bitter at times, and spent excessive time and energy dealing with those causing the conflict and their displeasure. In addition, I have not built up the current leaders God has sent our way.*

These churches are enthusiastic, idealistic, flexible, and focused on relational needs. Because of their talent for meeting people easily and making them feel comfortable, they have the ability to establish rapport with visitors quickly. Even though relatively few of their close friends with ideals similar to theirs will feel comfortable in these churches, they are likely to have acquaintances from all walks of life. These are warm and sociable churches that are keenly in tune with people's relational needs and perspectives and are generally accepting of most people. However, they have difficulty understanding people with strong rationalistic tendencies who do not respond to the enthusiastic warmth of their churches. Moreover, they feel threatened by individuals with a strong orientation toward rules, and usually resist those who want to implement policies, regulations, and procedures.

> *While it is easy for me to communicate with the dominant culture of our church, it would benefit the church if the relational people, including me, learn to follow through on promises. One of the things that came out during our interview time was that follow-through is a weakness of ours as a church. We come up with great ideas and begin strong but then get distracted easily.*

The Bible on Relational Ministry

John 13:34–35—"A new commandment I give to you, that you love one another: just as I have loved you, you also are to love one another. By this all people will know that you are my disciples, if you have love for one another."

John 15:13—"Greater love has no one than this, that someone lays down his life for his friends."

Energetic Ministry

Churches with this ministry style can inspire and empower any group of people. They have a wide range of personal contacts because they expend much effort in maintaining both career and personal relationships. For them, ministry is an opportunity to use their dynamism, creativity, and adaptability to initiate a variety of endeavors that provide solutions to problems experienced by people they care about.

> We have a lot of energy—a high degree of selflessness overall and a willingness to frequently get outside our comfort zone. Our youthfulness probably goes along with our high energy.

Some of these churches set up sports teams and leagues in which they are able to challenge themselves, release their energy, and maintain their physical fitness. Lack of stimulation and a constraining atmosphere can cause them quickly to lose interest and motivation. They must make these ideas and projects their own if they are to maintain interest. As the connection with their creative imagination diminishes, so does their characteristic enthusiasm, optimism, and vigorous approach to the ministry effort.

> The pastor is not the "be all and end all" in the church; the people are the church and they are more than capable of using the gifts that God has given them to serve the Kingdom.

Lively, friendly, and energetic, these are fun-loving, easygoing churches whose members seek to find meaning in all they do. Their ideal ministry provides diversity, novelty, challenge, and freedom from rigid oversight; it is idea-oriented and creative, and has lively, spirited people enjoying themselves and their efforts. These churches should develop a ministry plan in advance so they don't waste their inspiration and dynamism in ministries that don't fit them, and so they are able to stay focused on what they are uniquely called by God to do.

An overabundance of ideas can do a couple of things. One thing mentioned is that it can scatter our focus. I know this is true for me personally; I am a great starter but not always a great finisher. This is not tied to lack of industriousness but rather to the fact that something "better" has drawn my attention. As an institution this can be deadly. I think of this in light of Jim Collins' "hedgehog effect" in his book Good to Great. *We need to be clear on our vision and calling and stay focused on it.*

Relational church members are initiators of change who are keenly aware of possibilities and have a gift for invigorating people through their contagious fervor. They take their relationships very seriously and are revitalized by being around people. Having opportunities to use their creativity in a flexible, open, exciting environment as they interact with people is what stimulates them in ministry.

Our pastor took into account the other views that were expressed. And he recognized that we were not all in one accord on this issue, so we backed up a little bit and came at it with a different approach. A key aspect of our church culture is community and attendance to relational dynamics.

These churches are often called to act as leaders in the community because of their eagerness and passion for developing solutions for the problems people face. Their zest for their projects can be so compelling that they disregard their time and energy limitations, sometimes forgetting their need to take breaks from ministry activities for rest and nourishment. Therefore, ministry team development is an important solution to their tendencies toward physical and emotional exhaustion. They need to be zealous about helping members of their churches find places on ministry teams that fit their gifts and talents. In this way, the ministry responsibilities are shared more evenly.

We are very enthusiastic about getting involved with a lot of projects, but in reality it is a minority of people in the church that end up following through. In some senses this is a good complementarian way of ministry, because the majority of us have a bit

129

more derring-do and willingness to go outside of our comfort zone than other types. While those others are naturally better at systematic, persevering follow through—those characteristics can feel a lot like a root canal for many of the rest of us in our church. The danger comes in when one group in the church begins to feel burned out and withdraws; something that is possible for us if we are not careful.

Lively and vivacious, they can sometimes be smothering with their zeal, but nevertheless Relational church members are highly valued for their genuine warmth and high ideals. They lavish their love and affection on the people in their churches as they make every effort to help in gracious and compassionate ways. They use the same insight and zeal to identify options to help people that they use to get around the barriers erected by resistant people. However, they do not let obstacles discourage them; rather, they feel invigorated by the challenge.

At Citylights, church isn't just a once-a-week event—it is about relationships! Citylights is a place where people can make new friends, deepen existing friendships, and be loved and accepted as they are. We know that authentic relationships are hard to come by, and that's why we're making them a big emphasis!—Citylights Community Church, Long Beach, California

These are typically active, effervescent churches which conduct spontaneous ministries that adapt well to the rapidly changing environment of urban life. Meticulous work, time limitations, and unnecessary structure drain strength from these churches, and the longer they operate in such conditions, the more likely it will take its toll on their fruitfulness in ministry. These churches enjoy having a positive influence on people by inspiring and discipling them in ways that contribute to their growth and development.

At Citylights, they'll find real people—in other words, people just like them. It is not about a building, a place, or an organization—our church is about people! The people at Citylights are friendly, warm, non-judgmental, welcoming, and loving. Come as you are, and be yourself.—Citylights Community Church, Long Beach, California

These churches are stimulated by working in a team setting with ingenious and imaginative people who explore new ideas and opportunities for significant impact on other people. Because they are driven by ideas rather than the follow-up activities that develop ideas into programs, members can become bored and may neglect details once their thinking has moved past the inspirational stage. They take pleasure in creative problem-solving, especially as they brainstorm with others about possible solutions.

> *The great thing about this team ministry system is that it accomplishes tasks in an efficient manner, it gets different people involved (hopefully in an area where they are gifted), and it keeps decisions and happenings in the church at a more grassroots level, as people take their reports back to their primary groups.*

These churches are leaders in their communities as organizations likely to take charge when an initiative needs visionary people. Their strengths in ministry are undergirded by their boundless capacity to see a variety of options and develop innovative approaches to problems. These churches are catalysts in their communities because their warmth, eagerness, and resourceful ideas empower people to do more than they thought possible. They place a high priority on helping people achieve the potential God has placed within them.

Here is a grace-centered leadership principle—never say "no" to God.

The Bible on Energetic Ministry

Ephesians 1:17–19—"That the God of our Lord Jesus Christ, the Father of glory, may give you a spirit of wisdom and of revelation in the knowledge of him, having the eyes of your hearts enlightened, that you may know what is the hope to which he has called you, what are the riches of his glorious inheritance in the saints, and what is the immeasurable greatness of his power toward us who believe."

Colossians 1:28—29—"Him we proclaim, warning everyone and teaching everyone with all wisdom, that we may present everyone mature in Christ. For this I toil, struggling with all his energy that he powerfully works within me."

Small Groups

Because a primary characteristic of Relational churches is their interest in new possibilities for the lives of people, they are attracted to involvement in small groups. During group activities, people are exposed to new ideas, new people, and new opportunities to serve others. Interactive, vigorous, and energetic learning groups stimulate these people spiritually and intellectually—especially if the participants are involved in one another's lives outside of group times. The members of these churches involve themselves in these groups with trust and optimism—assuming the groups will be welcoming, safe, and uplifting.

> *Small group ministry is a high value for us. Currently we have close to 90 percent of our regular attendees (89 families) involved with small groups. But involvement is only half of the story. What I mean is that every person (couple) in a group has a job. The job may be leader or co-leader, it might be assimilation or mercy ministry, it may be children's ministry or missions.*

These churches are less fruitful when there is disharmony, because they depend more on healthy relationships among people in the church than they do on almost any other priority. Their desire for spontaneous, flexible structures is a significant aspect of the ministry style of these churches. However, churches with well-defined government structures will have an advantage if the nature of a small group turns destructive, because those churches are more empowered to enforce the relational values of the church.

> *Every decision, from church government to personal counsel, will be subjected to light of Scripture. We will set the church solely upon Scripture. We will choose to speak when the Scriptures speak*

and be silent when the Scriptures are silent.—Mercy Hill Church, Milwaukee, Wisconsin

These small groups give people an opportunity to talk about ideas with other members, along with an opportunity to ask questions and develop new ideas. Also, these groups provide the means for people to communicate their strongly held values and beliefs regarding the necessity of spiritual growth in one another's lives. Their attention is never passive or casual, never wandering in this regard, but always directed toward this purpose.

Believing intimacy in relationships to be a significant means of personal growth and development, these churches wholeheartedly embrace the opportunity for closeness with one another. Animated, positive, and inquisitive, they are eager to communicate with one another over new ideas and experiences as a means of developing close friendships. These interactions lead them to be increasingly transparent with one another and reveal how much they love each other.

We want to create a place that people look forward to going to where they can share the state of their soul, whether in a time of great joy and excitement, or great sorrow and darkness. We want to create a community that will encourage one another wherever we find ourselves and help build one another up.—Missio Dei Church, Portland, Maine

These congregations place a high priority on finding in their churches a few trusted people with whom to discuss problems and personal matters so that these friends become confidants and soul mates as well as those with whom they have fun. On the other hand, if their relational sensitivities are wounded, they become uncomfortable sharing themselves deeply even with their friends. This is because they tend to take any disapproval personally and become annoyed and upset when friends communicate negative judgments of them. They view this as communicating displeasure or dissatisfaction with them personally.

We want to encourage each other to keep pursuing Christ as the center of every aspect of our lives. Our desire is to create a group where we not only feel God shows up, but the real us shows up as well, not the character that we create who is always "fine."—Missio Dei Church, Portland, Maine

These churches develop small-group ministries that foster growth in people by building relational bridges. However, if their heartfelt concerns are discounted by some of the more analytical people in their groups, they can question their own insights, even though the majority of people may share their perspectives. This self-doubt occurs because they are easily wounded by negative remarks made toward them. Consequently, they can become preoccupied with what they perceive to be a breach in their relationships, resulting in the diminishment of the emotional strength necessary to put the critique in a more objective perspective.

We want to flesh out a context where we are comfortable sharing who we really are, we go out of our way to love one another, we can share the good and the bad, the bright and the dark, we not only look forward to coming, but we don't want to leave, those from the outside will be unconditionally welcomed, loved and immersed inside, the Spirit in our midst is not just a hope, it is a reality.—Missio Dei Church, Portland, Maine

These small groups provide their people with encouragement through the mutual sharing of personal stories of God's work in their lives, opportunities to know and be known by people in turn, and scriptural guidance in discovering their identity in Christ. They communicate these scriptural insights in ways that are enlightening, fun, and challenging. They are compassionate, resourceful, and fervent counselors to one another, helping people in their churches find scriptural solutions to problems. However, because of their relational sensitivity, they can be weighed down by the chronic, more deeply imbedded problems with which their people struggle. Therefore, groups might gradually shift into becoming champions of causes more than healers of troubled souls.

This context will take shape as we gather regularly for prayer, sharing, study, support, socializing, sharing good food and fun, lov-

ing and blessing those that God sends into our lives and edifying them that we might fulfill our mission as "sent ones."—Missio Dei Church, Portland, Maine

The leaders of these groups often find themselves surrounded by people who look to them for knowledge, good judgment, and courage—a reliance that can weigh on them. People in these churches tend to attribute more ability to their leaders than is actually present, which includes feeling that these leaders can see through them—a capability that is usually not present. These leaders feel this burden because they tend to seek new outlets for their creative ideas and approaches to ministry, and they worry that they may lead people astray. Nevertheless, they trust the validity of their insights from Scripture and therefore tend to launch out with zealous enthusiasm in whatever direction their innovative ideas point them. Since they are persuasive and possess good interpersonal skills, the leaders often are able to motivate others in their groups to join them in their creative endeavors.

We want to flesh out a context where we learn to filter life through the text, not filter the text through life; our mission is driven by the "who" not the "what"—Jesus is in the center, not in the periphery.—Missio Dei Church, Portland, Maine

Their style benefits from variety in the ways their small groups interact and learn, since these churches seek quite a bit of liberty in exercising their creativity. They usually seek some modification in the standard way of doing things by adding or subtracting aspects of their ministry approach. Because they look for a variety of opportunities to try original ways of doing ministry, they want freedom from normal constraints. Variety in ministry endeavors suits their talents well because they need quite a bit of latitude in exercising their adaptive ingenuity. They consider intense emotional experiences with the Lord in worship to be essential in their small-group experiences.

Our desire for our LifeGroup is to create a place where we can really incorporate Scripture into our lives and our lives into Scripture. We want to do more than read the text; we want the

text to not only read us, but to send us as well; to live in a con-
stant state of mission.—Missio Dei Church, Portland, Maine

Even though Relational churches have the ability to make strangers feel like old friends, their concentration on developing new and different ways of doing ministry can turn away new people who are looking for the church to be a haven from tumultuous changes. Nevertheless, they have an extraordinary ability to understand the motivations of people after knowing them for a brief period of time. They use these insights, and their ability to adapt quickly, to fashion their groups to relate to visitors on their own terms. However, if they neglect to follow through in developing the relational bonds with these new people, they will have problems with leading them to become dedicated, committed members of the group and church.

Community is to know one another, and to be truly known. All
Saints is a community of people getting to know one another while
we explore together what it means to be a Christ follower. All
Saints welcomes all who believe, doubt, and seek, no matter their
background, religious experience, or place on their life-journey.—
All Saints Church, Seattle, Washington

The Bible on Small Groups

Acts 2:46–47—"Breaking bread in their homes, they received their food with glad and generous hearts, praising God and having favor with all the people. And the Lord added to their number day by day those who were being saved."

Hebrews 10:23–25—"Let us hold fast the confession of our hope without wavering, for he who promised is faithful. And let us consider how to stir up one another to love and good works, not neglecting to meet together, as is the habit of some, but encouraging one another, and all the more as you see the Day drawing near."

Communication Style

These churches typically focus their studies on the concepts, ideas, and principles of the Scriptures, and especially emphasize the

136

teachings on choices and possibilities. If they are emotionally engaged by a subject, or can relate it to the concerns of people, then they will study the topic relentlessly with great intensity. On the other hand, Relational churches lose their motivation when the scriptural focus is on analysis of the details or when facts and figures, accuracy, precision, thoroughness, and adherence to rules are emphasized.

> *We believe that God's truth has the power to change people's lives. We ourselves have been transformed by the truth that we can be reconciled to God by trusting in his Son Jesus Christ and his death on our behalf on the cross.—Alathia Community Church, Issaquah, Washington*

They begin presentations, whether preaching or teaching, with the big picture, goals, and objectives. They present biblical information globally, first communicating its broad shape and the possibilities inherent in it before looking at the detail. This is their pattern, because they view learning as a way of expanding their horizons and a path toward growth and spiritual development. They prefer to interact with the broad ideas of the Bible by focusing on the promises and thinking through the implications and consequences of adherence to its truths.

> *He [the pastor] is a big picture guy, and we noticed that right off the bat when we first came here. And sometimes for people like me—I am much more of a detail kind of guy, so we would come at a Scripture differently. They are going to look at the overall picture of the Scripture and the covenants, and then they're going to interpret the details based on what they see in the big picture. Whereas I am going to look at the details first and try to paint the picture from what I see in the details.—Alathia Community Church, Issaquah, Washington*

These churches are able to grasp complex scriptural concepts and theological paradigms. They are zealous to apply the Scriptures, orally or in written form, to the issues faced by people in order to foster their growth. They are zealous to demonstrate how the truths they have gleaned from the Scriptures are beneficial to people's lives. Their interest in symbols, meaning, and human relationships often attracts them to Scripture passages that help people pursue new perspectives and possibilities for their lives.

> *Small groups are an opportunity for us to get together and support each other as we seek to follow Christ together. By meeting regularly in smaller groups, we can form deeper bonds with one another and better encourage, comfort, teach, and when necessary, confront each other as we strive to walk with Jesus and imitate him in our everyday lives.—Alathia Community Church, Issaquah, Washington*

The Bible on Communicating the Word

Luke 24:25–27—"And he said to them, 'O foolish ones, and slow of heart to believe all that the prophets have spoken! Was it not necessary that the Christ should suffer these things and enter into his glory?' And beginning with Moses and all the Prophets, he interpreted to them in all the Scriptures the things concerning himself."

Acts 8:32–35—"Now the passage of the Scripture that he was reading was this: 'Like a sheep he was led to the slaughter and like a lamb before its shearer is silent, so he opens not his mouth. In his humiliation justice was denied him. Who can describe his generation? For his life is taken away from the earth.' And the eunuch said to Philip, 'About whom, I ask you, does the prophet say this, about himself or about someone else?' Then Philip opened his mouth, and beginning with this Scripture he told him the good news about Jesus."

Characteristic Weaknesses that Bring Stress

When these churches are faced with the drudgery of researching details in order to communicate their vision, they tend to drop current projects in favor of exploring new and more exciting opportunities. Moreover, they may spend too much time in friendly but unfocused conversation, and they may ignore critical deadlines, or delay important decisions until the last moment. They may act prematurely or without hard data to support their decisions and occasionally implement change for the sake of change, without a sufficient rationale. Some projects may be dropped because the leaders try to juggle too many opportunities at the same time. They tend toward disorganization, inadequate follow-through, and inattention to the facts.

> *I think it is appropriate that we as leaders should govern with a certain amount of privacy, but I think what we found was that as much information as we can convey to our people and in as timely a fashion as possible, the better things are going to go. This is an important strategy in leading and communicating with detail-oriented people. I think this is a good rule in general, but I think it is particularly important with the dynamic of our church. When we are making big decisions for people, they should not feel like they are in the dark.*

It is not uncommon for the agitated emotions of their leaders to overrule good, practical sense when they become distracted by the attacks of people with significant personal problems. They can become especially upset when people are critical of them without also being appreciative, or when people reject their counsel without consideration of the impact on the people involved.

> *I think there was a general approachability which was a positive. I think it kept that situation from becoming a nightmare. Approachability is another key element in our church culture that should not ever be neglected. Those who are more task and "bottom line" oriented will find this frustrating about the church because approachability slows down the process.*

During times of relational tension, members of these churches can feel alienated from one another. When continual stress causes them to be anxious, they often become pessimistic about the future, and their faith in their capacity to deal with problems effectively weakens. When the pressure they are experiencing causes them to become self-absorbed, they find the experience to be strange and upsetting. During these times of conflict, they become increasingly anxious about what lies ahead to the point that they begin to expect disastrous events to engulf them.

> *The last month has seen great progress as I have believed the gospel, gotten outside of myself, and driven the vision for the church with grace and love. A few in the congregation have sensed a renewed enthusiasm and are likewise enthusiastic. One of the characteristics of our type of church is that conflict can wear us out. I had not been living in Christ and believing the gospel but rather living in worry, anxiety, and fear of failure.*

The diminishment of people's emotional strength leads to feelings of melancholy and sorrow, which leads them to become increasingly closed-minded regarding the future. They no longer possess the vision to expect anything that differs from their present problems. As relational conflicts continue, their negativity becomes overwhelming. Their dissatisfaction, resentment, and sense of despair over their ability to do anything as well as in the past becomes unbearable. Very little of their normal optimism, tolerant acceptance of innovative approaches to ministry, and amazing perception of future developments will be seen.

> *On the personal side, this battle is costing me sleep, stealing time, energy, and margin from the church and from my family. On the good side it is causing me to run to the cross constantly, to minister out of weakness in what might otherwise be an "Oh, look at what a great, vibrant, and growing church 'I' pastor." It is also causing me to more carefully communicate vision to the church.*

Under the influence of their despondency, the usual discernment of Relational church members becomes misguided and they begin to misinterpret the motivations and objectives of people they trusted in the past. They can become so self-absorbed that they feel compelled to draw attention to their accomplishments to reassure themselves that they are valuable and worthy. As they feel more and more frightened and overwhelmed, they become rigidly nonconforming—especially if they feel too much structure is being imposed on them. During these times, they feel gloomy and isolated, and become increasingly moody and withdrawn.

> *The principles of grace have taken me out of my strengths and weaknesses to a place where God gives me the motivation and the power to trust him, to love those he loves and to love myself as he has created me to be. It is fascinating how getting outside of self and depending on the Holy Spirit actually results in living a life of greater risk, humility, and courage, confidence, and joy.*

The Bible on Stress

Philippians 4:6–8—"Do not be anxious about anything, but in everything by prayer and supplication with thanksgiving let your requests be made known to God. And the peace of God, which surpasses all understanding, will guard your hearts and your minds in Christ Jesus. Finally, brothers, whatever is true, whatever is honorable, whatever is just, whatever is pure, whatever is lovely, whatever is commendable, if there is any excellence, if there is anything worthy of praise, think about these things."

Hebrews 12:1–4—"Therefore, since we are surrounded by so great a cloud of witnesses, let us also lay aside every weight, and sin which clings so closely, and let us run with endurance the race that is set before us, looking to Jesus, the founder and perfecter of our faith, who for the joy that was set before him endured the cross, despising the shame, and is seated at the right hand of the throne of God."

Outreach

These churches encourage their people to create new ideas, programs, services, or solutions to problems in ways that will genuinely help people to be transformed and grow. They want their members to meet new people, learn new outreach skills, and continually expand the kingdom of God by working with a diverse group of people in the community through a variety of outreach projects.

The essence of our vision for Missio Dei is to be a missional community. The heart and soul of who we are is produced by a self-interpretation that understands the church's role in society as a redemptive agent/force, as we live and love the way Christ did. We believe that God is birthing Missio Dei in order to redemptively navigate the pathways of Portland's culture with his counter culture.—Missio Dei Church, Portland, Maine

Outreach for Relational churches is motivated by creative insights, and rarely requires people to handle the routine details or maintenance of programs. Instead, they allow people the freedom to follow their inspirations and to participate in exciting and stimulating explorations into the genuine needs of people in the community.

There are many pathways to the culture of Portland: the arts, single parents (exceeding the national average by some 70 percent), a thriving music scene, stay-home mothers, the Old Port, recreation, immigrants, college campuses, and the list goes on.—Missio Dei Church, Portland, Maine

They want their ministries to be conducted in a friendly and relaxed environment with humor, goodwill, and a minimum of interpersonal conflict. At the same time, they want their programs to be fun, challenging, and always varied while remaining consistent with the beliefs and values of the church. Because they have a priority of ministering in an environment that appreciates enthusiasm, resourcefulness, and imagination, they encourage people to do outreach spontaneously at their own pace and schedule, with a minimum of rules or structure.

I see art studios opening as a place for artists to work, experiment, and connect with each other and God. I see bands forming who have mastered the art of telling redemptive stories. I see mothers starting play groups in order to be intentional about caring for and loving their neighbors. I see students coming together to study not only science, math, and art, but the teachings of Jesus. I see older men and women intentionally investing in the next genera-

142

tion. I see immigrants finding hope and rest in the homes of the Missio Dei community. In short, I see the people of Missio Dei becoming not a church, but a missional community, as we intentionally navigate the above-mentioned pathways of Portland with an authentic Gospel witness. This approach to life breaks down the divide between the sacred and secular, creating an incarnational church on the edge of both gospel and culture.—Missio Dei Church, Portland, Maine

Statements by Relational Churches on Outreach

My vision for Missio Dei Church is to be a redemptive force in Portland, Maine, as we navigate the pathways of Portland's culture with his counter-culture. Our goal is not to preface everything we do with the word "Christian," thus setting it apart from Portland. Our vision is to embody Christ as we create, work, and play with Portland. Our goal is not to start Christian art studios, but studios where the redemptive people of God live, love, and create with Portland. Our vision is not to create Christian music, but music, that tells both the human story and redemptive story well. Our vision is not to create Christian cafes, but coffee houses where people find and nurture relationships in a context that engages the heart and head redemptively. "Exposure" is a ministry created to facilitate the vision of Missio Dei to be a church "in and among" the culture of Portland. As many churches are detached from the culture around them, and subsequently struggle to make their redemptive story relevant, we desire to be the kind of church that encourages our people to be involved in culture and community. We plan to do a host of things together, from watching movies to attending AA meetings. Our desire is simply to think and pray through how we as his church can embody the life and love of Christ to Portland in an authentic way.—Missio Dei Church, Portland, Maine

Aestus is a Missional church, which means we deeply believe that the church was created by God under Jesus' leadership to

143

be a sent entity into the world (just like Jesus) to be his emissaries and messengers of hope, healing, forgiveness, and redemption. This missionality is demonstrated in the way in which we believe people come to a point of truly following Jesus. There first must be a sense of belonging in a Jesus-centered community in which a person must feel they are a participator and contributor regardless of where they may be in their spiritual journey. Through the experience of belonging, the gospel of Jesus is experienced as life, not merely doctrine, and the person is drawn by Christ to believe and embrace that gospel as a new creation. From this place of belief, life-transformation begins and continues for the remainder of our life. Belonging . . . belief . . . behavior—always in that order. Being missional is also seen in our strategy of bringing the life-giving news of Jesus to those who don't yet know him. We intentionally seek to pattern our life after Jesus' strategy of going into the world: Leaving our place of comfort and familiarity as God calls us. Our Mission: To permeate and infuse the world with the culture of Christ's kingdom by embodying the gospel. We see in the gospels that Jesus is sent by God into the world and nothing less is expected of us. And so we strive to be in the world, our neighborhood associations, softball leagues, PTAs, etc., because we believe that's where Jesus is, drawing people unto the Father. We also see that Jesus' message was not to leave the world and hide away in a separatist community, but a message of a kingdom whose values transcended every culture and every era. This kingdom, this spiritual vitality in Jesus, is brought to bear on everything we are and do and in so doing we strive to bless our city and neighborhoods."—Aestus Church, Kent, Washington

We seek to be people who are evangelistically bold. We have a deep passion to see all people come into a saving relationship with Jesus Christ. We will love and pursue the lost in tactful, loving, and relevant ways. We dream of being a church that loves, seeks,

144

and reaches the lost. Members of our church will be evangelistically bold, yet extremely loving. We will be a place where the unchurched will feel drawn to because of our uncommon love and compassion for them. We will be a church that will reach out to the "radically unchurched." We hope to see 50 percent of our membership be made up of formerly unchurched people. We expect to regularly hear testimonies of how people from lifestyles of drug addiction, prostitution, gangs, etc., were changed by God's grace. We dream of having far-reaching impact into our city. The city will see us as making a positive impact and a great ally. We will be a church that mobilizes every member into action to impact our neighborhoods. We will donate thousands of volunteer man-hours to the city each year. We will run an excellent community center that will offer relevant services, meeting needs of the community. We dream of being a multiethnic and economically diverse church. We will be a place that accepts and welcomes all people regardless of background, social status, or race. We believe that the local church should be a reflection of the kingdom of God on earth. We will strive towards unity as a testimony of Jesus' power to break down the artificial barriers society has put up.—Citylights Community Church, Long Beach, California

The Bible on Relational Outreach

Acts 4:32–35—"Now the full number of those who believed were of one heart and soul, and no one said that any of the things that belonged to him was his own, but they had everything in common. And with great power the apostles were giving their testimony to the resurrection of the Lord Jesus, and great grace was upon them all. There was not a needy person among them, for as many as were owners of lands or houses sold them and brought the proceeds of what was sold and laid it at the apostles' feet, and it was distributed to each as any had need."

Acts 13:49—"The word of the Lord was spreading throughout the whole region."

CHARACTERISTICS OF THOSE MOST RESPON- SIVE TO THE GOSPEL AS PRESENTED BY RELA- TIONAL CHURCHES

These people seek enduring relationships while holding to people-centered values. At the same time, they appreciate innovative approaches to meeting the deeper needs of people and are energized by personal contact and collaborative interaction with others. They are looking for a friendly, relaxed atmosphere that develops and maintains harmonious, inclusive relationships and seeks to involve people in projects that entail intense and challenging activity. These people look for and develop the talents in others, believe in and value teamwork, and appreciate the flexibility to make the most of last-minute opportunities. Because they are energized by starting something new, they highly regard people who act as catalysts, initiators, motivators.

> *[Our mission] is to immerse seekers and doubters into the redeemed community to experience the gospel first hand, cultivating faith experientially. . . . As we offer men and women a safe place to doubt and question without feeling pressure to conform or to believe, we provide people the opportunity to experience the reality of the gospel which transcends logic and reason.—Missio Dei Church, Portland, Maine*

VOCATIONS OF THOSE TYPICALLY ATTRACTED TO RELATIONAL CHURCHES

Relational church members are inclined to be employed in the vocations listed below because the requirements, design, and style of these occupations fit them well. Therefore, it follows that the people in the community in these vocations will be more responsive to the ministry style of the Relational church. The following material is adapted from:

- http://www.wsc.edu/advising_services/career_planning/ exploration/personality_careers
- Allan, Ross. *Connecting Personality Types with Careers and Jobs.* Washington, DC: United States Department of the Interior, 1999.[1]

146

Creative

- Artist
- Cartoonist
- Character actor
- Columnist
- Informational-graphics designer
- Interior decorator
- Musician/composer
- Newscaster
- Reporter/editor
- Screenwriter/playwright

The obvious appeal of these vocations is the opportunity to continually develop new and original approaches. Because Relational churches enjoy the creative process, especially if it offers opportunity for collaboration and to be inspired by serving with others, those in creative careers will feel at home. The more unconstrained and flexible the ministry environment, the more genuinely creative people will like it. They work well independently but need frequent and spontaneous interaction with others to keep their creative juices flowing and to keep their work fun; therefore, Relational churches are the best environment for them.

Marketing/Planning

- Advertising account executive and creative director
- Copywriter/publicity writer
- Editor/art director (magazine)
- Marketing consultant
- Public relations specialist
- Publicist
- Research assistant
- Strategic planner

Relational churches are effective vision casters and long-range thinkers, and can easily see the possible effects on others of an idea, program, or service. In order to devise innovative and humane solutions to problems, they often take the needs and concerns of people into consideration in their planning. They enjoy engaging in creative problem-solving, especially as part of a lively and energetic team. Therefore, it follows that those who find satisfaction in writing advertising copy for print or broadcast media and are engaged in the fast pace and constantly changing face of advertising will resonate with these churches.

Education/Counseling

- Alcohol/drug addiction counselor
- Bilingual education teacher
- Career counselor
- Child welfare counselor
- Development director
- Early childhood education teacher
- Ombudsperson
- Psychologist
- Rehabilitation worker
- Residential housing director
- Social scientist
- Social worker (elderly and child day-care issues)
- Special education teacher
- Teacher: art/drama/music/English

Relational churches are engaged in ministry with a positive relational impact on people. Among those who will resonate with these churches are compassionate and supportive psychologists and creative and enthusiastic career counselors who help clients find biblical solutions to their problems. Because these churches focus on possibilities for a new start in life, which they communicate with an infectious and energizing style, those in the helping professions will feel understood and appreciated.

Health Care/Social Service

- Dietitian/nutritionist

- Employee assistance program counselor
- Legal mediator
- Physical therapist
- Speech-language pathologist/audiologist

These fields in health care and social service are generally appealing to those who will resonate with the Relational church because of their desire to use creative approaches in helping people. Men and women in these careers tend to be those who can self-manage while remaining independent, flexible, and able to work outside more inflexible, traditional structures—characteristics that describe the ethos of Relational churches.

Entrepreneurial/Business

- Advertising account manager or account executive
- Conference planner
- Consultant
- Corporate/team trainer
- Employment development specialist
- Environmental attorney
- Human resources development trainer or manager
- Inventor
- Management consultant: change management/team building
- Marketing executive: radio/TV/cable broadcast industry
- Merchandise planner
- Outplacement consultant
- Restaurateur
- Sales: intangibles/ideas

People in these professions enjoy working for themselves because it gives them freedom and flexibility and the opportunity to choose their projects and the people with whom they want to work. They usually have an abundance of ideas they want to see turned into reality, particularly those that will affect other people. Many people in these careers will appreciate the way Relational churches do team building and conflict resolution, and increasingly grow in the effectiveness of their ministries.

THE CHURCH OF PETER

Peter, who ministered as a leader among Jesus' disciples and in the New Testament church, serves as an example of the gifts, values, and abilities descriptive of the Relational church. Observe Peter's spontaneous boldness, fervent devotion to Christ, and ability to adapt to the radical teachings of Jesus in the account that follows.

The choice of Peter as a leader among Jesus' disciples is reported in Matthew 16:18–19, where Jesus confers the nickname "Rock" on Simon as a sign of his future role as upholder and interpreter of the Lord's teachings. Peter was among the first to be called as a disciple; he was also one of the three, along with James and John, who formed an inner circle around Jesus (Mark 5:37; 9:2; 14:33).

The story in Luke 5:1–11 relates the model response to Jesus' call to follow him as his disciple. Overwhelmed with Jesus' divine power, evident in the huge catch of fish, Peter confesses his own sinfulness. When called to become one of the "fishers of men" (Matt. 4:19), Peter, along with James and John, leaves everything in order to follow Jesus (vv. 9–11). As a transformed disciple, Peter makes his possessions always available for Jesus' use. In one instance, Peter provides his house in Capernaum for Jesus to stay the night, and Jesus heals Peter's mother-in-law there (Mark 1:29–31). In another account, Peter offers his fishing boat to Jesus as a platform for preaching to the crowd at the lake of Gennesaret (Luke 5:1–3).

Spontaneous

Peter's spontaneous temperament is revealed on the occasion recorded in Matthew 14:22–33, when he and the other disciples are on the sea at night, tossed by the wind and the waves, and Jesus appears at a distance from them walking on the water. The disciples are terrified and think, "It is a ghost!" until Jesus says, "It is I. Do not be afraid." Peter puts Jesus to the test by asking, "Lord, if it is you, command me to come to you on the water." Jesus replies, "Come!" so Peter obeys by walking for a moment on the surface of the sea. But Peter loses his confidence and becomes fearful when he turns his eyes from Jesus to the storm and begins to sink. He cries out, "Lord, save me!" The Lord takes him by the hand, lifts him out of the sea, and leads him back to safety inside the boat where Peter falls at Jesus' feet and worships him, saying, "Truly you are the Son of God!"

In this story, we see the somewhat rash and impetuous character of Peter as he appears in many of the Gospel accounts. Another example is John 21:7: "When Simon Peter heard that it was the Lord, he put on his outer garment, for he was stripped for work, and threw himself into the sea" even though he was a hundred yards from the shore.

A third example is when Peter, with James and John, was a witness of the Lord's transfiguration. In the thrill of the moment, Peter blurts out, "Lord, it is good that we are here; if you wish, I will make three tents here, one for you and one for Moses and one for Elijah." But when he hears the voice of God, he is terrified and falls on his face (Matt. 17:1–8).

Represents the Disciples

In three ways, Peter is identified in the Gospels as a representative spokesman for the disciples. First, he receives from God special insight into Jesus' identity as the Messiah (Matt. 16:16–17). Second, he communicates the views of the disciples as influenced by Satan, which Jesus rejects (Matt. 16:22–23). Third, Peter requests information on behalf of the disciples, as in the question to Jesus about the reward for them as ones who have "left everything" to follow him (Matt. 19:27). Peter is the one, on behalf of the disciples, who requests clarification about the saying by which Jesus declared all things clean (Matt. 15:15) even though it means he receives Jesus' rebuke: "Are you also still without understanding?" In Acts 10:9–16 God reveals to Peter in a heavenly vision that all things are clean and thereby opens the way for Peter to baptize the first Gentiles into the church. Peter deals with the authorities on the question of paying the temple tax and then receives further instruction from Jesus, who provides for both himself and Peter (Matt. 17:24–27). Peter also receives special instruction on forgiveness on behalf of the disciples (Matt. 18:21–22).

Fervent but Impetuous

At their last supper together, Jesus begins to wash the disciples' feet; but when he comes to Peter, the disciple presumptuously declares, "You shall never wash my feet!" But when the Lord replies, "If I do not wash you, you have no share with me," Peter complies, and goes on to request that Jesus also wash his hands and head (John 13:3–9).

When the Lord declares, "Simon, Simon, behold, Satan demanded to have you, that he might sift you like wheat, but I have prayed for you that your faith may not fail. And when you have turned again, strengthen your brothers," Peter says to him, "Lord, I am ready to go with you both to prison and to death." Jesus says, "I tell you, Peter, the rooster will not crow this day, until you deny three times that you know me" (Luke 22:31–34). Nevertheless, Peter brashly insists, "Even if I must die with you, I will not deny you!" (Matt. 26:35).

His Spirit Is Willing but His Flesh Is Weak

Peter and the other disciples accompany Jesus to Gethsemane (Matt. 26:36–54), but when Jesus goes off in the distance to pray, Peter falls asleep. Jesus rebukes him, "So, could you not watch with me one hour? Watch and pray that you may not enter into temptation. The spirit indeed is willing, but the flesh is weak."

When Judas comes with a crowd bearing swords and clubs to arrest the Lord, Peter draws his sword and cuts off the right ear of Malchus, a servant of the high priest, for which he is promptly rebuked, "Put your sword back into its place. For all who take the sword will perish by the sword. Or do you think that I cannot appeal to my Father, and he will at once send me more than twelve legions of angels?" (Matt. 26:52–53).

When Jesus is arrested, Peter, along with John, follows him at a distance to the palace of Caiaphas and enters his court. While he is there, a servant girl says to Peter, "You also are not one of this man's disciples, are you?" Peter answers, "I am not" (John 18:15–17). Peter's second denial occurs at the entrance to the courtyard where another servant girl declares to the bystanders, "This man was with Jesus of Nazareth." Peter denies it with an oath, "I do not know the man" (Matt. 26:71–72). His third denial occurs an hour later, in reply to some who charge him with being one of the disciples of Jesus, saying, "Your accent betrays you." Peter probably had made some remark in his Galilean dialect. Then he begins to invoke a curse on himself and to swear, "I do not know the man." The crowing of the rooster and the look of the Lord convict Peter of his guilt, "and he went out and wept bitterly" (Matt. 26:73–75).

Restored and Commissioned to Lead the Church

In John 21:15–17 the risen Lord restores Peter by leading him through three questions to proclaim his love for Jesus, corresponding to his three denials. The Lord then commissions Peter to feed his sheep, which Peter does as one of the leaders of the church responsible for an expanding Christian mission, first to Jews, then to the Gentiles, as recorded in Acts 1–15.

In these chapters we see the immature Peter of the Gospels—impulsive, faltering, slow to understand the teachings of Jesus—contrasted with the same apostle who has grown spiritually to the point that he preaches the gospel on the Day of Pentecost and three thousand are saved (Acts 2:14–41), who is unwavering and bold in declaring he would "obey God rather than men" (Acts 5:29), who charges the rulers with the murder of Jesus (Acts 5:29), and who is willing to lead the church in a radically new direction in response to revelation from the Lord that Gentiles are to be baptized because they "have received the Holy Spirit just as we have" (Acts 10:47).

Because of the spontaneous boldness in the way he related to Jesus, because of his fervent devotion to Christ in his willingness to follow him anywhere, and because of his ability to adapt to the radical teachings of the Lord and lead the church accordingly, Peter serves as a good model for the Relational church.

8

The Entrepreneurial Church

* *

Outreach on the Cutting Edge

SUMMARY STATEMENT

Entrepreneurial churches desire to grow closer to God and to other people, and learn how to live practically in relationship with God through Christ. Because they see the needs of the community as an opportunity for trying something different with a positive impact for Christ, they create outreach events that are new, flexible, and responsive to the changing culture. They are especially adept at scanning the community to find connections with existing ministries so that when they add their creativity, a powerful outreach effort results. They want their ministries to reflect their resourcefulness and desire to solve problems while making fun, exciting, and adventurous things happen. Entrepreneurial churches flourish in communities where change, adaptability, calculated risk, and competency are valued. Often these churches build their ministries on small groups in which people really do know and care for each other. See Table 7 for a summary of these characteristics.

MISSION STATEMENT

Entrepreneurial churches are called by God to develop outreach efforts that anticipate the future and create new approaches to reach a

Table 7: Characteristics of the Entrepreneurial church.

Strong Points	• Handle crisis and problem situations adeptly • Are fearless risk takers, overflowing with optimism
Challenges	• So absorbed in action and the moment, they may lose sight of the long-term strategy • Can be so bored by routine that important day-to-day activities go unattended
Primary Ministries	• The new, the exciting, the adventurous, the risky • Involvement with new opportunities
Ministry Tempo	• Action oriented, rapid paced
What Inspires Them	• Spontaneity, autonomy, challenge
What De-motivates Them	• Rules, regulations, structure
Under Stress	• Become excessively pessimistic about the future • Become emotional • Decision-making capabilities erode
Decision-making	• Use logic, analysis, cause-and-effect reasoning
Desires	• A flexible, spontaneous, ever-changing environment
Priority	• Changing things for the good of others
Church Ethos	• Easygoing and cooperative; minimally structured, unregulated
Outward Appearance	• Concentration of attention and resources for quick, powerful impact
Gains Self-Assurance Through	• Connection first with the task
Fears	• Dealing with ambiguity and theory unconnected to reality

wide variety of people groups including the powerful and influential in the community.

Theme verse: "I can do all things through him who strengthens me" (Phil. 4:13).

ENTREPRENEURIAL CHURCH CHARACTERISTICS

Visionary

These churches are compelled by the optimism that theirs is the best of times and God's will makes anything possible. They are driven to impact people and the community through the development of flourishing ministries that overcome ministry problems and grow self-sufficient, stand-alone programs. Their hopefulness enables them to recruit people with the right gifts and talents and place them in the appropriate ministries. (Note: quotes in this chapter are from the web sites of Entrepreneurial churches as referenced.)

> *Buffalo Creek Community Church is a casual, contemporary church that seeks to glorify God by leading our generation to Christ and see them develop into fully devoted followers of Christ, impacting the world around them.—Buffalo Creek Community Church, Lancaster, New York[1]*

These churches encourage people's competency and ability to engage in creative problem solving that generates new and innovative approaches to challenges as they arise. They do not require follow-through with repetitious details over the long term in order to allow their people to focus on designing and starting projects that can be turned over to others. Since they place a priority on members engaging in fun, active, and exciting ministries, they establish an environment that is casual and unstructured in which people can experience a high degree of personal freedom and spontaneity.

> *We pursue placing people in areas of service in which they are gifted and passionate. We pursue the creation of organization and programs that functionally help us fulfill our mission.—The Seed Church, Bothell, Washington[2]*

156

These churches support their people in implementing innovative solutions through ministry systems that function competently—based on objective, commonsense goals rather than the personal preferences of a few individuals. They promote opportunities for people to increase their ministry effectiveness by interacting with resource people who are making an impact for the kingdom on the national level. In order to foster significant interaction with visionaries, they encourage their people to meet and relate with a diversity of people in rapidly changing, high-energy churches.

Changing Methods, Unchanging Message—We value innovation.—Buffalo Creek Community Church, Lancaster, New York

These churches are well suited to entrepreneurial ministry because of their foresight and adaptability. Planning and development require them to use their insight to see what God is doing and to formulate strategy accordingly. They create new ministry systems and models, sometimes putting their institutions at risk for the sake of their vision. They place a high value on their leaders seeking to discern a common direction from God. They value team contributions as long as the participants are focused and working toward the same goals.

Focusing on Things that Unite Us—Not Things that Divide us—We value unity and diversity. Expanding Our Influence and Reach—We value cooperation in worldwide church starting and missions.—Buffalo Creek Community Church, Lancaster, New York

Inspired by their picture of the future and focusing on possibilities with the courage of their convictions, these churches are architects of change. They are compelled to plan and lead new ministry projects with enthusiasm and energy, assuming the risks for their endeavors while advocating ministry strategies for the future. Since they are visionaries, refining and sharing their insights is a key part of how they garner support from the people who must be part of fulfilling the plan. Once the vision is communicated, they anticipate that everyone will be inspired to work independently with the same end in mind.

A church without a vision is like following an explorer without a compass. You'll never know where you're going! At The Highlands, we understand that the church needs God's vision in order to accomplish its mission. In other words, we need to know where we're going.—The Highlands Church, Gainesville, Georgia[3]

Their perceptive abilities cause these churches to see possibilities everywhere. Therefore, they are driven to start new projects and envision new ways of doing things. Because they are so stimulated by complexity and new problems to solve, they are often found in ministries where trouble-shooting plays a part. Their ability to understand people and situations intuitively is a distinct advantage in their ministries.

Vision is what we believe God is calling us to do and accomplish for his glory. It is a word picture of a future reality from God's perspective. In short, the vision is our destination.—The Highlands Church, Gainesville, Georgia

Entrepreneurial churches appreciate strong preaching and teaching, and attract excellent communicators who use theological concepts and expressive language to proclaim vision. They get excited and enthusiastic about ideas and are able to spread their passion to the people. In order to be all the more effective in preaching the Word of God clearly, they use their insight to predict cultural trends. They will often say yes to just about anything they can imagine; however, they may not fully recognize the scope of that to which they have committed if they have not stopped to map out the details and test reality. Development of their practical sense helps them attend to the down-to-earth aspects of making their dreams a reality.

Our dream is for a church, a church that strives to be a place where the people of North Hall County and the greater Gainesville area are accepted and shown the unconditional love of God, regardless of where on life's spiritual journey they find themselves. We dream of a church where worship isn't a dry, lifeless, long-faced service, but is regarded as a celebrative, mysterious, and reverent experience with an amazing God.—The Highlands Church, Gainesville, Georgia

These congregations are visionaries; creating and sharing their visions are key parts of their leadership role. This leads to constant debate, which allows them to explain and defend their visions and to convince others of the correctness of their solutions. They can become totally immersed in projects that will actualize visions, approaching these projects with great energy and excitement. Their visions are often based on a need to analyze and solve problems or to improve processes or systems. They create rational vision and compelling frameworks for action. These churches prefer to create and share their visions and assume others will be inspired to work. They want members who can work on their own to efficiently and competently complete pieces of work that tie into the overall vision, goal, or project.

> *Though somewhat non-traditional in style, The Highlands is deeply committed to the classic Christian faith as handed down through history. While doctrine is essential and important, the things that aid in defining a church are its values, vision, and mission. They shape who we are.*—The Highlands Church, Gainesville, Georgia

The Bible on Being Visionary

Daniel 3:17—"Our God whom we serve is able . . . and he will."

Ephesians 3:17–19—". . . that Christ may dwell in your hearts through faith—that you, being rooted and grounded in love, may have strength to comprehend with all the saints what is the breadth and length and height and depth, and to know the love of Christ that surpasses knowledge, that you may be filled with all the fullness of God."

Small-Group Ministries

Leaders in these congregations communicate with logical, analytical language that is precise and to the point. As they speak out for truth from Scripture, they communicate models and logical systems to meet the pressing needs of people. They are adept at using their verbal skills to lead groups and thereby communicate on a personal basis. Otherwise, some people in these churches may not receive enough information to understand the rationale behind actions and decisions of the church and have trouble "buying in." In this way, leaders can make sure their communications are not overly task-oriented but are sensitive to people.

> *In many ways, small groups are the backbone of The Crossing—they are the primary place where people connect with one another and develop genuine friendships. A good small group will offer a chance to explore the Scriptures, pray for needs, and share concerns—all with people you trust. And importantly, there will also be times to relax and simply have fun.—The Crossing, Columbia, Missouri[4]*

Exciting and stimulating, Entrepreneurial churches radiate a contagious enthusiasm for their ideas. Their inventiveness is attributable to their rich intuitive abilities, which give them a world of possibilities. Their favorite ministry activity is leading a small group of four to eight people in discussing a situation, problem, or issue in light of scriptural truth. They love to debate issues and brainstorm solutions in the group context. Their strength is bringing together and integrating the input of all the group members.

> *The Scriptures are clear: the Christian life is meant to be lived in community. We need others to help us apply the all-encompassing and ultimately satisfying truth of the gospel. As we remind each other about God's grace and all of its implications, we help each other experience the genuine spiritual growth that God desires to bring about in our lives. Small groups at The Crossing meet in their members' homes either weekly or every other week.—The Crossing, Columbia, Missouri*

It is important for these churches to share their ideas, because they are naturally skilled communicators. A "we can do it" approach inspires confidence externally and internally. They do not feel a need to conserve and preserve the old ways and realities. As leaders, they communicate by using logical analysis, and are precise and to the point. Constantly bombarding themselves—and others—with ideas, they burst with an excitement that leads to tackling one exciting challenge after another. Since everything is open to new possibilities, formal procedures and

160

structures don't get much serious attention in these churches. Their small groups are where growth occurs.

> *The Highlands believes that people best experience Christ, develop as leaders, and grow spiritually in a small group of people. Therefore, we are a church of small groups and not just a church with small groups. Small groups are where people study the Scripture together, pray for each other, tackle the tough questions of faith and life, care for one another, and it's also where you are missed if you don't show up.—The Highlands Church, Gainesville, Georgia*

Being verbally fluent and valuing personal expression, the leaders share their biblical perspectives in their small groups as a key part of their leadership role in these churches. Discussion, inquiry, criticism, and challenges are all part of life in these churches, and the people learn to interact in the small group context if they want to grow. The small group times allow the leaders to explain and defend the scriptural world and life view, and to convince others of the correctness of their solutions. In these ways, the people are constantly taking in new information from the Scriptures and shifting their mental models to fit the data.

> *We are convinced the best place for spiritual growth is in a small group of caring people. In fact, it is the best place for a lot of things: friendship building, encouragement, prayer, spiritual growth, support, and service . . . just to name a few. During the hectic pace of a crazy week, small groups are a breath of fresh air! Every group provides an opportunity to step away from the isolation of anonymous Christianity into an experience of real biblical community. Newcomers are warmly welcomed.—The Highlands Church, Gainesville, Georgia*

These churches strive for knowledge and insight for solving the complex problems in their lives. In their small groups, they discover innovative solutions and find the courage to take action based on the insights provided through interaction with Scripture. Because of their growing confidence in the rule of God in their lives, they learn to find alternative solutions and reframe problems as opportunities. They contribute to the group when they are able to help others discover strategies to solve problems or capitalize on opportunities.

> *My wife Amy and I have been members of the Highlands for over a year. We were a couple looking for a church to inspire us, help us grow in our faith with Christ, and each other. I had no idea where it would take us until now. I host a small group on Wednesday nights and have been blessed so much to have people that really care. I realize that life is not about me, but when I really do have a problem, I have eight guys that do care.—Chris Badura, The Highlands Church, Gainesville, Georgia*

A goal for these Entrepreneurial churches is to bring people to the point that they can see problems as opportunities. Their natural focus on challenge, pursuit of ideas, and independent thinking characterize all aspects of their ministry style, with the result being consistent growth in the lives of their people. Their philosophy is that there's always another approach; if something fails, then try, try again.

> *I know my life was not going to fix itself overnight, but when you can share it with people that are willing to listen, it makes it a whole lot easier. Some call you, pray for you, inspire you, and help you grow. Isn't that what life is about? Growing in a relationship with Christ and having friends to support you. Without the small group it would be just another day, but because of them it's not. If you're not in a small group, join one—your life won't be the same!—Chris Badura, The Highlands Church, Gainesville, Georgia*

Through relationships in these churches, one can expect to be challenged—usually by scriptural perspectives that may seem to be new and different, or on the cutting edge. The leaders think about their audience before they speak, remembering that some people prefer straight talk and can become lost and frustrated if they must interpret the metaphors and symbolic language more natural to these churches. Leaders try to be quiet and allow pauses in conversations for others who may need time to process their innovative ideas. They remember that even though their ideas are scriptural, they are still new to the experience of most people, so they accept that it will take time for people to get on board.

> *After the first Sunday at The Highlands, I was hooked. God used Jeff to give me messages that I could relate to and understand. The messages made me hungry for God's Word. The people were friendly and welcoming and I didn't feel that I had to dress or act a certain way to be accepted and embraced. I couldn't wait to go back the next Sunday and the next and. . . . It was exactly what I had been looking for and I knew it was where I needed and wanted to be. Although I was involved in a Bible study with a group of friends before visiting The Highlands, we all went our separate ways after the study with very little contact during the rest of the week. My small group is so much more than that. Not only do we study God's Word, we also have wonderful fellowship that has created new friendships.—Denise Jackson, The Highlands Church, Gainesville, Georgia*

The Bible on Small-Group Relationships

John 13:34–35—"A new commandment I give to you, that you love one another: just as I have loved you, you also are to love one another. By this all people will know that you are my disciples, if you have love for one another."

1 John 4:7–8—"Beloved, let us love one another, for love is from God, and whoever loves has been born of God and knows God. Anyone who does not love does not know God, because God is love."

Creative-Innovative

The application of truth in creative, stimulating, and authentic ways to people's experience is the basic driving force of these churches. Entrepreneurial churches are stimulated to develop creative solutions in order to help people work through difficulties in their lives. Clever, curious, and intuitive about any ministry endeavor, they see a broad range of possibilities. The opportunity to use their creativity in a flexible, open, and stimulating environment energizes them in ministry.

I had come to a place where I could no longer digest the stifling, restrictive role I was required to play. Where was the room for the Holy Spirit to work creatively among us?—Chuck Smith, Calvary Chapel, Costa Mesa, California[5]

Because they enjoy interacting with people, these congregations are motivated to refine their ability to read the social environment. They prefer ministries that offer variety and the opportunity to find creative solutions to dynamic problems. Since they view rules as distractions that impede the creative process, they quickly become bored with routine and structure. These factors, added to their enthusiasm and creative ideas, energize them. In the long run, these churches will be wise to develop ministry opportunities in which their people have autonomy over their work and have the fellowship of like-minded, creative people who also appreciate good ideas and prefer to work in less-structured and less-confining ministries.

It seemed that our church, like so many churches, was artificially bound by extra-biblical rules and formalities, and run by men who acted as employers rather than brethren bonded together in the love of Christ.—Chuck Smith, Calvary Chapel, Costa Mesa, California

Doing outreach to the community allows Entrepreneurial church people to be involved with other creative people in developing and implementing ideas in resourceful and inventive ways. Such outreach ministry requires them to use their abilities to identify innovative ways to communicate biblical truth so the unchurched can hear and understand. Because difficulties are likely to stimulate rather than discourage their creativity, they will evangelize people who might be dismissed by other churches.

We dream of a church where people are equipped, encouraged, and empowered to discover their God-given spiritual gifts in service to God and community, where all people use the gifts and talents God has given them to ensure that the entire church functions like a well-oiled machine or a well-tuned orchestra; a church where everyone contributes his or her part to the beauty of the whole.—The Highlands Church, Gainesville, Georgia

Since the people of these churches have a lot of options open to them, the leaders will do well to choose ministries that allow people the freedom to use their creativity to generate new ideas and solve problems. However, as entrepreneurial people, they do face the challenges of creating a workable structure and dealing with details while serving in accordance with their creative and flexible style.

Little wonder it [the church] lacked the explosive dynamism, relevance, and love of the early Church as reported in the New Testament. It seemed that we had lost something on the way as these past twenty centuries went by.—Chuck Smith, Calvary Chapel, Costa Mesa, California

Some ministries are more appealing to these churches: outreach, counseling, community development, and other efforts that allow them to be on the cutting edge. In addition, outreach efforts using innovative communications and technology lead them to develop their creativity and problem-solving skills. Their remarkable insight and ability to create solutions to problems catalyze their ministries.

It is interesting to see that no one formula works, but that different fellowships seem to find innovative approaches as God directs.—Chuck Smith, Calvary Chapel, Costa Mesa, California

By their nature, these churches value new approaches and are interested in a wide range of unconventional ministry endeavors that are ahead of the times. While they appreciate status and approval, they ultimately want to be judged by their innovative accomplishments. If they can delegate the follow-through of the details to others, they enjoy strategic planning that focuses on the development of innovative solutions to problems in the church and community. Because they excel at adaptability and expansion, they respond adeptly to the shifting values of the surrounding community. They encourage the interaction and participation of a variety of people in order to create new ministry approaches that engage in innovative methodologies to reach the culture.

> *When God moves in our lives, without our hindrance, doubt, resistance, or manipulation, he can achieve astounding things. It is always greater than any of our own ambitions or visions for what is possible in our lives.—Chuck Smith, Calvary Chapel, Costa Mesa, California*

In their effort to see the big picture, these churches use their insight to process information quickly and accurately. Because they value and develop skills that enhance problem-solving, they are especially adept at resolving difficulties. In a disciplined manner, they logically analyze opportunities that focus their ministry direction. They make honest, objective critiques of their past ministry endeavors and their current methodologies so they can avert failure in the future.

> *We envision a church that refuses to be ingrown or self-focused, but instead one that channels its redemptive power into the world by understanding that community service is not optional. Rather, it's understood as a spiritual mandate from Christ and lived daily through acts of service, which show God's love to others through involvement with local, national, and world missions, along with the planting of new churches.—The Highlands Church, Gainesville, Georgia*

Entrepreneurial ministries appeal to these churches because of their inherent talent for creating a ministry environment that is fresh, flexible, and always changing. They want to be known for their ideas, perceptiveness, and capacity to understand and communicate with people. As they work with the practicalities of various situations, they display an unusual talent for overcoming any challenges through improvising as they go along. Planning and development require them to envision what the Lord is doing in the advancement of the ministry in order to anticipate opportunities to reach the unchurched.

> *Our mission answers the question, "How do we accomplish God's Dream?"—The Highlands Church, Gainesville, Georgia*

These churches' intuitive ability to understand the nature of people and events enables them to adapt their strategies when they recognize trends, themes, and opinion shifts. Because of their knack for seeing relationships and connections between seemingly unrelated things, they are able to identify the potential in opportunities that lie ahead. Their vision makes them confident and drives the skill to accomplish that which is within the will of God.

> *We envision a church where the diversity of God's creation is cel-ebrated in spite of age, race, ethnic origin, or station of life. We dream of a church where help, hope, and healing are offered freely so that others can experience for themselves the life-altering grace of God. We dream of a church that stands firmly on the founda-tion of God's Word as contained in the Bible, depends on prayer and fasting as its source of power, and looks to the Holy Spirit as central to all its activity—filling, guiding, and empowering our lives.—The Highlands Church, Gainesville, Georgia*

Being skilled at integrating information from a number of sources, these congregations tend to be generalists rather than specialists. They focus on knowledge of the big picture, and the strategies and competen-cies that will develop their skills. Any competency that facilitates their insight about situations is valued and developed because their success is driven by their talent for solving problems. Their logical abilities provide them strength and purpose, but may also hinder them from empathizing with people in the community. Because they are able to use their charm and people skills to communicate their ideas, they enjoy the fast-paced, sometimes unpredictable nature of evangelism.

> *We can whistle while we face the aggravating responsibilities of life because even in the midst of a dirty job, our joy is in the Lord.*

> *There is a sense of peace, a depth of understanding, a patience, a kindness, a gentleness that comes from walking in the Spirit. There is a strength and power to cope with the persistent desires of the flesh. We suddenly are able to see the big picture and find the wisdom to deal with our fallen nature in a realistic and rational way.—Chuck Smith, Calvary Chapel, Costa Mesa, California*

The Bible on Creativity and Innovation

Acts 1:8—"But you will receive power when the Holy Spirit has come upon you, and you will be my witnesses in Jerusalem and in all Judea and Samaria, and to the end of the earth."

Ephesians 4:11–12—"And he gave the apostles, the prophets, the evangelists, the pastors and teachers, to equip the saints for the work of ministry, for building up the body of Christ."

Energetic and Competent

Enthusiastic, adventurous, and confident, these churches form strong ministry teams that energize one another with their challenging and sometimes unconventional ideas. They focus on new ideas and theories that require a great deal of energy, patience, and fortitude when solving new problems. While assuming the risks for their visionary endeavors, they like to plan and lead new ministry projects with enthusiasm and energy. However, because of their ingenuity and energy, they often manage to avoid some of life's setbacks and don't always recognize the severity of problems that lie ahead. Therefore, effort spent in sorting out priorities and values is a good investment of their time.

> *There has to be a guard against presumption. A lot of people who test the waters to see what God might want to do make a serious mistake by falling back on human effort when God's hand obviously is not in it. Sometimes we can get so committed to something that our reputation seems to be on the line. Then we start pumping extra energy and effort into a program that wasn't of God to begin with.—Chuck Smith, Calvary Chapel, Costa Mesa, California*

These congregations read their surrounding communities well and are energized by interacting with people. Their ministry projects tend to be increasingly large in scale, requiring the development of big budgets and the participation of energetic and influential people. Their enthusiasm for a current project can be so compelling that they may be oblivious to their time and energy limitations, sometimes ignoring the need to rest. They may find that it takes considerable concentration and energy to employ their relational sense while making decisions because their rational abilities are so strong. They should continue to critique their many ideas and inspirations; otherwise, they may waste their energy by being involved in too many projects or in an endless succession of new interests.

Centered in Jesus and compelled by his mission, we dream of being a church that fully experiences the rugged depths of life and fights and bleeds for the raw authenticity of Jesus. We dream of being an instrument for awakening the spiritually marginalized of our community, nation, and world.—CityView Church, Fort Worth, Texas[6]

Participating enthusiastically in dialogue and discussions, members of these congregations will express their views in a straightforward manner because they like to challenge people and demonstrate their skill with concepts. Both within and outside the church, they frequently discuss the pros and cons of various options because they prefer to learn about a subject by participating in lively, informed conversation or discussion, rather than through private study or reflection. In these churches, everyone is expected to digest information rapidly and become an active part of ongoing discussions.

In difficult doctrinal matters, may we have gracious attitudes and humble hearts, desiring most of all to please him who has called us to serve him in the body of Christ. Discussion - YES! Disagreements - YES! Division - NO!—Chuck Smith, Calvary Chapel, Costa Mesa, California

Their competitive nature as a church, combined with their desire to grow in their expertise, may prove to be overwhelming for highly relational people and can lead to hurt feelings and conflict. Their love for discussion of issues may even prompt them to employ debate tactics to the disadvantage of others, even when the "opponents" are valued friends in the church. Through development of their relational perceptions, they can become more aware of their impact on others and of the sometimes negative consequences of continual intellectual challenge and debate.

> *This is not to say that we do not have strong convictions. When the Bible speaks clearly, we must as well. But on other issues we try to recognize the scriptural validity of both sides of a debate and avoid excluding or favoring those in one camp over the other.—Chuck Smith, Calvary Chapel, Costa Mesa, California*

Focus on details and step-by-step procedures can frustrate these churches and even make them feel incompetent in their ministries. Because they value the development of expertise in the most important areas of ministry, they can be particularly intimidated when others question their competency or uncover details they may have overlooked. It helps these churches to recognize that they are not detail-oriented and, in fact, that too many details can depress them when they have to double-check and triple-check what they have done. On the other hand, discipline in getting the facts and details right can create an anchor for them during the storms of ministry and even help them to go deeper in their spirituality.

> *We at CityView believe that our story is accurately portrayed in the Scriptures. As a credible story of how we got to where we are and where we eventually will end up, this narrative informs and motivates the very details of our lives.—CityView Church, Fort Worth, Texas*

Entrepreneurial churches flourish in environments where change, flexibility, risk, and competency are valued. Leaders inspire their people to outdo one another in good deeds, and take risks with boldness, audacity, and daring. They appreciate creativity, excellence, working in a group setting, and a nonstructured ministry environment. Since they know they will always have to do something that is potentially boring, they think of creative and fun ways to make things more interesting. In this, their imagination is the only limit.

> *At The Highlands, we strive to explore the powerful, timeless truths of the Bible to find down-to-earth solutions for real life dilemmas. We do so through multimedia, live music, drama, and solid biblical teaching. Our dream for The Highlands is that we would be a place where a genuine faith in God is lived in a meaningful way. We invite you to join us on Saturday evenings because we just might change your mind about what it means to be a part of a community of faith. A new day requires a new church.—The Highlands Church, Gainesville, Georgia*

These churches feel it is important to be seen as capable, possessing skills and ingenuity to accomplish ministry tasks with excellence under a variety of circumstances. Although they may be intolerant of those who are incompetent or do not meet their expected standards, they are tolerant of diversity. They want to have an impact on their surroundings by understanding, controlling, explaining, and predicting events. They are driven to consistently improve by increasing their knowledge as much as they can so they can fit what they experience into a comprehensive ministry system.

> *Our church is more than a building, an organization, a man, or a Sunday. Elevation Church is a group of missionaries, a body of believers, and a population of diverse individuals united by a common relationship with Jesus Christ.—Elevation Church, Auburn, California[7]*

Working on new projects and developing novel ways of doing ministry energize the Entrepreneurial church. Because they are motivated to search for excellence and to make some specific and tangible difference in the world, their focus is on developing their ministry competency. These churches do more than develop creative ideas; they put their insights into action in order to make a genuine difference

171

by bringing innovative ideas to life. These churches are driven by the desire to keep growing in their knowledge of the deeper things of the Spirit and eternity, no matter how competent they might be in other matters of the mind and heart.

> *As Way of Grace Church, it is our desire to walk according to the new way made possible by Jesus and by the grace of God. Our purpose as a church is the same purpose Jesus had: to call follow-ers. You see, all of us are followers. The question is, "Who are we following?" Jesus came to take us in the right direction: God's direction. So we express our purpose and personal commitment to Jesus' leadership this way: we're about* calling followers *and* fol-lowing his call. *This is about making disciples and being disciples of Jesus.—Way of Grace Church, Buckeye, Arizona*[8]

The Bible on Competence

Proverbs 24:5–6—"A wise man is full of strength, and a man of knowledge enhances his might, for by wise guidance you can wage your war, and in abundance of counselors there is victory."

1 Corinthians 2:6–7—"Yet among the mature we do impart wis-dom, although it is not a wisdom of this age or of the rulers of this age, who are doomed to pass away. But we impart a secret and hidden wisdom of God, which God decreed before the ages for our glory."

Optimal Ministry Environment

Entrepreneurial churches flourish in communities where change, adaptability, calculated risk, and competency are valued. Interacting with resourceful people and having opportunities to use their creativity in a flexible, open, stimulating environment energize them in ministry. Their spirit of "I can do all things through him who strengthens me" creates a fast-moving, invigorating ministry environment.

> *We want to return to the church's roots that started with 12 young men that led a movement that continues to change the world.—CityView Church, Fort Worth, Texas*

Entrepreneurial churches have a deeper understanding of their neighborhoods than almost any of the other types of church because they enjoy interacting with the community, and they accurately read the people who live there. They continually scan their surroundings, absorbing and integrating information to form new ideas and connections. Discussion, inquiry, criticism, and challenge are all parts of their church culture, and those who appreciate high involvement and commitment will fit in.

> While many people cling to the promises of John 10:10, we believe that "abundant life" does not mean "the good life" or the American Dream. We believe the abundant life is filled with highs and lows . . . and we want CityView to be the kind of place where people can experience both the highest highs and the lowest lows in a community where mourning and celebration take place simultaneously.—CityView Church, Fort Worth, Texas

Entrepreneurial churches are most fulfilled when they can conduct ministries that involve significant events and bold concepts that do not entangle them in details and precise facts. They instinctively look for ministry opportunities that are important, ambitious, noteworthy, momentous, and substantial. The bigger and more consequential the projects, the more these churches respond with a generous expenditure of their time, talents, and resources. They like to initiate ministries of grand magnitude that are extensive and vital for the good of the community.

> At Mars Hill, we desire to cultivate communities on a mission. To accomplish this mission—the mission of the gospel of Jesus Christ—community groups offer support, leadership development, and spiritual growth with the intention that members will branch out and replicate these efforts, changing thousands of lives in the process.—Mars Hill Church, Seattle, Washington[9]

More interested in understanding *why* things work, rather than perceiving *how* they work, these churches are inclined to look beneath the obvious facts in events and situations in search of deeper realities. On the other hand, because they are especially capable at conceptualizing and abstract reasoning, the facts may stimulate them to form new theories or models. Discussion, analysis, brainstorming, fast-paced teaching, multimedia, workshops, topical sermons, and small groups are useful to them in getting at the deeper meaning of things.

> We were designed for significant, God magnifying lives. We find the most pleasurable, adventurous life when we operate within our design.—Providence Church, Little Elm, Texas[10]

The Bible on Ministry Potential

Matthew 19:26—"But Jesus looked at them and said, 'With man this is impossible, but with God all things are possible.'"

Mark 9:23—"And Jesus said to him, 'If you can! All things are possible for one who believes.'"

Worship Style

These churches begin their services by communicating the big picture, goals, and objectives of the worship of God, and make it known that everyone is expected to be an active part of worship. In worship, they seek new ways of looking at God through the Scriptures. They have a thirst for knowledge and enjoy exploring truths, beliefs, and theology in the Bible.

> Because worship is a response to God, our passion is to help people delight in his holiness and grace, trust in his unfailing promises, and rely on his incomparable power. In this way, our worship will be both an acceptable offering before God and a witness of his glory, so that "many will see and fear and put their trust in the Lord" (Ps. 40:3).—The Crossing, Columbia, Missouri

These churches help worshipers focus on the possibilities and potential of the presence of God in their lives and everyday experience,

174

which encourages the people to launch into new challenges beyond their current level of experience. They communicate a powerful vision of what can be, and are able to motivate people to act, change, and develop in new and healthy ways. Their worship is centered on biblical ideas for the future that act as catalysts for inspiring people to be all God intended for them to be.

> *True worship is the right response to whom God—Father, Son, and Holy Spirit—has revealed himself to be in the Scriptures. Because worship is a response, our ministry will seek to engage hearts and minds in order to encourage faith and love in increasing measure.—The Crossing, Columbia, Missouri*

These congregations create an open and lively worship atmosphere that provides the opportunity to question and explore assumptions, presuppositions, and the reasons behind things as they are. Their preaching and teaching is logical, with coherent arguments that set challenges that the people are encouraged to achieve in their own way. Their worship services offer variety and the opportunity to find creative solutions to dynamic problems.

> *We're a church of people just like you—real people on a real journey to connect with God. We don't have all the answers and we're not sure we know all the questions, but we're on the journey.—Veritas Church, Decatur, Georgia[11]*

The pastors of these churches are respected for their intellectual and leadership abilities. Skilled at integrating information from a number of sources, these pastors are generalists rather than specialists. They ask searching questions and go beyond assumptions.

> *Who is God? Perhaps the better question is: "Who is God and what do we have to do with him?" We believe that the God of the Bible can be known because he has revealed himself both historically and relationally. In fact, it is the Bible that allows us to know who God is. Biblical, Christ-centered teaching is one of our passions.—Lake Ridge Church, Cumming, Georgia[12]*

These congregations believe an ideal worship service allows for creativity and originality. Since they become bored or frustrated when doing the same thing over and over, they keep blending various worship forms to create new and exciting means of focusing on the Lord. They resonate with inventiveness and improvisation, change, innovation. These churches are attracted to creating new or improved forms of worship. Because they appreciate variety, their worship will cover a range of topics regarding the attributes of God, often jumping quickly in a stream-of-consciousness manner. They are stimulated by ideas and quick to grasp possibilities, enjoy challenges, engage in problem-solving, and adapt to new worship forms.

> *The worship at Lake Ridge Church will combine the best of emerging music and melody with the most cherished practices of ancient Christianity. You will hear music in a style that is familiar to the modern ear. You will also experience those practices that have been used for centuries. The one thing you will not experience: boredom. Our worship is passionately about the One who is worthy of our worship and our goal is to connect you to him.—Lake Ridge Church, Cumming, Georgia*

These churches are certain of the value of their inspirations, and any difficulty along the way is a stimulating challenge. They appreciate exposure to solid biblical theology as a means to acquire knowledge of God and his purposes. They want their services to be times of using Scripture to solve complex and intellectually challenging problems.

> *Who we are: More than who WE are, the description of our church must be centered on who GOD is. We are a church who believes that our own personal stories and experiences as individuals and as a community make sense only when we see ourselves in light of God's story. This is a story that begins with creation, is complicated by the rebellion of humanity, and culminates with Jesus Christ the God-man who died that we might be initiated into the reality of what it really means to be human. It is a story of freedom and the creation of a new community—a community*

reconciled to God and to one another. And the hero of the story is God!—Lake Ridge Church, Cumming, Georgia

Small groups that encourage sharing and individual expression are satisfying for these congregations, because they are assertive, outgoing, and verbally fluent. Following worship, these churches encourage discussion, inquiry, and reflection. Churches with this ministry style learn best by studying, exchanging, and analyzing ideas. They want to learn in an intellectually stimulating atmosphere in which interaction and problem-solving are encouraged.

Small groups are intentional efforts to create an atmosphere that causes believers and non-believers to grow in their understanding and application of God's direction in our lives. Small groups help create Biblical community . . . . In Acts 2, the first-century church met in temple courts (Sunday morning worship) and in house-to-house (small group) settings. These new church communities began as small groups, just as Jesus had modeled with the Twelve (Mark 3:14; Luke 6:12–19). —Providence Church, Little Elm, Texas

The preaching and teaching in these churches communicate insights through logical, cause-and-effect reasoning that is energetic, clear-cut, and colorful. They are often concise in conveying goals and strategies regarding how problems can be solved. The people appreciate when enthusiasm and imagination are communicated.

We at CityView believe that our story is accurately portrayed in the Scriptures. As a credible story of how we got to where we are and where we eventually will end up, this narrative informs and motivates the very details of our lives. As 2 Timothy 3:16–17 asserts, "All Scripture is inspired by God and profitable for teaching, for reproof, for correction, for training in righteousness, so that the man of God may be adequate, equipped for every good work." We see even our contemporary story emanating from the ancient story of the Bible. Yet we simultaneously

177

THE EIGHT CHURCH PERSONALITIES

gain momentum from its insight into our current and future situation.—CityView Church, Ft. Worth, Texas

These churches seek creative ways for worship services to develop in people the qualities of listening to the Lord, reflecting on his purposes, and exercising patience for the fulfillment of his will. Leaders are adept at using their skills of expression to lead worship through their preaching, teaching, counseling, influencing, and intercession, through which they give information rather than mandates. Because they want to adapt to what people need in their relationship with the Lord, leaders prefer to have worship unstructured so they are free to experiment from week to week.

Resurgence means to rise again or surge back into vibrancy. The gospel of Jesus Christ must resurge in every generation to meet the needs of people and their continually changing cultures. Resurgence (a "Missional Theological Cooperative") encourages this movement for our day, and will be a resource for future generations to engage the culture of their day. Resurgence is an international nonprofit of Mars Hill Church equipping Christians in sound doctrine by rightly handling Scripture and its application to culture in the fulfillment of the Great Commission.—Mars Hill Church, Seattle, Washington[13]

Structured, authoritarian worship is tedious and too routine for these churches. They tend not to accept a pastor's authority without question—readily pointing out any inconsistencies in an argument or method. They find their motivation diminished when worship is essentially passive, i.e., observing others, listening to how something "should" be done, taking notes. The people want to be more involved.

Too often our worship is an exercise in cultural imperialism. We develop a complete culture of worship that has no connection with the world people live in. This culture is carefully crafted with its own language, customs and rituals and then exported as a universal culture of worship. Over time these songs, prayers, and routines become how worship is done.—Tim Smith, Mars Hill Church, Seattle, Washington[14]

The Bible on Worship

John 4:23–24—"But the hour is coming, and is now here, when the true worshipers will worship the Father in spirit and truth, for the Father is seeking such people to worship him. God is spirit, and those who worship him must worship in spirit and truth."

Acts 2:42, 46–47—"And they devoted themselves to the apostles' teaching and fellowship, to the breaking of bread and the prayers. . . . And day by day, attending the temple together and breaking bread in their homes, they received their food with glad and generous hearts, praising God and having favor with all the people."

Learning Style

Eager for growth and wanting to learn, Entrepreneurial churches have an inner drive toward spiritual development. They grow best by studying, analyzing, and exchanging ideas in a spiritually stimulating atmosphere in which discussion and problem-solving are encouraged. They are more responsive when the training is unstructured and they are free to follow their own interests. With an analytical style that drives them continually toward growth, they challenge one another through spirited study disciplines.

Our worship gathering presents the timeless truths of faith in Jesus in a way that's true to ancient history but relevant to people in twenty-first-century Gainesville. Worship leader Carlene Archer and our talented praise team lead us in our musical response to God through a mix of modern music and hymns. This gathering is a vehicle designed to bring you into the mysterious yet loving presence of God and assist you in making a genuine connection with the One who offers forgiveness, while learning to apply the Bible to your daily life. No matter where you are on your spiritual journey or how many twists and turns you have had along the way, you will be accepted and cared for as you grow in your

179

understanding and experience of Jesus Christ in this community of faith.—The Highlands Church, Gainesville, Georgia

These churches approach disciple-making with a fun-loving attitude that is undergirded by the goal of making everything an educational exercise that promotes people's development as fully committed followers of Christ. They challenge one another to spiritual growth through their enthusiasm and energy, though follow-through may be a problem. Because they want to become all God intends for them to be, they consistently progress spiritually and develop ministries that go beyond what would seem possible.

We all secretly desire to grow closer to God, other people, and learn how to practically live in relationship to God through Christ. The Highlands is a church of small groups where people really do know and care for each other. Each small group is made up of, at least, 6–12 people who are dedicated to helping each other grow deeper in their relationship with Christ. We also offer other opportunities of spiritual enrichment including short-term studies, weekend retreats, and one-day intensive seminars, among others. We hope you will discover the many ways that you can grow in your relationship with God as you seek opportunities to develop your own spiritual roots.—The Highlands Church, Gainesville, Georgia

These churches are not oriented to private study and reflection as means of spiritual growth. They prefer to investigate issues by participating in stimulating dialogue led by knowledgeable people, which enables them to learn as they critique new ideas. Discerning relationships among large amounts of information, the people of these churches are quick learners who test out the theories and models that result.

As we reach the greater Gainesville/North Hall county area we attempt to live out our mission of "Inviting people to seek, encounter, and grow in a real relationship with Jesus" by being a place where faith is lived out in practical ways. In the

midst of living life and living faith, we try not to take ourselves
too seriously. Therefore, we laugh, we worship, we serve, we care,
we study, we pray, and we simply enjoy being a God-built faith
community.—The Highlands Church, Gainesville, Georgia

The Bible on Learning

Psalm 78:1-4—"Give ear, O my people, to my teaching; incline
your ears to the words of my mouth! I will open my mouth in a
parable; I will utter dark sayings from of old, things that we have
heard and known, that our fathers have told us. We will not hide
them from their children, but tell to the coming generation the
glorious deeds of the Lord, and his might, and the wonders that
he has done."

Communication Style

Providentially, these churches are adept at training people to
examine and explain the biblical world and life view, because effective
outreach requires the identification of creative ways to present biblical
truth so that the unchurched can understand. Because they are verbally
fluent and enjoy expressing themselves in a discussion format, these
congregations excel at small-group ministries—an optimal setting for
them to communicate truth on a personal level.

You may choose to investigate what membership (partnership) is
like here by participating in Orientation. This two-hour course
is taught by our pastor on Sunday afternoons at least every quar-
ter and is structured to be a life-giving, soul-refreshing time of
encouragement, learning, and laughing together. In Orientation
you'll find answers to your questions concerning our vision, val-
ues, and mission of The Highlands, plus a few other distinctives
that make this congregation unique.—The Highlands Church,
Gainesville, Georgia

The basic motivation of these churches is to communicate truth
in a creative but faithful manner that applies to people's lives in

helpful ways. They emphasize ideas for the future by using their discernment to anticipate cultural trends so they can speak the Word of God appropriately and accurately into people's situations. They enjoy communicating to audiences on both the intellectual/cognitive and the emotional/visceral levels.

> *Being a member at The Highlands means you are a missionary. You are a missionary to your community in the sense that you learn their language, their values, their philosophies, and furthermore you learn how to build bridges into their world and communicate the story of Jesus.—The Highlands Church, Gainesville, Georgia*

Their inspiring preaching and entertaining teaching focus on goals, strategies, and problems to be solved. They plan meetings that feature discussion about "what if" scenarios, and everyone is expected to participate. Because they can see multiple points of view in almost any discussion as new insights or perspectives are communicated, they are sensitive to contrary opinions. However, when given the opportunity to provide critique and offer suggestions for improvement, they communicate directly and straightforwardly.

> *We strive to worship Him with every aspect of our lives, as we enjoy our city and its culture, as we laugh and eat good food with friends, and as we serve each other, our neighbors, and our Lord Jesus.—Mars Hill Church, Seattle, Washington*

At times their communication can be overly task-oriented rather than people-focused, so these churches need to work consistently on the relational dynamics of good communication, trust, and mutual respect. Otherwise, lack of church-wide communication will bring people-management problems that result in underachievement.

> *We see a church where the Christian faith is lived honestly, simply, and with integrity. Where being a follower of Jesus is more than memorizing words on onionskin paper. A place where all people are ultimately transformed by Jesus Christ through lov-*

ing, laughing, living, and learning together in small groups, who in turn, mentor and develop new generations of fully devoted followers of Christ.—The Highlands Church, Gainesville, Georgia

The Bible on Preaching

Matthew 10:7—"And proclaim as you go, saying, 'The kingdom of heaven is at hand.'"

Luke 4:18–19—"'The Spirit of the Lord is upon me, because he has anointed me to proclaim good news to the poor. He has sent me to proclaim liberty to the captives and recovering of sight to the blind, to set at liberty those who are oppressed, to proclaim the year of the Lord's favor.'"

Outreach

When Entrepreneurial church members face the challenge of winning over skeptical people in the community, they let the discussion be driven by their enthusiasm for the gospel and its power for positive change in the lives of people. Their childlike enthusiasm and genuine interest in people makes them willing and able to develop redemptive relationships with the significant people in their lives.

All Christ-followers must be involved in "reaching out" to the world so that they can exhale the power of Jesus Christ and his Word into the church and world.—The Highlands Church, Gainesville, Georgia

When describing the benefits of entering the kingdom of God through Christ, they will use their powers of communication persuasively. In their enthusiasm, however, they may communicate a more glowing picture of the Christian life than is generally true.

True North Community Church exists to create environments where God can draw people to Jesus and be centered on how amazing he is.—True North Community Church, Port Jefferson Station, New York[15]

Resistance to the gospel stimulates their creative thinking. Spurred on by the challenging ideas and new perspectives communicated to them by people in the community, they employ their ingenuity, logic, and rational insight in developing an enthusiastic and stimulating response. Evangelistic opportunities inspire and challenge their active minds and insatiable curiosity about ways to communicate concepts that relate to people. They look for new approaches that may stimulate fresh perspectives and models in how to communicate effectively.

> *All God needs is one person in harmony with his purpose. God can accomplish his desires through one man. All he needs is just one man. That's both a challenging and exciting thought. That thought kept Jonathan awake until he finally woke up his armor bearer and said, "Let's go over and see if God wants to deliver the Philistines to Israel today."—Chuck Smith, Calvary Chapel, Costa Mesa, California*

As long as their challenges produce new opportunities, these churches bounce back quickly from setbacks and are persistent in pursuing their goals. Since they are self-assured and confident in communicating with others, they assertively seek performance-based feedback. Because they easily disclose themselves on a personal level, they are engaging and responsive to different ways of doing things. Since they are adept at creating a rational vision and compelling framework for action, they like to be active in solving problems.

> *Like the early church, those first communities of Jesus' followers, we want to be faithful in growing spiritually together ". . . from house to house . . ." (Acts 2:46; 5:42; 20:20). Our home groups are times to do just this. Through discussion, encouragement, sharing, and prayer, our hope is to grow in our love for God, one another, and all people.—Way of Grace Church, Buckeye, Arizona*

The Bible on Outreach

Acts 10:42—"And he commanded us to preach to the people and to testify that he is the one appointed by God to be judge of the living and the dead."

Romans 1:16–17—"For I am not ashamed of the gospel, for it is the power of God for salvation to everyone who believes, to the Jew first and also to the Greek. For in it the righteousness of God is revealed from faith for faith, as it is written, 'The righteous shall live by faith.'"

CHARACTERISTICS OF THOSE MOST RESPONSIVE TO THE GOSPEL AS PRESENTED BY ENTREPRENEURIAL CHURCHES

People most likely to be attracted to these churches value an intellectual approach that demonstrates competence and a zest for envisioning good things for the community. Since they are attracted to a challenge to do the impossible, they respond to a take-charge type of church that communicates long-term vision. Because they welcome a rational and objective perspective regarding sensitive issues, they are impressed with churches that communicate straightforward, innovative solutions for difficult problems in the community.

> *We are a church full of love and amazed by grace, that people cannot constrain themselves from sharing generously of their resources and material possessions with those in need.—The Highlands Church, Gainesville, Georgia*

THE INVITATIONAL STYLE OF OUTREACH

The most effective outreach strategies for Entrepreneurial churches will build on the example of Jesus in John 4, where we read about the Samaritan woman drawing water at the well of Sychar. When Jesus took the initiative to speak with her, she was amazed by his knowledge of her life story. Soon she learned that he was the long-awaited Messiah sent from God, so she hurried to her village and announced to all who would listen that she had met the Christ, the Son of the Living God. Then she invited them to follow her to the well so they could hear the proclamation of the gospel by Jesus. After two days of being with Jesus, "They said to the woman, 'It is no longer because of what you said that we believe, for we have heard for ourselves, and we know that this is indeed the Savior of the world'" (John 4:42). Through this invitational style of outreach, the church in Samaria was planted.

VOCATIONS OF THOSE TYPICALLY ATTRACTED TO ENTREPRENEURIAL CHURCHES

Entrepreneurial church members are inclined to be employed in the vocations listed below because the requirements, design, and style of these occupations fit them well. Therefore, it follows that the people in the community in these vocations will be more responsive to the ministry style of the Entrepreneurial church. The following material is adapted from:

- http://www.wsc.edu/advising_services/career_planning/exploration/personality_careers
- Allan, Ross. *Connecting Personality Types with Careers and Jobs*. Washington, DC: United States Department of the Interior, 1999.[16]

Communications

- Attorney
- Editor
- Journalist
- Newscaster
- Reporter
- Social scientist
- Speech pathologist

Entrepreneurial church members are adept at expressing themselves in words, and resonate with those in the field of communications, whether it be interpersonal communications, writing, or helping others to communicate or to present a viewpoint.

Marketing/Creative

- Advertising creative director
- Advertising director

186

- Information-graphics designer
- International marketer
- Magazine art director
- Producer
- Public relations specialist
- Publicist
- Radio/TV talk show host
- Researcher/planner
- Sports marketer

Entrepreneurial churches are often attractive to those in the fields of marketing, advertising, and public relations because these churches are comprised of creative people who develop and implement ideas, often in creative and exciting ways. These churches enjoy the fast-paced, fascinating world of public relations and advertising, and are able to use their charm and people skills to spot trends and to sell their ideas and concepts—all characteristics appreciated by those in marketing and the creative fields.

Planning and Development

- Computer analyst
- Conference planner
- Consultant
- Financial planner
- Industrial design manager
- Inventor
- Investment banker
- Logistics consultant (manufacturing)
- Network integration specialist (telecommunications)
- Personnel systems developer
- Real estate agent/developer
- Research assistant
- Special projects developer
- Strategic planner

Careers in planning and development require the ability to use vision and anticipate trends and formulate creative plans—all characteristic of Entrepreneurial churches. Developers work on speculative projects, often needing to convince others of their merit and potential for success—activities these churches enjoy and at which they often excel. Developers also need to remain flexible, adapting to new opportunities, ready to put together new approaches and programs without much planning or notice—skills that Entrepreneurial churches appreciate and welcome.

Politics

- Political analyst
- Political manager
- Politician
- Social scientist

Occupations connected to politics allow people to use their ideas, knowledge, and personal sophistication in a highly charged, fast-paced, and powerful arena—which is quite appealing to Entrepreneurial churches. These churches are able to use their abilities to see trends, themes, and public opinion shifts and adapt to those changes—skills that are appreciated by those who enjoy working with a variety of people. Entrepreneurial churches often attract pastors and Bible teachers who are excellent orators, using figurative, expansive language and expressing great vision—skills that are attractive to those in the political realm.

Entrepreneurship/Business

- Actor
- Diversity manager/trainer
- Inventor
- Literary agent
- Management consultant: marketing/reorganization/compensation
- Outplacement consultant
- Photographer

- Restaurant owner
- Technical trainer
- Venture capitalist

The appeal of these careers is the ability to create an environment that is new, flexible, and changing, and that involves the interaction and participation of many people in creating new concepts and approaches, thinking in innovative ways, and engaging in risk-taking. These characteristics are all appreciated by Entrepreneurial churches. The projects developed by these churches are often large-scale, requiring the development of big budgets and the participation of powerful and influential people—which appeal to those in entrepreneurial businesses.

THE CHURCH OF JOSEPH (GEN. 37-50)

Joseph, who became the vice-regent over all of Egypt, serves as an example of the gifts, values, and abilities descriptive of the Entrepreneurial church. Observe in the account that follows Joseph's extraordinary visionary gifts and leadership skills.

As a young man, Joseph experienced the resentment and wrath of his brothers for several reasons, but near the top of the list was *his visionary gift* (Gen. 37:5–11): *"Now Joseph had a dream, and when he told it to his brothers they hated him even more."* One day, Jacob sent Joseph into the countryside to check on his brothers' shepherding work. When they saw him at a distance coming toward them, the brothers schemed about killing him. Because his brother Reuben intervened, they sold him instead to some Ishmaelite traders for twenty shekels of silver.

These merchants sold him in Egypt as a slave to Potiphar, an officer of Pharaoh, "the captain of the guard" (Gen. 39:1). *"From the time that he made him overseer in his house and over all that he had the Lord blessed the Egyptian's house for Joseph's sake; the blessing of the Lord was on all that he had, in house and field"* (Gen. 39: 5). When Potiphar's wife made a false charge of rape against Joseph, he was thrown into prison (Gen. 39:20), where he remained for at least two years.

189

Again, God was with Joseph during his years in prison, granting him favor with the warden, so that he entrusted all the prisoners to Joseph's care, leaving everything to his supervision. "The Lord was with him. And whatever he did, the Lord made it succeed" (39:23). After a while, the chief cupbearer and the chief baker of Pharaoh's household were put in the same prison (40:2–3). The cupbearer and the baker each had a dream one night, and Joseph was able to interpret them. These interpretations were fulfilled three days later on the birthday of the Pharaoh (40:20–22), just as Joseph had foretold.

Joseph's ability to interpret dreams led to his being remembered by the cupbearer two years later when Pharaoh had dreams. When Joseph interpreted the dreams, Pharaoh was impressed with his ability and with his wise counsel regarding the events he foretold. "Then Pharaoh said to Joseph, 'Since God has shown you all this, there is none so discerning and wise as you are. You shall be over my house, and all my people shall order themselves as you command'" (41:39–40).

During the following seven years of plenty that Joseph had predicted from the dreams, Joseph gathered massive stores of grain to prepare for the years of famine that he also predicted would come. When the famine came, Joseph supplied food for Egypt and the surrounding nations. He made use of this opportunity to put all Egypt under Pharaoh—first all financial reserves, then the cattle and the land, and finally the Egyptian people themselves.

With five more years of famine still ahead, he brought Jacob and his extended family (seventy men, women, and children—all the Jewish people in the world at that time) to Egypt for safety. When his first child was born, Joseph called him Manasseh, which sounds like the Hebrew word for "forget," saying, "God has made me forget all my hardship and all my father's house" (41:51). Though many would have taken revenge against the brothers, Joseph discerned God's sovereign work in his life through the suffering they inflicted on him. His two statements to his terrified brothers revealed his ability to see the big picture regarding God's sovereign control over all that had happened as a result of their sin: "You sold me, . . . God sent me" (45:5; cf. 45:7–8), and, "You meant

190

evil against me, but God meant it for good" (50:20a). Joseph recognized that God allowed the latter, but also controlled the former so that his purpose in protecting and then building the Old Testament church might not be hindered.

No matter how discouraged Joseph must have become during the many setbacks he experienced at the hands of evil people, his faith in the Lord never wavered. In moments of crisis he chose to focus on the sovereignty of God at work. Rather than being eaten up with bitterness against his brothers or returning hatred for their evil, Joseph looked beyond them to see that the hand of God was on him "for good."

In faith, Joseph instructed his children not to leave his bones in Egypt when he died (50:24–25). As Hebrews 11:22 states, "By faith Joseph, at the end of his life, made mention of the exodus of the Israelites and gave directions concerning his bones." He was certain that the Lord would fulfill the promises he had made to his forefathers to return his people to the land of promise.

Because of his visionary abilities, leadership skills, and faith in the sovereign workings of God, Joseph serves as a good model for the Entrepreneurial church.

9

The Strategizer Church

*Outreach and Assimilation Driven by
the Sense of Calling and Destiny*

SUMMARY STATEMENT

Strategizer churches focus on ministry projects that require thorough research and structured plans leading to clear outcomes in order to move the ministry forward. Their determination is to conduct ministries that harmonize with their theological and ministry values so that people do not question the direction of the church or the integrity of their leaders. In order to solve troublesome problems in the church and community, these churches are zealous to develop creative approaches that continually improve the way they do things. When a strategy does not work as planned, they are adaptable enough to change direction after objectively analyzing pertinent programs and structures. Because these churches place a high priority on helping people to develop spiritually and in other areas of their lives, they focus on intense interaction with people on a one-to-one basis. They believe in the equipping model, which teaches that God is calling all laypeople of the church to be engaged in ministries that fit them uniquely, while the role of the staff is to serve as equippers

Table 8: Characteristics of the Strategizer church.

Strong Points	• Pioneers in the development of new ministries and outreach opportunities • Focused on completing tasks at the level of excellence
Challenges	• Can get bored with routine activities and leave them unattended • Can ignore the present for the future
Primary Ministries	• Developing theories and vision • Solving complex problems
Ministry Tempo	• Rapid pace
What Inspires Them	• Creating plans, developing prototypes and designing strategies
What De-motivates Them	• Unpredictable delays and postponements that slow them down in attaining their goal
Under Stress	• Loses objectivity • Raw emotions exposed • Becomes overly sensitive
Decision-making	• Logical and clear-thinking
Desires	• Visualize where the church is going and then communicate that vision to others
Priority	• Staying current to ensure the ideas they communicate are well validated
Church Ethos	• Energetic, task-oriented people organized around a clear vision
Outward Appearance	• Reserved, unassuming, unceremonious
Gains Self-Assurance Through	• Being deemed competent
Fears	• Failure • When emotion rules

and trainers of the people. If these churches are doing their job, they expect that growth will result in the lives of individuals and in the number of members in the church. See Table 8 for a summary of these characteristics.

MISSION STATEMENT

Because they place a high priority on helping people grow spiritually and in other aspects of their lives, members of Strategizer churches focus on intense interaction with one another. They believe that God calls all his people to be engaged in ministries that fit them uniquely, while the role of church staff is to serve as equippers and trainers of the people. In order to apply the gospel to the unchurched and to troublesome problems in the community, Strategizer churches are zealous to develop creative ministry approaches that continually improve the way they do things. They believe that if they are fulfilling their mission, then growth will result in the lives of members and in the number of people drawn to the church's fellowship.

Theme Passage: "Enlarge the place of your tent, and let the curtains of your habitations be stretched out; do not hold back; lengthen your cords and strengthen your stakes. For you will spread abroad to the right and to the left, and your offspring will possess the nations and will people the desolate cities" (Isa. 54:2–3).

STRATEGIZER CHURCH CHARACTERISTICS

Vision-Oriented

Strategizer churches live in a world of possibilities where they see all sorts of challenges to be surmounted, and they want to be the ones responsible for surmounting them. They have a drive to lead that is well served by their quickness to grasp complexities and their ability to absorb a large amount of strategic information with quick and decisive judgments. They are "take charge" churches. (Note: the Perimeter Church quotes are from two in-house publications: *Perimeter: The First Ten Years* and *Attempting Something So Great for God*.)

> *Our mindset is this: If a program isn't accomplishing its objec-*
> *tive, we need to let it die and mourn its passing—then get on*
> *with the business of trying something new.—Perimeter Church,*
> *Atlanta, Georgia*

Strategizer churches have many upfront gifts and talents among their members, which makes it possible for them to exercise a great deal of influence. They are assertive, innovative, long-range thinkers with an ability to translate theories and possibilities into solid plans of action. They are usually a collection of forceful personalities and have the tools to accomplish whatever goals they set.

> *Our church would "find a way to impact the whole of the city—*
> *reaching far beyond the influence of one church in one loca-*
> *tion."—Perimeter Church, Atlanta, Georgia*

Strategizer churches have a discerning view of their ministries and their environments. They frequently see patterns that other churches do not, and proceed confidently to develop and implement their long-range goals accordingly. After some time to analyze and grasp the possibilities and then to integrate them with their perspective, these churches move quickly to create a comprehensive system to meet the challenges of the future. Their systems are logical and wide-ranging, though they can sometimes overlook some of the steps necessary for implementation and fail to recognize the extent of their negative impact on some people. When the resistance of people opposes their intuitive picture of what the future requires, they can become tough and stubborn.

> *Our church "has had a vision greater than itself. This is the essence*
> *of faith. A vision not just to grow in numbers or build facilities,*
> *but to truly reach a sick and dying world."—Perimeter Church,*
> *Atlanta, Georgia*

While other types of churches may present the facts of the gospel, Strategizer churches convey the rich meaningfulness of biblical truth with greater depth by presenting the symbols, signs, and images of Scripture that convey spiritual vision and truth. In these ways, they

195

motivate the people by presenting an inspiring purpose and a sense of meaning for the service they render in the church and through the church to their families, community, and marketplace.

> *I changed from preaching at people to communicating with people. I began talking about issues that people were facing right now.—Dennis Slavens, Antioch Family Worship Center, Overland Park, Kansas*[1]

In a comprehensive manner, these churches focus on ways that people can grow in every aspect of their lives: spiritually, intellectually, emotionally, and socially. They typically communicate a picture of what can be accomplished through the transforming power of the gospel, and then repeatedly convey that vision to the people. They are especially adept at presenting the potential people have in Christ to tackle today's problems and challenges. This means of communication empowers transformation in people's lives that is continuous and durable.

> *For many years, we were not an inviting church. People would not invite their friends and neighbors. They loved their church, it worked for them, but they did not think it was relevant to invite someone from the office or home. . . . People begin to bring unsaved friends and relatives, and when they do that and the gospel is presented, many of them find Christ. That was an enormous breakthrough.—Dennis Slavens, Antioch Family Worship Center, Overland Park, Kansas*

These churches are compelled to help all their members discover and fulfill the calling the Lord has placed on their lives for serving in their homes, community, and marketplace according to their individual uniqueness. As a result, people do not become bogged down by the mundane and ordinary because they are regularly presented fresh challenges in serving the Lord.

> *We envision neighborhoods where Willow Creek is not just a building where people go to church, but where we are the church in the community—devoted to thinking, acting and being like*

Jesus. Our hope is to simplify people's lives by giving them the free-dom to grow and serve together as a community. The expressions and experiences of each community will be different, depending on the unique passions and gifts of the people there.—Willow Creek Church, South Barrington, Illinois[2]

Strategizer churches are comprised of people who are gifted as analysts, revisers, planners, and innovative change agents. A driving motivation is their desire that their church's ministry grow in competence and excellence for the glory of God.

Since the earliest days of Willow Creek, when we were 125 people strong, our vision has been abundantly clear—to become a bib-lically functioning community where there's transformational teaching, committed relationships, genuine prayer and worship, humble servanthood, help for the poor, and the ongoing miracle of people being revolutionized by Christ. And after more than 25 years, this goal still makes our hearts beat fast.—Willow Creek Church, South Barrington, Illinois

Strategizer church pastors teach about the challenges of the present in light of the promises of God, and preach about experiencing the reality of the "not yet" in the "here and now." They proclaim the potential of each person in Christ to meet each day's problems and challenges. What others may view as problems become the Strategizer pastor's opportunity to disciple. They believe any mountain can be moved through the power of Christ working in and through transformed lives.

It has been rewarding to look back over these years and engage in all of the "remember whens" of God's beyond belief bless-ings as well as his seeing us through even daunting circum-stances.—Perimeter Church, Atlanta, Georgia

These churches are at their most inspired and energized when they are creating plans, developing models, and developing strategies. These types of churches are all about boldness. They have willpower and imagination. They demonstrate how people's lives are fed and nurtured by the Savior to produce fruitfulness as they exercise faith in him. They elaborate on the Spirit's transforming power, Christ's spiritual authority, and the depth of the Father's love for his people.

> *It has been refreshing to recall God's tireless hand at work in our midst and his amazing ability to always be on time, but never, ever early or late!—Perimeter Church, Atlanta, Georgia*

The Bible on Vision

2 Kings 6:17—"Then Elisha prayed and said, 'O LORD, please open his eyes that he may see.' So the LORD opened the eyes of the young man and he saw, and behold, the mountain was full of horses and chariots of fire all around Elisha."

Zechariah 4:2–6—"And he said to me, 'What do you see?' I said, 'I see, and behold, a lampstand all of gold, with a bowl on the top of it, and seven lamps on it, with seven lips on each of the lamps that are on the top of it. And there are two olive trees by it, one on the right of the bowl and the other on its left.' And I said to the angel who talked with me, 'What are these, my lord?' Then the angel who talked with me answered and said to me, 'Do you not know what these are?' I said, 'No, my lord.' Then he said to me, 'This is the word of the LORD to Zerubbabel: Not by might, nor by power, but by my Spirit, says the LORD of hosts.'"

Skilled and Competent

Strategizer churches establish ministry environments with clear expectations. They can be spirited and want to know exactly what they need to do to excel. The members like to work with other competent and goal-driven individuals, especially in a structured ministry environment where achievement and independence are valued. Efficient and decisive, they will be sure to accomplish the ministry at a high level of excellence.

> *The unchurched unbeliever and believer alike are looking for something worthwhile to commit themselves to. Any organization of great worth will have high standards for membership—and of*

all organizations worthy of high standards, the church is the most worthy.—Perimeter Church, Atlanta, Georgia

Strategizer churches are natural leaders within the community, as their competence and strength inspire confidence and respect in others. Their power lies in their ability to take command of problem areas, impress others with their competence, and inspire them by their confidence. With their skill and resourcefulness, they are usually able to accomplish or even exceed their goals.

The goal of our ministry is to transform people into fully devoted followers of Christ . . . fully devoted followers who make an impact on their families, friends, neighborhoods, schools and workplaces.—McLean Bible Church, McLean, Virginia[3]

These churches can be aggressive in their zeal, and find it stressful to deal with incompetence, illogical behavior, and ill-defined criteria. With their emphasis on truth, accuracy, and productivity, Strategizer churches are unusually focused in commitment to their mission. They pursue leadership opportunities very directly, and have difficulty accepting other strategies unless those approaches provide more effectiveness than what they already experience. They are likely to be tolerant of diversity, but unaccepting of those who do not adhere to high standards of ministry excellence.

Everything we do for Christ must be done with excellence. "Whatever you do, work at it with all your heart, as working for the Lord, not for men, since you know that you will receive an inheritance from the Lord as a reward." Colossians 3:23–24—McLean Bible Church, McLean, Virginia

These churches focus on the task to be achieved in order to keep the ministry on track, while shaping the ministry structure to best serve the agreed objectives. They use their analytical and critical skills to solve problems so that short-term tasks are in harmony with the overall strategy. Because they are mission- and goal-oriented, they may become impatient with decision-making that seeks consensus and agreement, desiring instead to lead through directing. Once the expectations are made clear, they want people to take responsibility for their parts of the ministry as much as possible.

> *We believe that learning to identify the leading of the Holy Spirit, yielding our will to his, and responding in obedience requires discipline. Specifically, we believe that four spiritual disciplines are essential to becoming a fully devoted follower of Christ. Therefore, we encourage and challenge every believer to practice these four disciplines: Grow in your relationship with Jesus Christ, Connect in biblical community, Serve in your God-given ministry, Share the message of Jesus Christ.—McLean Bible Church, McLean, Virginia*

The Bible on Skill and Competence

Exodus 28:3—"You shall speak to all the skillful, whom I have filled with a spirit of skill."

Exodus 31:3, 4, 6—"I have filled him with the Spirit of God, with ability and intelligence, with knowledge and all craftsmanship, to devise artistic designs. . . . And I have given to all able men ability, that they may make all that I have commanded you."

Planning

Essential to the direction of Strategizer churches is a plan. They are able to design systems only when they have developed a clear plan. These churches are most inspired and energized when they are creating their plans, developing prototypes, and designing strategies.

> *I love creating new ways to do church better.—Perimeter Church, Atlanta, Georgia*

Then these churches develop policies that are subordinated to that plan, and help people fit into those programs and to understand their importance. They believe that whenever a plan goes awry, it is usually due to problems regarding follow-through on the plan.

Purpose Statement: To bring people to Jesus and membership in his family, develop them to Christlike maturity, and equip them for their ministry in the church and life mission in the world, in order to magnify God's name.—Saddleback Community Church, Lake Forest, California[4]

Administratively, Strategizer churches organize themselves into a smooth-functioning system, planning in advance, keeping both short-term and long-range objectives well in mind. Because the church leadership works at understanding human behavior in order to plan realistically, these churches usually succeed in a wide variety of ministries.

It is the dream of developing people to spiritual maturity through Bible studies, small groups, seminars, retreats, and a Bible school for our members.—Saddleback Community Church, Lake Forest, California

For Strategizer churches, the ministry is an opportunity to use their analytical and planning skills to reach out to the world in an organized fashion. Behind any plan of these churches, there is always a theological worldview of reality that explains how things work.

It is the dream of sending out hundreds of career missionaries and church workers all around the world, and empowering every member for a personal life mission in the world. It is the dream of sending our members by the thousands on short-term mission projects to every continent. It is the dream of starting at least one new daughter church every year.—Saddleback Community Church, Lake Forest, California

Strategizer churches are energetic planners and builders, projecting themselves into the future with ease. Since Strategizer churches strategically analyze alternatives and possible outcomes, they easily convince others that they have the wherewithal to make the future happen now. They usually will make it happen; they will set a goal and achieve it, even at great cost.

It is the dream of welcoming 20,000 members into the fellowship of our church family—loving, learning, laughing, and living in harmony together.—Saddleback Community Church, Lake Forest, California

The Bible on Planning

Proverbs 15:22—"Without counsel plans fail, but with many advisers they succeed."

Proverbs 16:3—"Commit your work to the LORD, and your plans will be established."

Proverbs 19:21—"Many are the plans in the mind of a man, but it is the purpose of the LORD that will stand."

Decisive

Leaders of these churches incorporate their vision of possibilities into their decision-making. Then they are able to analyze problems logically and objectively, weigh the pros and cons, and make efficient, sensible, and often tough decisions in light of the vision.

Jesus said, "I have come that they might have life, life to the full" (John 10:10). Jesus also said, "As the Father sent me, so I am sending you" (John 20:21), so we believe that our mission as a Christian church should be an extension of his—helping people learn to live in the fullness God intends, a fullness too many of us miss too often.—Christ Lutheran Church, Bethesda, Maryland[5]

Potential drawbacks in ministry for Strategizer churches may include making decisions too quickly and without enough information, a tendency to ignore the interpersonal climate in the church, failure to communicate diplomatically in interactions with others, and impatience with the details of implementing decisions. The Strategizer church may be tempted not to focus at all on the personal side, and to see only the overall logical good of a decision.

Rick Warren (pastor of Saddleback Community Church, Lake Forest, CA) found his own purpose at the end of 1980, when he was the young minister of a 150-member congregation that had no building and held services in whatever high school gym he could rent. Burned out from trying to keep his flock together, Warren collapsed in the middle of his sermon one Sunday and fell into a depression. He spent the next year soul-searching for a way to help people without getting overwhelmed again. "I needed to figure out what mattered most and not worry about the rest," says Warren, 50.—Time *Magazine, "The Man with the Purpose," Sept. 29, 2004*

Strategizer churches are proactive and decisive, which makes them effective in a changing situation where clear action is necessary and delay would be damaging. Because these churches are strongly dependent on their logical decision-making abilities, they usually get right to the point without mincing words.

Warren writes that God has five purposes for people's lives: to bring enjoyment to him, to be a part of his family, to become like him, to serve him, and to share him with others. The payoff for abiding by these precepts, Warren promises, is reduced stress, sharper focus, simplified decisions, greater meaning, and better preparation for eternity. —Time *Magazine, "The Man with the Purpose," Sept. 29, 2004*

The Bible on Decisiveness

Isaiah 11:2–5—"And the Spirit of the LORD shall rest upon him, the Spirit of wisdom and understanding, the Spirit of counsel and might, the Spirit of knowledge and the fear of the Lord. And his delight shall be in the fear of the LORD. He shall not judge by what his eyes see, or decide disputes by what his ears hear, but with righteousness he shall judge the poor, and decide with equity for the meek of the earth; and he shall strike the earth with the rod of his mouth, and with the breath of his lips he shall kill the wicked. Righteousness shall be the belt of his waist, and faithfulness the belt of his loins."

Isaiah 16:3—"Give counsel; grant justice; make your shade like night at the height of noon; shelter the outcasts."

Personal and Church Growth

Strategizer churches are quite intent on turning new ideas and approaches into practical ministries. When they have a good idea, they usually find a way to make it work. A thirst for knowledge makes them good teachers as well as innovators in ministry development. They have an insatiable curiosity, and desire to learn about life from a spiritual perspective.

We also believe God continues to speak to us in this day through the words of the Bible. There is no secret code, no extra books you need to understand God's words. There is no additional truth hidden for the ages and made plain only later that you need to find God.—Kingstowne Community Church, Kingstowne, Virginia[6]

Strategizer churches are especially adept at analyzing people and relationships within the body of Christ in light of biblical teaching. This enables them to implement innovative solutions regarding individual and corporate problems through finding creative ways for people to accomplish God-ordained tasks while making the process of individual and church growth fulfilling.

*Says parishioner William Nared: "At most churches they just preach and preach about how I ought to be a good Christian man. But what's so powerful about the Purpose-Driven ministry is that it teaches me how to do it."—*Time *Magazine, "The Man with the Purpose," Sept. 29, 2004*

Strategizer churches consistently focus on ways they can help people grow. This leads to a search for deeper knowledge of Christ and spiritual development, and can also lead to laypeople going into vocational ministry.

*Warren wants each of Saddleback's 2,000 small groups to adopt a village in a developing country, make mission trips there, and send educational and medical supplies, along with spiritual and financial support, to its residents.—*Time *Magazine, "The Man with the Purpose," Sept. 29, 2004*

Strategizer churches enable people to serve well by consistently providing a compelling purpose and a sense of meaning for the ministry. They think it not helpful to motivate with, "It's your duty," or, "Do it because you're supposed to." In this manner, they keep the inner fire of their people burning in the midst of the sometimes-difficult challenges of life.

Warren says, "I wanted to be guided by purpose and not by pressure." Through prayer and Bible study, he rediscovered the Christian doctrines that formed his blueprint for living a life of purpose and meaning.—Time *Magazine, "The Man with the Purpose," Sept. 29, 2004*

Strategizer churches view life as a spiritual and intellectual pilgrimage. They are zealous to keep improving the way they encourage people toward greater depth in both aspects of their lives.

One of the most unusual aspects is the leadership given by [the] Music Minister in the worship services. He provides spiritual education to the congregation on the what, how and why of worship and helps individuals grow in their worship of God.—Perimeter *Church, Atlanta, Georgia*

Strategizer churches are usually comfortable applying their clear sense of what is correct, efficient, and effective to all aspects of their ministry. Their focus is on finding what is preventing them from doing what they believe they need to do. If it's lack of confidence or motivation, then the solution is in building up those character qualities in their people. If it is rules or other inhibitors, they strive to eliminate them.

We will also use our resources to help the people who attend continually grow in their spiritual lives. As a church we are committed to acting in ways to increase our effectiveness in reaching new people with the Good News of Jesus.—Kingstowne *Community Church, Kingstowne, Virginia*

These churches like to discover new approaches. They prefer creating and beginning things, organizing projects and programs, and then teaching others how to do them and handing them off. Their strengths are patience, wisdom, and discipline—wisdom to focus on the right priorities, and correct decisions and patience to implement the plan.

> Our church "believes in a model in which God is calling each person . . . a model in which the staff are the equippers of ministry, not the assigners of ministry . . . (but) . . . leader-equippers."
> —Perimeter Church, Atlanta, Georgia

The Bible on Personal and Church Growth

Mark 4:30–32—"And he said, 'With what can we compare the kingdom of God, or what parable shall we use for it? It is like a grain of mustard seed, which, when sown on the ground, is the smallest of all the seeds on earth, yet when it is sown it grows up and becomes larger than all the garden plants and puts out large branches, so that the birds of the air can make nests in its shade.'"

1 Corinthians 3:10–15—"According to the grace of God given to me, like a skilled master builder I laid a foundation, and someone else is building upon it. Let each one take care how he builds upon it. For no one can lay a foundation other than that which is laid, which is Jesus Christ. Now if anyone builds on the foundation with gold, silver, precious stones, wood, hay, straw—each one's work will become manifest, for the Day will disclose it, because it will be revealed by fire, and the fire will test what sort of work each one has done. If the work that anyone has built on the foundation survives, he will receive a reward. If anyone's work is burned up, he will suffer loss, though he himself will be saved, but only as through fire."

Strategy Characteristics

As they seek to enable people to accomplish what the Lord intends for them, these churches work especially well with structured plans that point to clear biblical outcomes. They like to formulate innovative, well-organized goals that move the mission forward. In addition, they work hard to maintain an environment that is friendly and relatively free of interpersonal conflict through adhering to biblical principles of ministry. (Note: quotes in this section are from the Oak Bridge Community Church, St. Louis, Missouri.[7])

> *Jesus Christ had a mission. He came to earth from heaven knowing his purpose. Even at the age of 12, he told his parents, "didn't you know I had to be about My Father's business?" (Luke 2:49). His single-mindedness, determination, and reliance on his heavenly Father's guidance ensured that at the end of his ministry, he could pray confidently, "I have accomplished the work which You gave me to do" (John 17:4).*

Strategizer churches are particularly effective at considering options thoughtfully without rushing to judgment. Using their ability to conduct research, they analyze a variety of alternatives in order to enhance the quality and competency of the church's programs. In this manner, they create new approaches to a variety of challenges for the purpose of helping people grow and develop.

> *Jesus had a plan. His ministry unfolded in stages, and he said "No" to many opportunities when they were the right things at the wrong time. With no shortage of need, he had to be selective about the people and possibilities in which he invested.*

Because they understand that people will adopt new methodologies only if they are constructive and useful toward accomplishing well-defined goals, leaders work hard to search for the appropriate words that describe to the people the opportunities at hand. The leaders do not force conformity to their innovative ideas because they believe people will adopt new ministry approaches when they see the proposed improvements are aligned with the church's mission.

> *Jesus recognized that some "ministry growth" would be detrimental to his long-range plan, so he stifled it—he told certain people he'd just healed not to go public. The control he exercised in relation to his ministry was always in response to the leading of his heavenly Father—and as the appropriate way to facilitate his mission and vision in accordance with his values.*

Strategizer churches demonstrate a problem-solving leadership style that is willing to realign the church operation toward its goals when they encounter overlapping functions, duplication of effort, and inefficient use of human and material resources. They dislike messiness, wastefulness, or anything that is muddled, unclear, or confused in the way the church is organized.

> *Whenever we implement a plan, we keep one eye on our effectiveness, and the other on the next step God seems to be showing us. On a human level, three groups of people direct the ministries of Oak Bridge. Those bodies are the elders, the staff, and ministry leaders.*

Devoting themselves to rigorous study and preparation, these churches systematically examine the Scriptures and theological principles in order to communicate the truth in a manner that people can understand and apply to their lives. These congregations are determined in the face of opposition, because their study of the Scriptures enables them to be committed deeply to what they believe in and to lead accordingly. They recognize and speak to cultural trends in a way that is sharp, quick, and biblically attuned. Because of their gifts of discernment that enable them to detect broad developments in the church and community, they foresee where their leadership is needed for the greatest impact.

> *Grounded in the eternal Word of God, ministry must be adapted to be relevant to the hearers. Jesus' unchanging gospel must go forward in the language familiar to the people we're trying to reach. That includes familiar elements of culture.*

These churches value clarity and efficiency and will put considerable time and energy into helping people develop their ministry passions through structured programs that are beneficial to the fulfillment of each individual's sense of calling as well as the overall mission of the church.

> *All believers must have the opportunities to learn about and develop their spiritual gifts; we structure our ministry to imple-*

ment this value so that everyone can participate in some aspect of the Church based on their SHAPE (Spiritual giftedness, Heart's passion, Abilities, Personality temperament, life Experiences).

Strategizer churches hold themselves accountable to accomplish a well-defined quota of tasks that are completed within a definite time frame. Although they take enough time to formulate and process their ideas so that they are realistic, Strategizer churches move the decision-making process along efficiently because they want their structures to be functional as soon as possible. In order to operate with a high degree of hands-on influence to develop opportunities for their people, they organize the infrastructure of their churches to exert significant control over both the process and result of their efforts.

The New Testament is clear that the church is to be led by a plurality of Godly leaders under the oversight and watch-care of elders. They continually evaluate the teaching ministry of the church and review major ministry decisions and strategic initiatives.

These churches continue to grow in their ministry competencies through establishing realistic expectations about their program development and potential outcomes. Organizing their ideas into thoughtful and systematic plans, they identify and formulate goals that translate into actions to achieve well-defined policies that enable programs to run smoothly and efficiently. They accomplish their plans by staying on top of their ministry projects—which means following up with the people involved.

The elders are given responsibility and authority to see that the church remains on a true course biblically, that its members are being appropriately shepherded, that the body is being fed through insightful and accurate biblical teaching, and that the life of the church is being well managed with the assistance of other competent and Godly leaders. Scripture indicates that the ultimate decision-making authority in the church rests with its leaders (Acts 20:28; Hebrews 13:17; 1 Peter 5:1–2).

The Bible on Missional Strategy

Matthew 28:18–20—"And Jesus came and said to them, 'All authority in heaven and on earth has been given to me. Go therefore and make disciples of all nations, baptizing them in the name of the Father and of the Son and of the Holy Spirit, teaching them to observe all that I have commanded you. And behold, I am with you always, to the end of the age.'"

Mark 3:14—"And he appointed twelve (whom he also named apostles) so that they might be with him and he might send them out to preach."

Leadership Style

Strategizer churches respond positively to their leaders because those leaders exhibit insight, devotion, originality, and interpretive skill in their preaching, teaching, and counseling ministries. They serve in an orderly, self-paced manner in the context of structured, well-calculated plans that are based on solid theological models. In addition, they are able to summarize what they discern as potential difficulties in the church and community and then explain how the church can effectively meet the challenge.

Key Leaders at Pleasant Valley Baptist Church, Kansas City, Kansas:

- *Serve in their gifted and passion areas*
- *Are familiar with the overall ministry*
- *Are members of the church*
- *Collaborate with staff in defining mission and vision of the ministry*
- *Provide feedback, invite, equip, encourage, and delineate expectations for volunteers (in partnership with staff)*
- *Build into the lives of the volunteers with whom they serve.*[8]

Strategizer churches resonate with leaders who function within structured ministry plans that point to clear outcomes based on solid theological models. These preachers and teachers absorb solid biblical material and then communicate it in a manner understandable to the people. Studying, reflecting, and conceptualizing as a means of enhancing the quality and competency of the church, these leaders communicate insights and vision that are compelling in the ways they inspire trust. The leaders exhibit high standards for personal ministry performance, which are applied first to themselves and then to members of the church.

> *Because Jesus came to seek and save the lost, we feel compelled to do the same. But Jesus went beyond rescuing people from hell; he wanted to make them fit for heaven. Through the various sub-ministries of the church, we desire people not only meet Jesus, but also over time, to grow in their faith so that they live obedient to his commands and become conformed to his character.—Oak Bridge Community Church, St. Louis, Missouri*

These churches proclaim the Word of God in a straightforward manner and stand for what is right, good, and true in the church and the lives of the people. They are single-minded in their sense of purpose and not willing to settle for peace at any price. On the other hand, they genuinely desire harmony and order in the church, because they are serious about their relationships.

> *Although we are a collection of diverse individuals, certain common values unify our efforts and define our distinctives. We can summarize our core values using the following nine words: love, invite, grow, honor, prayer, joy/fun, authenticity, stories, excellence.—Oak Bridge Community Church, St. Louis, Missouri*

Strategizer churches are characterized by management teams that meet regularly to evaluate in a constructive manner how well volunteers in the church fit in their ministries, so that no one is burned out. These teams analyze their ministries and programs with objectivity to discover barriers that frustrate volunteers and block implementation of the mission, and then change plans when a strategy does not work as planned.

> *Whatever level or area of service, Pleasant Valley tries to ensure that volunteers' lives are in balance. Organizationally, this is referred*

211

to by the acronym TAFERR: Training; Affirmation; Feedback; Evaluation; Reflection; and Recognition.—Pleasant Valley Baptist Church, Kansas City, Kansas

The Bible on Leadership

1 Timothy 3:1–2—"The saying is trustworthy: If anyone aspires to the office of overseer, he desires a noble task. Therefore an overseer must be above reproach, the husband of one wife, sober-minded, self-controlled, respectable, hospitable, able to teach."

1 Timothy 5:17—"Let the elders who rule well be considered worthy of double honor, especially those who labor in preaching and teaching."

Communication

Strategizer churches tend to believe they are right. Some Christians and unchurched people may have a difficult time accepting this characteristic because they see it as a "superior attitude" or "snobbery." Their independent demeanor sometimes gives Strategizer churches an aura of superiority that slows down development of in-depth relationships with people in the community. At both ministry and play, Strategizer churches can seem aloof and argumentative.

> *Unchurched people today are the ultimate consumers. We may not like it, but for every sermon we preach, they're asking, "Am I interested in that subject or not?" If they aren't, it doesn't matter how effective our delivery is; their minds will check out.—Bill Hybels, D. Stuart Briscoe, and Haddon W. Robinson,* Mastering Contemporary Preaching *(Portland, OR: Multnomah, 1990, c1989), 26*

Perhaps the most significant characteristic of Strategizer churches in the interpersonal area is their capacity and desire to "work at" relationships. They can often synthesize the probable meanings behind such things as tone of voice, turn of phrase, and facial expression. This ability can then be honed and directed by consistent, repeated efforts to understand and support those whom they want to enfold into the church.

How do people couch their resistance? "You're being too harsh. You're being unrealistic. We're not ready for that yet." What about "God loves you as you are?" If I didn't have support from my elders, I couldn't keep it up, because sometimes the resistance gets too strong.—Bill Hybels, D. Stuart Briscoe, and Haddon W. Robinson, Mastering Contemporary Preaching *(Portland, OR: Multnomah, 1990, c1989), 122*

Generally, Strategizer churches place a priority on preaching, teaching, and evangelism, because through these ministries their enthusiasm, insight, devotion, originality, and interpretive skills can all be put to good use. They thrive in ministries that involve reaching out with the gospel to the community as well as nurturing the spiritual development of their people.

We have to teach people to engage in conversations with those who believe differently than they do or maybe don't have any spiritual beliefs at all. Personal evangelism, or having conversations about God, with people far from God should eventually become as natural to us as breathing.—Bill Hybels, interview by Lindy Lowry from Outreach *magazine, November/December 2006*

This church insists that its people protect the unity among the members by acting in love toward another through following their leaders and refusing to gossip. They emphasize Scripture passages such as the following:

- Romans 15:5—"May the God of endurance and encouragement grant you to live in such harmony with one another, in accord with Christ Jesus."
- Hebrews 13:17—"Obey your leaders and submit to them, for they are keeping watch over your souls, as those who will have to give an account. Let them do this with joy and not with groaning, for that would be of no advantage to you."

It's easy to feel tentative when I realize I may be asking a man to give up a six-figure income, or a woman to forsake a relationship she depends on,' or a teenager to be rejected by his peer group. The Evil One clouds my mind and makes me think I shouldn't lay such heavy challenges on people. Then I remember: It's in total commitment that we find the blessedness, peace, thrill, and adventure we were meant to enjoy.—Bill Hybels, D. Stuart Briscoe, and Haddon W. Robinson, Mastering Contemporary Preaching *(Portland, OR: Multnomah, 1990, c1989), 124*

Strategizer church leaders are sometimes portrayed as being inflexible and stubborn. This observation may result from their tendency to express their views directly and with conviction. Misinterpretation of their forthright communication style as being obstinate will discourage some from attending. This is unfortunate because Strategizer church leaders willingly engage people with questions about the faith in a warm and winsome manner.

When I speak about total commitment, people think I'm from Mars.—Bill Hybels, D. Stuart Briscoe, and Haddon W. Robinson, Mastering Contemporary Preaching *(Portland, OR: Multnomah, 1990, c1989), 112*

These churches have a well-developed ability to identify and formulate concepts and then translate them into useful plans of action for achieving ministry goals. They understand that the majority of their church members will adopt their ideas only if they are constructive in working toward accomplishing well-defined goals that are in alignment with the church's calling from God.

Church can be irrelevant. It can be boring. It may have nothing to do with everyday life. Not University Praise.—University Praise Church, Fullerton, California[9]

Only ideas that make sense to these congregations are ever adopted. Those that are not applicable are not acceptable, no matter who is the author. These churches are not impressed by authority that is based solely on degrees, credentials, titles, or celebrity; they are, however, submissive to biblical authority.

The pastors usually speak for about 30 minutes, and do their best to make the messages interesting, enjoyable, and relevant to daily life. The message will be based on the Bible.—University Praise Church, Fullerton, California

Strategizer churches tend to be more confident than most other churches—having developed their strong resolve by being lifelong learners. Decisions come rather easily to them; indeed, they can hardly rest until they have things settled and decided. They exhibit a drive to completion, always with an eye to long-term consequences.

Giftedness in leadership should be evident in this person's (lay leader candidate's) life and ministry. That is affirmed by their tested decision making in the past. They have shown an ability to listen to God, spend time in prayer, time in the Word, time in reflection, and have the ability to come to a God-honoring decision. This decision does not have to be shown to be perfect, but one of faith, understanding, and consistent with God's character.—First Family Church, Whittier, California[10]

These churches dislike messiness and inefficiency—anything that is muddled, unclear, or confused in the way people minister. They value clarity and efficiency, and will put considerable time and energy into helping members to develop their ministry passions into structured programs that are beneficial for fulfillment of their personal calling and the mission of the church.

The church I see has a process to assist people in spiritual development by helping them discover their shape for life and ministry. At FFC, we believe that a Christ follower will not be content in their relationship with the Lord until they learn and occupy the spiritual gifts that God has placed inside of them. Therefore, we are intentional about helping our attendees identify their spiritual gifts so they can grow past the infancy stage into full development.—First Family Church, Whittier, California

Their skill at taking a broad, long-range view of things contributes to Strategizer churches' reputation as being visionaries. Their recognition of cultural trends tends to be sharp, quick, and sometimes uncannily accurate. It is as if they have long antennae that enable them to detect broad developments before other churches do. They are able to use their intuitive abilities to anticipate trends in the culture's direction so they foresee where their leadership is needed.

> *The church I dream of functions as a biblically-based community of believers, working together as a team to fulfill Christ's redemptive purposes in the world. This church is not built on any one personality or individual, but on depth and breadth of participation, to reach a diverse culture with the love of Christ.—First Family Church, Whittier, California*

Strategizer churches have an unusual ability to comprehend theological concepts. Abstraction is not a problem for them, and explanation of the theoretical through logical means comes easily. They enjoy studying, learning, and growing in a formal educational context.

> *The requirements for recommendation to the Leadership Core of UP are as follows: . . . 3. Faithful and fruitful stewards and the desire to be a life-long learner (Luke 16:10, John 15).—University Praise Church, Fullerton, California*

These churches have a strong desire to contribute to the biblical education of their people, and genuinely enjoy guiding them toward greater spiritual fulfillment. The teaching abilities of their pastors are important to members because they appreciate presentations of in-depth theology with a global application.

> *We believe that accurate and anointed Bible teaching serves as the catalyst for life change. True Christ-followers possess a yearning to know God more and grow in faith and testimony.—First Family Church, Whittier, California*

The Bible on Communication

Mark 16:15—"And he said to them, 'Go into all the world and proclaim the gospel to the whole creation.'"

2 Timothy 2:1–2—"You then, my child, be strengthened by the grace that is in Christ Jesus, and what you have heard from me in the presence of many witnesses entrust to faithful men who will be able to teach others also."

Ministry Characteristics

These churches appreciate teachings that communicate theological systems, biblical patterns, and concepts that help make sense of the world and probe the basic assumptions, logic, and methodology behind ideas that predominate in the general culture as well as in the community in which they live. Sermons that present provocative ideas and perspectives that enable them to step back from current events to listen, observe, and analyze are highly valued.

> *The Scriptures provide the necessary and appropriate instructions for abundant life here on earth and in the preparation for the world to come. We are committed to the discovery and development of the spiritual and practical truths of the holy Scripture in the life of every person.—Grace Church, Fairview Heights, Illinois[11]*

Strategizer churches respond positively to a well-supplied church library, biblical counseling ministries for members of their church, and community that includes guidance regarding crisis intervention. These churches value a spiritual and ministry development plan for members that is created by the leadership team, which regularly holds them accountable for growth.

> *Jesus saw the preferable future, the new humanity his mission would make. He knew what he had to be like—and what his followers had to be like—if the world was to sit up and take notice. He built a community of believers—only twelve at first—that would be the foundation of a vast network of followers who would fulfill his vision.—Oak Bridge Community Church, St. Louis, Missouri*

Especially appreciated is a program that leads every member of the church through the process of identifying his or her unique calling from the Lord that points toward an optimal ministry niche in the church, or through the church to the community and marketplace. This program, headed by a lay leader or staff person, enables every member to experiment with a variety of ministries within the church in order to find an appropriate place. Follow-up opportunities are available to assess each participant's progress in an orderly and self-paced manner.

> *Spiritual gifts are revealed to you by exploring ministry opportunities, evaluating how the Holy Spirit worked through you and the impact you had on others. As you serve, look for the spiritual impact on others that you cannot attribute to your own efforts and talents. Also notice when the people you serve or serve with tell you that God worked through you in specific ways.—Willow Creek Community Church, South Barrington, Illinois*

The Strategizer church culture operates in the world of ideas and concepts which recognizes the value of intelligence, knowledge, and competence that questions and probes the basic methodology, assumptions, and logic behind the direction of the church's programs. Moreover, a high-quality church newspaper is valued as a forum for members to write about current events and other issues from a biblical perspective.

> *Ministry leaders are members chosen to assume responsibility for ministry tasks and specific care of the people. Wherever special ministry tasks were needed, since the beginning of the church, ministry leaders were appointed to carry out those tasks. As in Acts 6, our servant leaders assume responsibility for numerous ministry tasks throughout the life of the church. These godly leaders increase the quantity and quality of the church's mission and ministry.—Willow Creek Community Church, South Barrington, Illinois*

These churches are good at strategy development—regularly searching for new ideas and concepts to weigh against their current approaches. They operate best with structured ministry projects with clarity of direction. Able to analyze objectively their ministries and adaptable enough to change direction when plans don't bear fruit, they quickly discover barriers that block their implementation.

No decision is ever made that would knowingly contradict any of Jesus' teaching. In addition, through the guidance of the indwelling Holy Spirit, we endeavor to discern God's program for us as a church.—Oak Bridge Community Church, St. Louis, Missouri

Ministries supported by the Strategizer church members are organized, well-thought-out Bible training programs, self-teaching lessons, and high-quality discipleship courses. These congregations value being exposed to new information and opportunities that allow them to increase their ministry proficiency and confidence, as well as a strong Christian education program for themselves and their children. They appreciate sermon and Sunday school series that apply Scripture to tough issues in the culture such as: "Biblical Perspectives on Business Ethics," "Bio-medical Ethics: How the Bible Applies to the Issues of Life and Death," "Just War Theory," or "Current Events in Light of Biblical Truth."

Feedback is tied into training, helping volunteers discover how well they are implementing what they've learned. "I discovered in my staff development work that less than three percent of what people learn is applied if there isn't any follow up."—Pleasant Valley Baptist Church, Kansas City, Kansas

These churches encourage their members to create initiatives to improve the surrounding community by giving them freedom to transform existing programs and influence people for the sake of Christ. They give people control over their ministry projects and show them appreciation for their problem-solving while allowing them to minister alongside other capable and knowledgeable members of the church whom they respect.

Together, we're striving to become the kind of church described in the Bible—a church with relevant teaching, heart-felt worship,

219

honest friendships, constant prayer, and compassionate care for those in need. In short, we'd like to have the kind of contagious Christianity that can influence and encourage the entire community, one life at a time.—Willow Creek Community Church, South Barrington, Illinois

The Bible on Ministry

Psalm 51:12–13—"Restore to me the joy of your salvation, and uphold me with a willing spirit. Then I will teach transgressors your ways, and sinners will return to you."

Psalm 119:34–37—"Give me understanding, that I may keep your law and observe it with my whole heart. Lead me in the path of your commandments, for I delight in it. Incline my heart to your testimonies, and not to selfish gain! Turn my eyes from looking at worthless things; and give me life in your ways."

Pathways to Outreach

Strategizer churches network extensively by helping their members develop lists of friends, relatives, associates, and neighbors who know them and their commitment to Christ. Then they develop outreach programs that will resonate with those specific people.

ENCOUNTER services are built with our attendees' unbelieving friends and family in mind. These services are built around topics and issues that make it easy for our attendees to invite people who are seeking out the claims of Jesus Christ. It is our goal to partner with the FFC believers during these services to assist them in reaching their friends. During ENCOUNTER services, our leadership team is committed to using the arts; drama, music, video, dance, art, to help our unbelieving friends encounter God.—First Family Church, Whittier, California

These churches are good at developing practical training programs for their people to help them develop the skills, experience, and confidence to engage in fruitful outreach. They are convinced that the spiritual growth of their members depends on regularly engaging their network of relationships with the gospel.

> *We have to teach people to engage in conversations with those who believe differently than they do or maybe don't have any spiritual beliefs at all.*—Interview with Bill Hybels by Lindy Lowry from Outreach *magazine, November/December 2006*

These churches are good at strategy development—regularly seeking new ideas for outreach and weighing them against their current approach. They are objective in looking at ministry opportunities, and adaptable enough to change plans when current programs are not working well.

> *Looking at the Master Evangelist and the ease with which he had conversations with people outside the circle of faith becomes catalytic in the lives of church leaders. From there, we explain to pastors that lost people really do matter to the Father, and if they matter to him, they ought to matter to us.*—Interview with Bill Hybels by Lindy Lowry from Outreach *magazine, November/ December 2006*

The outreach strength and talent of Strategizer churches lie in their ability to take command of the process, impress new people with their knowledge, and inspire them by their vision. To avoid being perceived as overbearing, they make a conscious effort to listen and ask questions as well as give answers.

> *Training people on how to have conversations naturally, how to listen to others' stories before telling your own and then how to tell your story is essential to making this neighborhood ministry really work.*—Interview with Bill Hybels by Lindy Lowry from Outreach *magazine, November/December 2006*

Because they solve problems creatively, these churches approach obstacles as challenges rather than as roadblocks. By preparing an assessment of the community's greatest problems and then using their creativity to develop innovative strategies to help solve them, they rise to the challenge of overcoming barriers.

> *We have a relationship with one of the schools near us. So when we heard about the budget cuts, we said, "Let us paint it." They agreed and we had 250 volunteers help out! The school district said it was the best and fastest job they've ever had done.—Pleasant Valley Baptist Church, Kansas City, Kansas*

These churches conduct demographic research on the Internet, and then talk with people in the community and key organizations to find out as much as they can about their challenging issues. This information enables churches to create a relational bridge to the community over which they are able to walk in to the lives of the people.

> *Journeying towards relational, formative, missional, authentic, transformative, meaningful, kingdomic and communal faith in the redemptive Spirit of Christ.—Sherman YL Kuek, Seminari Theoloji Malaysia[12]*

Outreach is conducted in a well-organized environment where people serve according to a clear and definite set of guidelines as they are mentored by intelligent, creative, motivated, and goal-oriented individuals whose competencies they respect. These churches give people opportunities to meet and interact with a variety of other capable, interesting, and influential people within the church and community.

> *Entry Level: Serve alongside a mentor who understands all aspects of the ministry.—Pleasant Valley Baptist Church, Kansas City, Kansas*

Strategizer church outreach programs enable laypeople to work with complex and difficult problems in the community in order to challenge and stimulate their intellectual curiosity. They encourage volunteers to set and meet goals, and thereby use their organizational skills to focus on larger goals while accomplishing their objectives in a timely and efficient manner.

Core Volunteers Level: Serving in their gifted and passion areas; Trained to function effectively in their ministry role; Encouraged to develop their God-given potential as it relates to their skills.—Pleasant Valley Baptist Church, Kansas City, Kansas

Outreach opportunities for lay leaders give them responsibility for broader ministries within the church as they demonstrate their abilities and commitment. Laymen lead the organizing and development of the outreach ministry system of these churches, so that they run efficiently and attain their goals on schedule. Moreover, laypeople engage in long-range strategic planning and creative problem-solving that generate innovative approaches to reaching the community. Lay volunteers supervise others in the church by implementing sound methodologies that utilize each person's strength.

Key Leaders Level: Collaborate with staff in defining mission and vision of the ministry; Provide feedback, invite, equip, encourage and delineate expectations for volunteers (in partnership with staff); Build into the lives of the volunteers with whom they serve.—Pleasant Valley Baptist Church, Kansas City, Kansas

The Bible on Outreach
2 Corinthians 5:20–21—"Therefore, we are ambassadors for Christ, God making his appeal through us. We implore you on behalf of Christ, be reconciled to God. For our sake he made him to be sin who knew no sin, so that in him we might become the righteousness of God."

Ephesians 4:11–12—"And he gave the apostles, the prophets, the evangelists, the pastors and teachers, to equip the saints for the work of ministry, for building up the body of Christ."

CHARACTERISTICS OF THOSE MOST RESPONSIVE TO THE GOSPEL AS PRESENTED BY STRATEGIZER CHURCHES

The kinds of people attracted to Strategizer churches are those who are compelled to investigate the truth through focused study. More objective than subjective in their understanding of the truth, they have a great desire for clarity and are willing to spend time organizing their thoughts and beliefs. Patiently willing to ask hard questions, they develop strong convictions and opinions based on investigation of facts.

> *It is an environment where people can study God's Word together and tackle the tough questions and challenges of life.*—First Family Church, Whittier, California

Stimulated by interesting ideas and perspectives, they are willing to be challenged by searching questions, and to change their opinions when new evidence emerges. Concerned about meaning and refusing to be satisfied with unclear explanations, they have a strong internal motivation to understand truth. Possessing a deep desire to investigate the truth, they will spend whatever time is necessary with someone who can communicate truth to them.

> *Our Purpose at FFC is to bring people through a process of change that will allow them to answer two questions. One, Who am I? And Two, Where do I belong?*—First Family Church, Whittier, California

People attracted to these churches enjoy debating, challenging, and questioning ideas and theories with a cool, logical, and detached approach. Because they think through issues at greater depth than many others, they value long-term vision, breakthrough concepts, and plans. They desire to receive clarity regarding changes in the culture that defy normal analysis.

> *It is in the attempt to answer these questions that we have developed a process that will challenge and bring life change to the lives of seekers, new believers, and committed followers of Christ.*—First Family Church, Whittier, California

VOCATIONS OF THOSE TYPICALLY ATTRACTED TO STRATEGIZER CHURCHES

Strategizer church members are inclined to be employed in the vocations listed below because the requirements, design, and style of these occupations fit them well. Therefore, it follows that the people in the community in these vocations will be more responsive to the ministry style of the Strategizer church. The following material is adapted from:

- http://www.wsc.edu/advising_services/career_planning/ exploration/personality_careers
- Allan, Ross. *Connecting Personality Types with Careers and Jobs.* Washington, DC: United States Department of the Interior, 1999.[13]

Leadership/Managing People

- Administrator—wide range of organizations
- Corrections officer
- Manager—wide range of organizations
- Probation officer

Those attracted to the ministry style of Strategizer churches have often moved into leadership positions in their vocations. They like to take charge, so they gravitate to opportunities to manage and organize people and projects.

Arts and Design

- Actor
- Designer
- Fine artist
- Photographer

Strategizer churches often have an artistic flair to their ministry style. If they cultivate their creativity, they are attractive to those in arts and design. People in the community in the artistic vocations provide these churches with opportunities to use their wealth of ideas. The field of arts and design is very broad; think about specific skills and media enjoyed by people in the church, and match those interests and talents with the artistic vocations of people in the community.

Business

- Administrator: health services
- Advertising account manager
- Corporate trainer
- Executive
- Financial planner
- Franchise owner
- Human resources people
- Information services-new business developer
- International sales and marketing
- Logistic consultant (manufacturing)
- Management consultant: computer/information, marketing, reorganization
- Marketing executive: radio/TV/cable broadcast industry
- Marketing professional
- Media planner/buyer
- Network integration specialist (telecommunications)
- Sales manager
- Technical trainer

The ministry style of Strategizer churches is attractive to people in business careers—especially those with an entrepreneurial or leadership focus. People in human resources and corporate training positions may fit the Strategizer church personality if the church has developed competency in organizational development and a focus on performance, development, and effectiveness in organizational systems. Business executives appreciate churches that use long-range planning skills to develop contingency plans and map out the best course to meet their goals. Strategizer churches, using a style of direct management, fit those in these vocations because they are usually able to make tough yet fair decisions and set policies for the members and employees of the church. In general, independent, results-oriented people who can work without a lot of supervision or intervention tend to gravitate to the ministry style of the Strategizer church.

Professional Vocations

- Architect
- Biologist
- Chemist
- Consultant—general or in education, business, or management
- Economic analyst
- Psychologist
- Research scientist
- Social scientist
- Teacher—science, social science, university, English

People responsive to Strategizer churches are especially drawn to the abstract and theoretical nature of university education. Therefore, Strategizer churches serve especially well in academic communities.

Finance

- Corporate finance attorney
- Credit investigator
- Economic analyst
- International banker
- Investment banker
- Mortgage broker
- Personal financial planner
- Stockbroker

Those who excel in the field of finance are drawn to Strategizer churches. They enjoy the competition of the field, and take charge quickly and easily. These careers enable them to use their ability to forecast trends and design ingenious ways to take full advantage of opportunities for their clients. They do best when they have little work that involves detail and follow-up, but instead can delegate to a competent support staff. These characteristics fit the Strategizer church ethos.

Consulting/Training

- Business consultant
- Corporate team trainer
- Educational consultant
- Employment development specialist
- Labor relations
- Management consultant
- Program designer
- Telecommunications security consultant

The variety and independence offered in consulting careers appeal to those naturally attracted to the ministry style of Strategizer churches. Consulting vocations give people the opportunity to satisfy their entrepreneurial spirit, work with people in a variety of business settings, and be appreciated in proportion to the work they put in. They can be stimulating trainers who appreciate a structured and challenging environment with creative design and high-energy gatherings. They prefer to take on new projects and enjoy teaching other motivated people the ways to increase their competence. These characteristics fit the Strategizer church ministry style.

Professional

- Attorney
- Biomedical engineer
- Chemical engineer
- Environmental engineer
- Intellectual property attorney
- Judge
- Science/social science teacher

Those in the field of law, including practicing and administrative attorneys and judges, are attracted to the influence that Strategizer churches attain in the community. For those in the fields of chemical engineering as well as the emerging field of environmental and bio-medical engineering, the ministry style of Strategizer churches is appealing because they both resonate with intellectual challenge. In education, those attracted to these churches usually prefer teaching in the upper grades, especially secondary education, adult education, and at the college level. They like to apply their knowledge in the world around them, and often have careers that let them expand their teaching responsibilities into other areas—such as politics or political consulting.

Data Management and Analysis

- Analyst
- Auditor
- Banker
- Computer analyst
- Credit investigator
- Telecommunications worker

Many work in data management and analysis. They especially enjoy making logical analyses and managing details, and are attracted to Strategizer churches that are competent in the same ways.

THE CHURCH OF PAUL

Paul demonstrates significant characteristics of the Strategizer church in his ministry as a theologian, Christ's apostle to the nations, and master builder of the church. He was a man of passionate heart, vision, self-awareness, willpower, boldness, genuineness, energy, nuance, skillfulness, diplomacy, brilliance for organization, strength for authority, communication, and leadership.

The planter of at least thirteen churches, the writer of thirteen inspired letters, the man who experienced "far greater labors, far more imprisonments, with countless beatings, and often near death" (2 Cor. 11:23), the man who said, "I will most gladly spend and be spent for your souls" (2 Cor. 12:15) and who counted all things "as loss for the sake of Christ" (Phil. 3:7); the man who could truly say, "For to me

229

to live is Christ, and to die is gain" (Phil. 1:21) and who truly felt that he was "the very least of all the saints" (Eph. 3:8)—this was the man to whom God gave the special grace and privilege of building his church.

Paul could be as gentle as a father—warmly charming, so as to persuade the people: "I have become all things to all people, that by all means I might save some" (1 Cor. 9:22b)—but then become passionate and demanding if that was what it took to win people to Christ. For instance, Paul looks "intently at" men in Acts 13:9 and Acts 14:9, which indicates that Paul had a penetrating, commanding presence that also was apparent in his gestures (Acts 26:1). He rebukes the Corinthians (1 Cor. 4:8–14) with cutting sarcasm. He compares their pride, their self-satisfaction, their feeling of superiority with the experiences of an apostle. He chooses a vivid picture, comparing the Corinthians in their barefaced arrogance to a conquering Roman general exhibiting the trophies of his conquests, while he as an apostle was among the little group of captives at the end of the procession who were doomed to execution. To the Corinthians, the Christian life meant displaying their trophies and adding up their accomplishments; to Paul, it meant unassuming service and a willingness to sacrifice his life for Christ.

Paul was willing to endure much persecution for the sake of the gospel. To Timothy he wrote, "Indeed, all who desire to live a godly life in Christ Jesus will be persecuted" (2 Tim. 3:12). He says, "For it has been granted to you that for the sake of Christ you should not only believe in him but also suffer for his sake" (Phil. 1:29). He wrote to the Christians at Thessalonica, after a period of persecution in that Macedonian city, "that no one be moved by these afflictions. For you yourselves know that we are destined for this. For when we were with you, we kept telling you beforehand that we were to suffer affliction, just as it has come to pass, and just as you know" (1 Thess. 3:3–4). In Acts 14:19–20, Paul displays astounding courage. Immediately after surviving a stoning in Lystra, his response was to go right back into the city where his executioners were still celebrating what they thought was his demise. On the other hand, Paul describes his bewilderment with his many persecutions: "We are afflicted in every way, but not crushed;

perplexed, but not driven to despair; persecuted, but not forsaken; struck down, but not destroyed" (2 Cor. 4:8–9).

In Acts 21:3–4, 7–14, Paul demonstrates his resolve to persevere no matter what lay ahead. Nothing could have been clearer than the admonitions of the disciples at Tyre and Agabus at Caesarea, but their warnings could not dissuade Paul from the course he believed the Lord had chosen for him.

The gospel bestowed on Paul a great sense of authority. He was a representative of Jesus Christ. Paul never thought of his authority as coming from his own accomplishments. Rather, it was in the authority of Christ that he spoke. In Galatians chapters 1–2, Paul sets forth his apostolic authority and defends his ministry. To curb their conceit and brazen self-confidence, he recounts his experience in Antioch when he stood against the apostle Peter. He was daring enough to rebuke Peter, a leader of the apostles: "But when I saw that their conduct [Peter and "certain men … from James"] was not in step with the truth of the gospel, I said to Cephas before them all, 'If you, though a Jew, live like a Gentile and not like a Jew, how can you force the Gentiles to live like Jews?'" (Gal. 2:14).

In 2 Corinthians 9:1, we see how practical was Paul. He knew that enemies would charge him with stealing part of the offering, so he took steps to ensure that it would be impossible to accuse him by enlisting others to share the responsibility of delivering the money to Jerusalem. He determined always to be above suspicion by handling everyday matters in a manner that was transparent and above board.

In summary, Paul was the leader of those devoted followers of Jesus who went forth during the first century from Jerusalem into Judea, Samaria, and the uttermost parts of the earth, and turned the world upside down for their Lord. This statement describes, as well, the mission of the Strategizer church.

10

The Organizer Church

*Quality, Educationally Based Outreach
that Challenges People to Submit to the
Eternal Truths of the Bible*

SUMMARY STATEMENT

Organizer churches have high expectations for themselves regarding the efficient and timely delivery of programs. Organizer churches do quite well in managing ministry structures, such as their Christian education departments, and making sure that programs run well. Because Organizer church leaders are good communicators with strong opinions, people seldom have to guess where they stand on any given issue. They conduct their decision-making on the foundation of trustworthy facts and evidence of achievement, and seek knowledge that assures them of being accurate in their presentation of truth. Organizer church strengths include correctness, reliability, self-control, continuity, management, and the gaining of understanding through analytical abilities. They want truth presented in a logical manner so they can apply it to concerns in their personal lives, church, and community. When serving in the community, Organizer churches are likely to communicate clear standards and expectations. See Table 9 for a summary of these characteristics.

Table 9: Characteristics of the Organizer church.

Strong Points	• Preparation • Troubleshooting • Managing
Weak Points	• Obsessive • Fault-finding • Unsympathetic
Primary Ministries	• Program Development • Planning and Management
Ministry Tempo	• Deliberate • Systematic
What Inspires Them	• Orderly Procedure
What De-motivates Them	• Randomness • Disorder
Under Stress	• Reserved
Decision-making	• Calculated
Desires	• Exactness
Priority	• The Method
Church Ethos	• Efficient • Proper
Outward Appearance	• Conventional
Gains Security Through	• Attention to Detail • Research
Fears	• Embarrassment

MISSION STATEMENT

Organizer churches are called by God to take a solid, educationally based approach to ministry that enables them to establish quality programs which appropriately challenge people with the eternal truths of the gospel. The focus on scriptural truth through their preaching and teaching ministries and their desire for solid conversions enable these churches to reach and disciple those who want transformation in their lives so they might accomplish the purposes of the Lord.

Theme Verse: "All things should be done decently and in order" (1 Cor. 14:40).

ORGANIZER CHURCH CHARACTERISTICS

Sense of Responsibility

Being efficient and zealous about following through, these churches use their organizational skills to manage ministry projects. These churches have the capability for developing relationships with the community that will continue for decades. They seek solidity and predictability in church life, which lead them to accept responsibility for advocating God-honoring causes in the surrounding community. (Note: quotes in this chapter are from Organizer churches that have been promised anonymity.)

> *Our denomination has a distinct organizational structure that is very well defined and is responsible. And it is good to be able to talk to people in terms of accountability. While we may stumble, we have a clear organization and if we follow it, it works. And that's a comfort. The responsibilities are communicated in the denomination's Book of Order for the local governing board, as well as the regional and national governing bodies.*

These churches are especially trustworthy, consistent, firm, and conventional in their willingness to sacrifice themselves for the best interests of their children. They take this duty seriously, and appreciate the tasks and obligations that their responsibility involves.

We admire the couple in our church who saw a need with their nephews. They have invited them into their home and informally adopted them as their children and are raising them as their own. They took the responsibility very seriously that they were not going to let these kids wander because their biological father has not stepped up to his responsibilities.

What may not be obvious at a casual glance is the passion of these churches for organizing biblical truth and relating it to their past and present experiences. They take on the responsibility of ensuring that others are following these standards as well.

We were not sure we were going to have Vacation Bible School this year because of the lack of resources, and the church was rather tired because of what we had been through over the previous year. The new pastor made an announcement saying that the leadership was not sure if we would have VBS this summer. If anyone wants to have it then we need some volunteers immediately. Two of the women stepped forward to fill that gap, demonstrating [that] this is a concern and a value for the church and [they] were not going to let it fall this year because we were too tired.

The church's standards and guidelines communicate to members what the Organizer church expects of them. However, these responsibilities can create an overwhelming workload that becomes a significant stressor in the lives of members. Eventually, their sense of obligation to their families, which for them ranks above all else, creates an agonizing tension within, and even guilt when they have to draw back from church activities.

One characteristic of our church is that we tend to have clear expectations of what's right and what ought to be done and will offer unsolicited advice to those who don't fall in with those same characteristics.

These churches are especially adept at accomplishing ministry tasks and improving their high-priority programs.

Some of the programs we see moving in the right direction include the youth program and worship program. The goal we set to pay off the church mortgage we pursued aggressively. But other things which are not as high a priority, such as the nursery, we don't seem to improve.

The basic driving passions of these churches are duty, service, and the desire to belong. They have an especially strong sense of responsibility to take of "their own."

It's so important to me that we don't have any members who have to rely on the state to pay their bills. We give to help them and our deacons do a great job.

Once these churches take on a responsibility, they persevere with it as long as necessary.

We take responsibility, we take seriously our roles in the church, we are committed to those responsibilities. Once we do say we are going to support a missionary, for example, they are on there for decades.

The diligence and sincerity with which Organizer churches accept responsibilities are among their distinctives. To their members, they communicate clear responsibilities and procedures that are consistent and logical, and indicate that when they make a promise, it is irreversible.

I can't tell you how many times I've heard lay leaders—multiple lay leaders—in the hearing of the very people they are talking about, say, "The problem with all these young people is they are just here for a little while, they don't do anything for the church, and they don't give enough money." And they then leave and never come back because you've just told them their value is how they can support our programs and they don't support our programs enough.

The Bible on Responsibility

Ezra 10:3–4—"Therefore let us make a covenant with our God . . . according to the counsel of my lord and of those who tremble at the commandment of our God, and let it be done according to the Law. Arise, for it is your task, and we are with you; be strong and do it."

1 Timothy 5:21–22—"In the presence of God and of Christ Jesus and of the elect angels I charge you to keep these rules without prejudging, doing nothing from partiality. Do not be hasty in the laying on of hands, nor take part in the sins of others; keep yourself pure."

Driven by Duty and Tradition

When serving in the community, Organizer churches are likely to communicate clear standards and expectations. When commitments are broken within the community, they become upset because they hold others to the same standards of steadfastness to which they hold themselves. They can sometimes be very demanding and critical because they have such strongly held beliefs about what is right. These churches dread the prospect of a morally bankrupt nation that abandons its Christian legacy and its commitment to biblical values. They are likely to express themselves passionately if they feel that officials are ignoring biblical standards.

> *A passion of our previous pastor was to take a stand against gambling being introduced into the area. Since he's been gone this has not been so much on the church's agenda. We do host the blood drive at the church which is a community value issue that is very good. We are also the voting location for the area. The Community Mother's Club meets at the church building once each month. Our church building is open to the community. We have strong values regarding the education of children. The church has been strongly involved in the pro-life movement in the community.*

As a result of difficult high-stress experiences, older and more mature Organizer church members tend to recognize and incorporate a broader, more flexible perspective for their lives. They are better able to stand back from the consuming tasks and responsibilities of daily living and consider what is most important.

Our people are in different places on the pro-life issue. Therefore, some of our older leaders take a more sensitive approach that has developed from their life experience and a concern for how the issue is going to affect the body as a whole.

Ceremonies and rituals are significant ways in which Organizer church members bond with one another. They naturally desire to uphold and pass on to succeeding generations the biblical ways of thought and behavior for the family and community. They stress moral obligations, submission to the Lord, and biblical standards as the best ways to fulfill their calling to develop productive and thriving members of society.

Rituals and traditions are an important way this church stays connected with its members. Outsiders may not always understand the reason we do these things but members are expected to participate out of a sense of loyalty.

It is important for these churches to develop ministries that pass traditional values and doctrine on to the young, especially through catechism classes and other courses of instruction.

For me, ours is the best church in town because we help train up our children in the faith. So many churches we tried before entertained the kids—ostensibly to educate them—but the kids only remembered the fun. Here we have only as much entertainment as necessary to help them get the real meat of Scripture.

Driven by their values of loyalty and faithfulness, these churches take seriously their responsibility to their children and marriages.

When we were considering calling our current pastor, I remember seeing a picture of him hiking with his kids with their backpacks and hearing him tell stories going back to his Boy Scout days. So this tradition of the pastor demonstrating commitment to his own family continues with our new pastor. There is a continuity which we see there. So we are headed in the same direction: loyalty to family and church.

238

In the church members' relationships with their children, they emphasize duty, accountability, and biblical standards as the best ways to fulfill their responsibility to raise independent and successful members of society.

> *We have a commitment to our children and families. The dynamics of the youth being so visible in the church is impressive. Especially one of the junior high school Sunday school teachers has had a terrific impact on many of our children.*

Esteem for the laws and traditions of the faith may lead Organizer churches into conflict with teens (and their parents) who are happy-go-lucky types. Moreover, because of their desire to "do what is right" with what they have been given, these churches tend to involve themselves in efforts to safeguard societal standards and ethics such as taking a stand against the introduction of immoral elements to the community.

> *When the church as a whole has been engaged with issues that are important to us and about which we are passionate, we are not too understanding with those who have a different thought. For instance, we are pretty passionate about the gambling and pro-life issues and we are not very understanding of those with a different mindset.*

The basic stability and reliability of the church's ministry systems—which it creates and protects unconsciously—are reinforced by this church being sometimes closed to outsiders.

> *We are very loyal among ourselves—very close to each other. When you look at our officers, most of us go back many years. So it can be intimidating for new people to try to break into a culture like ours where so many people have been part of the church for so long. Even if someone comes from one of our sister churches in our same denomination it is difficult. So what is an outsider going to think about this dynamic in our church?*

Publications such as bulletins and newsletters are usually produced at a high level of quality.

I love that the publications and printing from the Sunday worship guide to the newsletter to even simple letters are always printed professionally. I'm proud to pass out our newsletter to friends.

Organizer churches value the traditional, hierarchical system of government, and believe there is a sensible effectiveness in a clearly defined chain of authority. Leaders are so in tune with the long-established ways of conducting ministry within the church that they cannot understand those who might want to discard or drastically alter church customs. Standard operating procedures keep variance from the rules to a minimum. Leaders carefully supervise staff and members to ensure they attain agreed-upon levels of quality in their work and achieve worthwhile goals. Even moderate nonconformists may be viewed as demanding and difficult to please. On the other hand, these churches give special honor to those who adhere to traditional ways of doing things.

We rely on our denomination's constitution to instruct and direct us. We made a call recently to the denominational headquarters to get clarification on a discipline procedure. This is important to us in that we are part of a connectional governmental system.

Organizer churches tend to preserve and protect standard procedures to ensure that programs and events occur as promised. When apprehensive about events that seem out of control, these churches look for connection to reliable institutions, trust authority figures, and aspire to positions of influence to provide themselves safeguards from the unexpected. They take credentials seriously—especially those that designate firm orthodoxy. These churches hold to definite values, and work hard to maintain their authority and control. They are especially proficient at handling details, administering justice, initiating practical procedures, and developing a smooth flow of programs for the people.

Our sense is that the people are happy to have us, as the leaders of the church, work with the policies and procedures and do not inquire about those issues because they do not want to be involved. If you were to poll the members of the church regarding our policies and procedures you would receive a lot of blank looks.

The Bible on Duty and Tradition

Ezra 10:11–12—"'Now then make confession to the LORD, the God of your fathers and do his will. Separate yourselves from the peoples of the land and from the foreign wives.' Then all the assembly answered with a loud voice, 'It is so; we must do as you have said.'"

1 Corinthians 11:2—"Now I commend you because you remember me in everything and maintain the traditions even as I delivered them to you."

Programs and Principles

Organizer churches have high expectations for themselves regarding the efficient and timely delivery of programs. Dependable and consistent, these churches take a solid, businesslike approach to ministry that enables them to establish quality ministries and keep them going at a high level of excellence.

Before our present pastor came, we had so much conflict because for years our church wanted to make itself out to have something for everyone. We avoided distinctives like the plague. But rather than keep us free from conflict, this really caused more because everyone felt like all opinions and preferences were equally desired. We had to find ourselves; we had to figure out why we're not just another church on another street in a city with tons of churches. I've been in this church for over 20 years, and we've never had so many people and so little conflict. That's because we know who we are now.

These churches are usually ready and eager to take charge and run things in a dependable, consistent manner. Bottom-line results are very important to them. In these churches, rules are made to be followed—not broken.

As we look back on our pastoral search process, organizing our mission trips and other ministry opportunities, we have not gone into them blindly but have collected the necessary information. For instance, with our building campaign we brought in a professional firm that "held our hand" through that process. During the pastoral search process we took time to collect information from people whom we considered experts. So we did not take a cavalier approach to any of these efforts. We do well at gathering all the facts but do not do a lot to consider all the other possibilities out there.

Convinced that their methods represent the right way of doing ministry, Organizer churches may fail to recognize or acknowledge the complaints of members and staff who are not satisfied with playing by the rules of the church. Because they thrive on order, continuity, and consistency, they may not naturally be in tune with what others are feeling, and tend to be very unobservant in these respects.

Some people seem to indicate that the governing board makes decrees so that the people are not considered. This stems from a disagreement on the type and amount of communication necessary in the life and governance of the church.

Organizer churches do quite well in managing ministry structures, such as Christian education departments, and in making sure that programs run well. They are conscientious about maintaining the programs that serve and care for their people. These churches especially appreciate people for their practical efforts, their common sense, and their work in keeping children and families on track. Because the idea of the church going bankrupt is unthinkable, they are efficient and thorough in keeping track of income and expenditures. They do not allow errors or omissions to go unchecked or uncorrected.

But we do things so deliberately and carefully that when we "got socked in the gut" in the abuse situation then we were able to do well.

These churches prefer traditional, established programs because their continuity provides a stabilizing effect.

Another tradition is an evening of music that the church has conducted for years. Recently we had a music appreciation for the musicians in our worship service, which is something we try to do every year. This was an activity of the Appreciation Committee. These kinds of activities may go unnoticed but these are traditions.

These churches can be counted on to conserve their resources and to bring to the ministry a practical point of view.

We set the goal of paying off the mortgage and we achieved it.

Organizer churches are competent at producing programs and methodologies to accomplish the tasks for which they are responsible—especially those that concern concrete and pragmatic issues. Because they fervently focus on attaining their goals, these churches act rapidly in their decision-making. They dislike disorganization and inefficiency, and will manage people and supplies as resourcefully as possible to enhance the quality of their efforts.

If you've got somebody with an expertise you let 'em go ahead and do that—there's a real trust for that. . . . And that helps the decision making so that you know you don't have somebody that's inexperienced or somebody that's looking out after themselves; they're really doing it because they want to serve God and doing it to the best of their abilities. You trust people who have those particular abilities and so that helps when we're making decisions.

However, these churches may have a tendency to make decisions without considering the practical impact on people. As a result, they may fail to notice the desire of some people in the church to conduct ministry differently from the way the Organizer church has done it in the past. Additionally, in their zeal to achieve their objectives, they may pass over new factors, unusual methodologies, or other atypical options.

One of the decisions facing our church is whether to have a pro-life newsletter. When one of our leaders mailed out to the full membership such a newsletter, it did cause some upset reactions from some of our members. In discussing whether to continue this or not, we heard a number of older, more mature voices encouraging us to look at the broader picture: "a broader, more flexible perspective."

These churches like to engage in rational investigation of facts and figures so they can direct people more effectively and competently handle specifics of programs. Their matter-of-fact approach to ministry can make it difficult for them to envision opportunities that vary from past ways of doing things, because they are more comfortable making commonsensical decisions based on previous experiences.

We're spreading the decision making out a little bit. And I think our leaders are trying to improve communication with the congregation as we finalize decisions. In the past, the communications were probably something we needed to work on improving.

The Bible on Principle-Driven Ministry

Psalm 119:44–45—"I will keep your law continually, forever and ever, and I shall walk in a wide place, for I have sought your precepts."

Proverbs 6:20–23—"My son, keep your father's commandment, and forsake not your mother's teaching. Bind them on your heart always; tie them around your neck. When you walk, they will lead you; when you lie down, they will watch over you; and when you awake, they will talk with you. For the commandment is a lamp and the teaching a light, and the reproofs of discipline are the way of life."

Decision-Making and Change

Organizer churches generally dislike change because they think that issues and events in the future will differ substantially from past experience. They assume these incidents will be unstable variations that will drive them to commit errors; so they feel they have little control.

We apparently have a number of complainers in the congregation who watch the worship service like hawks and are quick to point out everything that was outside the status quo. Since I've been here, any change that was implemented has always included people saying, "You never told us that was going to happen" (even though we had mentioned it in our publication, Our Church at Work, *and in the announcements on Sunday morning), and "Why are you doing it differently?"*

It is important for the board to strategize about changes in advance so it can plan for and manage any primary issues that its discernment can foresee. In this way, the board can consider what may occur in the future in a more disciplined manner and be more adaptable to inevitable fluctuations and the discord they may create.

Things don't seem to me to change very much. Most of the members of our congregation do not like change very much. Change is best achieved incrementally, backed by a very well-reasoned philosophy and plan.

Organizer churches conduct decision-making on the foundation of trustworthy facts and evidence of achievement. They want certainty to guide their judgments rather than personal perspectives or preferences. When the board of this church indicates it wants to ponder a decision, it is not being evasive—the board members sincerely mean it.

That comes out in how we make decisions and handle change. We don't follow our gut very often. We tend to plan and discuss.

Organizer churches tend to make decisions and then act by concentrating on the available information, data, and practical applications. They are especially adept at collecting, sorting out, and evaluating the facts and employing inductive reasoning. These abilities are what make them skilled at directing programs, procedures, and tasks. They enjoy deliberating over facts and figures, but may be less capable at conceptualizing and abstract reasoning. Concentrating only on the facts without putting them together into some kind of coherent whole will sometimes immobilize them.

The most dramatic change we've done in the last couple of years is to bring the sixth grade kids in with the seventh graders in our Sunday school program. That decision got talked about quite a bit; and evaluated a lot as to why we should do this. I think it was the nature of the people involved; they wanted to chew on the data and get really comfortable with the purpose behind it so that we not do this just for the sake of change.

Rapidly changing events are difficult for Organizer churches because their optimal way of making decisions involves gathering principles from concrete experiences that serve them as a frame of reference. They rely on data gleaned from their five senses and trust facts gathered from the past and present to confirm their assumptions and guide their decision-making.

We are a pretty consistent, fundamental bunch. I don't have a problem with tried-and-true conservative traditions so long as they are cases of us dealing with fundamental issues of the faith.

With their focus on the reality of the present, these churches trust the evidence of their senses, relying on carefully accumulated past and present evidence to support their conclusions and planned course of action. These churches do not handle well any rapid change or new models of ministry because they normally draw upon their past experiences to make sense of present events.

Some of us by nature are planners and we want to know where the resources are not only for tomorrow but also six months down the road. And some of what we are doing now, even what we did a few years ago, was stepping out in faith that we are going to do these things because we see this as where God is leading us but we are not quite sure where the financial resources are coming from. So there is this financial stress, and I think that is something that is not only apparent to the leaders but to a larger group within the church, and that's most evident to me when we have our annual congregational meeting where we talk about the budget and there are always some people who you can tell their blood pressure is up.

246

Situations in which they have no experience can seem confusing and out of control to these congregations. They need time and the opportunity to use their expertise to understand and structure the process to work through new situations.

We've been faced with a number of discipline situations, and when they came we did not know exactly what to do and to respond to that took a lot of energy and effort. But we tried to do the research in order to figure it out and gather as much information as possible to figure out how to manage through the situation. We did have a lot of people resources to draw on to whom we looked for counsel.

Organizer churches appreciate and encourage program changes that are supported by reliable data and cautious analysis, but they dislike alterations that are done only to "shake up things." New events or circumstances in which they have no familiarity tend to disorient them and make them feel that events are unmanageable. These churches like to improve and build on what they have rather than create something from the ground up.

We are a very conservative group, whereas you've got some of the megachurches out here that would love to go with anything.

Spontaneous idea-sharing with no attention to realistic limitations is irritating to these churches, especially during times of rapid change. They need time to reflect on their circumstances so they can use their ability to comprehend the nature of the events, organize their thoughts, and develop a strategy that fits the new situation.

People are coming to the church and I'm in charge of this program and I had no idea that there was this ministry going on. So that struck me that there are a lot of things I bet we're not even keeping track of.

When there are no clear rules to guide a decision, these churches may continually reexamine the past rather than consider new models. However, principles will guide the decisions of this church rather than personal feelings that might be involved. Therefore, the leadership will deal with the members in a fair, logical, and impartial manner.

> *Major decisions at our church are based on a scriptural foundation, and prayer seems to always be a part of them. Our doctrine, Book of Church Order, systems of discipline, etc., are all solidly scriptural.*

Because they want to consider and understand all of the implications of changing a program or policy, Organizer churches are usually more deliberate in reacting to change than other churches. This is especially true if they believe the change is unjustified or imposed on the church by a denomination or legal entity. These churches are likely to see more value in making small, gradual improvements and revisions than in launching into a completely new way of doing things. By their nature, these are very stable institutions to the point that when they are struck by a large and sudden change they can become emotionally paralyzed and behave erratically.

> *I remember when I first started and I came to the governing board and what I wanted was to take some money that was in the budget and use it specifically to train some people to lead small groups. And there was a 30-minute vocal disagreement on the governing board . . . heated disagreement over whether or not we would spend this money that is already in the budget because of all these reasons. . . . And I just remember thinking, "This is insane . . . it's entirely insane." It's just because "we've just never done it that way before."*

Organizer church leaders assess all elements of any issue or potential program. They identify all the possible variables with clarity. Simultaneously, they recognize the barriers and solutions necessary to move forward. Their ability to investigate the possibilities enables the church to make good, solid decisions that minimize risk.

> *There was a resistance to the prospect of this change from the teacher because she said she was not comfortable having those sixth graders come in because they were so much less mature.*

There was never change just for the sake of change. There is incremental change that can be seen over the course of years.

While an inclination for inspection and analysis can be a constructive attribute, when it recurs habitually, people may ignore the Organizer church leaders' vigilance as exaggerated.

Because these church leaders recognize many of the complications of ministry that elude others, they can become obsessive and fretful with themselves and others.

Example of that was back when we looked at buying that church building on the West Side—and had all the meetings and going along and . . . inspected . . . everybody's excited . . . looked it over and then the decision was made not to buy.

Order of Decision-making

- Sort out the plan, participants, and procedure.
- Discern defects of the plan in advance.
- Get to the heart of the problem in a businesslike and straight-forward manner.
- Apply and adapt past experiences to the problem.
- Assess the program in a rational and objective manner.
- Proceed toward solutions in a systematic way.
- Move at a rapid pace in deciding on a course of action.
- Check back to determine whether the plan went well.

Because of the structure of our church as an organization, there are many checks and balances to provide for the opportunity to make good decisions. Committees report to ministry teams, who report to the governing board. And each ordained staff member is responsible to a ministry team. While this can be cumbersome at times, I think it works to provide a minimum of false starts.

The Bible on Decision-making

Psalm 37:3–5—"Trust in the LORD, and do good; dwell in the land and befriend faithfulness. Delight yourself in the LORD, and he

249

will give you the desires of your heart. Commit your way to the LORD; trust in him, and he will act."

Proverbs 3:5–7—"Trust in the LORD with all your heart, and do not lean on your own understanding. In all your ways acknowledge him, and he will make straight your paths. Be not wise in your own eyes; fear the LORD, and turn away from evil."

Strong Christian Education Program

Organizer churches seek the knowledge that assures them of being accurate in their presentation of truth. They strive for precision. Their basic apprehension is about making erroneous statements that bring derision and disparagement on them. They often raise issues and assess basic assumptions to determine whether they are heading in the right direction. As a result, this church focuses on the analysis of scriptural truth to satisfy its standards for excellence and correctness.

The church has a good reputation in the community and especially our denomination. Our commitment to Scripture and theological precision makes us a model. We have a good number of ruling elders serving on denominational boards and committees.

Because they strive to keep argument and antagonism to a minimum, these churches want their presentation of the truth to be unquestionable. Therefore, the Organizer churches' greatest strength is in thoroughly studying the Scriptures until they have learned its principles. They conduct the educational process in a methodical manner so there are no gaps in their knowledge.

Truth teaching—there always is a focus on God's truth—He is always true and always will be—there are no apologies for teaching the truth.

Organizer churches take satisfaction in the thoroughness of their Christian education programs. They make sure their curriculum covers all pertinent issues of the faith. Before they put into operation their system of study, they search zealously for any cracks in it that may raise questions. Precision, exactness, rightness in their presentation of the truth are the highest priorities.

> *In our Sunday school classes, we've been comfortable as long as it has been orderly, logical, organized with a good teaching sequence, and is clearly stated what we are going to accomplish. We have had some in the past who have not been as systematic as we thought it should have been and were more free flowing. We would talk with the teacher about the problem and ask him to work on some of these deficiencies.*

The Bible on Christian Education

Deuteronomy 6:6–7—"And these words that I command you today shall be on your heart. You shall teach them diligently to your children, and shall talk of them when you sit in your house, and when you walk by the way, and when you lie down, and when you rise."

Proverbs 22:6—"Train up a child in the way he should go; even when he is old he will not depart from it."

Desire for Accuracy

Organizer church strengths include correctness, reliability, self-control, understanding, analytical abilities, continuity, and management. They often center on quality control through the development of guiding principles, rules, methodologies, and results. They create rules of operation that govern how their programs should function so they can be sure whether their ministries are being conducted properly. The tendency toward meticulousness may impede the progress of these churches in expanding their programs. Because the desire to be careful can deepen the fear of conducting ministry improperly, their tendency to be overly cautious may intensify.

> *One characteristic of our church is that we tend to have clear expectations of what's right and what ought to be done and will offer unsolicited advice to those who don't fall in with those same characteristics.*

251

Organizer churches are vigilant, capable, and observant. Because they want to be accurate, they like to examine the procedures themselves. This inclination toward precision can immobilize the church. These overly vigilant tendencies may create anxiety that the procedures are not being followed correctly, which further spurs the temptation to act in a more analytical, impersonal manner.

> *It isn't uncommon for somebody new to come up and say, "So and so just said something to me and I feel horrible." And they explain that they were told to do something differently, don't blow out the candles that way . . . blow out the candles this way. Be sure to wash your hands. . . .*

The Bible on Biblical Accuracy

Acts 18:26b—"But when Priscilla and Aquila heard [Apollos], they took him and explained to him the way of God more accurately."

2 Timothy 2:15—"Do your best to present yourself to God as one approved, a worker who has no need to be ashamed, rightly handling the word of truth."

Goal-oriented

Organizer churches demonstrate their commitment by setting and meeting realistic targets, and will put forth tremendous effort to accomplish important goals. They are skilled at organizing resources and people toward that end.

> *Our church has the ability to organize itself to do whatever we consider to be a high priority.*

These churches are persevering with their programs, although they may not always be supportive of the goals of individual members.

> *The scouting program is supported in general by the church but when particular volunteers are needed then that specific support is not always there. If it's an individual's goal that someone wants to see done but the broader church does not especially want to encourage it, then it won't necessarily be supported.*

252

Organizer churches care more about substance than compliments. They structure specific, prearranged learning conditions so the educational process and the results can be correct. Since their passion is truth, sentiment will usually be a secondary consideration. Their perspective is that feelings are personal and may misrepresent the facts. Their concerns about unrestrained sentiments and illogical conclusions communicate their purpose. In other words, these churches think that irrationality may hinder the understanding of scriptural truth. Similarly, they dislike subjectivity and unreasonableness in other people. This church desires to prevent humiliation, so its people try to manage both themselves and their feelings.

> We have a leader in our church with a passion for the congregation to have access to information that is correct on the issue as opposed to information that is available to the congregation through the general media. Someone said that he thinks the man's passion is deeper than that in that he sees this as a truth issue and he wants to be sure that people are educated regarding the truth.

Organizer churches are inclined to favor the mission over the sentiments of people. They prefer well-communicated objectives with a steady tempo of activity that includes schedules and time limits. They give attention to rational and careful procedures to ensure that they make the best possible decisions. Their thinking is that the better defined they can make the process, the more likely the results will be of high quality.

> The congregation is composed primarily of very intelligent, capable, and highly successful people. They are good thinkers and not afraid of taking action when they feel competent in a particular area. Most members are not prone to being swayed by their emotions as they think carefully about everything that they do.

When Organizer churches take a stand, they do so because they are confident of their facts and data. They can be self-assured when they perceive that their case is unassailable. Having established in their minds the low probability of a mistake or potential for miscalculation that might weaken their case, they will speak out.

We are strong at gathering the facts and examining the consequences but are neutral on considering the impact on the people. And not much attention is paid to generating all the possibilities that could result. This is why we are not as strong in developing a vision statement. We can do it, but it is more difficult and time consuming than it would be for some churches.

The Bible on Goals

Philippians 3:14–15a—"I press on toward the goal for the prize of the upward call of God in Christ Jesus. Let those of us who are mature think this way."

1 Timothy 1:5—"The aim of our charge is love that issues from a pure heart and a good conscience and a sincere faith."

Application of Scriptural Truth

Organizer churches want truth presented in a logical manner that enables them to apply it to the concerns in their personal lives, church, and community. They are conscientious and exacting about truth, and direct their lives in accordance with their understanding of it in a reflective and scrupulous manner.

Whether the topic is tithing, suicide, baptism, divorce—there is no ear-tickling at our church by our senior pastor or any of the other pastors.

Working with people whose ways of thinking deny absolute truth creates a negative emotional response to whatever such people might put forward. On the other hand, their focus on truth and the desire to accomplish tasks ordained by God enables Organizer churches to be fruitful among people who appreciate a straightforward, authoritative presentation of the Scriptures.

I think in terms of the apostle Paul talking to the people of Galatia, recorded in Galatians, where he pointed out that he was given the gospel by God, directly . . . and not by man. We want to keep ourselves centered on what is God's purpose for our church. The question is: "What is the truth of God?"

254

Analyzing comes naturally to Organizer churches, and they typically receive criticism offered by respected authorities and peers as an
appropriate means of promoting excellence in their ministry. However,
these church leaders may neglect to give positive feedback to people
before offering negative criticism, not recognizing that people can be
offended and put off by their negative comments.

> *It's harder for people like us to be nice because we tend to be very,
> very critical. We always see the glass half empty instead of half
> full. I have to work so hard at remembering to be positive and to
> give the positive feedback before I give the negative stuff because
> what we do is we see everything that's wrong, all the problems, and
> immediately we jump to what has to be done. And it's part of the
> personality, it's the real down side, I think, of our personally type.
> I mean there are some other positive things, but it's the way I say
> it. . . . It's harder for us to be nice, and if that is characteristic of the
> church, that's something to really keep in mind.*

The Bible on Application of the Truth

Galatians 1:11–12—"For I would have you know, brothers, that
the gospel that was preached by me is not man's gospel. For I did not
receive it from any man, nor was I taught it, but I received it through
a revelation of Jesus Christ."

2 Timothy 3:16–17—"All Scripture is breathed out by God and
profitable for teaching, for reproof, for correction, and for training in
righteousness, that the man of God may be competent, equipped for
every good work."

Sermons and Teachings

Organizer church preachers are motivated to deliver an exceptional, unique, masterful sermon. They want the congregation to
think, "What a masterful sermon" or "I've never heard a better
presentation!" The preachers of these types of churches meticulously prepare themselves to make an unforgettable presentation
of each sermon.

I find that our people are here FOR the sermon and what they're going to learn.

Preaching/Teaching Style

Here are some characteristics of preachers and teachers in the Organizer church:

They make clear-cut and consistent presentations that are moderate in tone.

The preaching and order of worship are what grabbed me when I visited our church, and they are what have kept me. Our pastor has done many fine series, but it has been his biblically firm, yet compassionate treatment of the day's social issues that I have appreciated the most. I am thankful to have a pastor that addresses things like abortion, secular humanism, and homosexuality—and never misses the mark.

Excellence and thoroughness in the preaching/teaching ministry rank higher in priority to this church than creativity, vision, and inspiration. Outlines are provided in advance for all sermons and teachings, and then followed carefully.

But some characteristics that come to mind are good organization in the sermons, helpful note outlines, numerous Scripture references, and the ability to personalize the topic without making the sermon about you (the preacher).

They move verse-by-verse in sequential fashion through passages and books of the Bible. They present logical and well-reasoned points that build a case, as well as structured and well-organized follow-up exercises that stimulate the learning process.

Our sermons are not only Bible based and true, but they are usually very scholarly as well. Being a life-long learner, I love how we just keep learning.

They illustrate the way biblical truths function in real-life situations, make abstract principles real for the people, and avoid speculative theories that do not directly apply to everyday life. Instead, they provide concrete examples for every principle the sermon presents.

> *I appreciate those sermons that told stories, and showed me things in Scripture that I had not seen before. I especially like the ones where our pastor tells a personal story. I enjoy both topical and expository preaching, but I can't say either one is my favorite.*

They describe clearly the steps necessary to become proficient in the use of the content presented, and communicate the concrete outcomes that will result.

> *Clearly organized, scholarly, good applications so we know what to do with it all when we leave.*

They should provide ample evidence or proof from Scripture when presenting truths or methods new to the people.

> *The organization and the focus on the Scripture is important. When you visit other churches, I'm amazed at how little is from Scripture. I mean, it's just topical.*

The people respond well to a challenge to achieve particular goals.

> *I think one of the sermon series that was most convicting to me was the one about gossip. I'm not sure—I think it was for me because I don't think I'd ever heard such clear, practical preaching on gossip. In general, you know we're not supposed to gossip. But that was new information to me and I like hearing new things and like getting something out of it.*

All sermons and teachings are prepared thoroughly in advance, with careful attention to all of the details of the Scripture passage and the presentation.

> *I've never heard one of his sermons or lessons that weren't utterly prepared. I never have to wonder if he's going to wing it or that he'll stumble around, but he knows what he's going to say and*

he's passionate to get it out. This makes learning enjoyable and worth coming to hear.

Each sermon/teaching should convey substance, significance, and solidity. Depth of knowledge, reasoning, and comprehensiveness communicates to these churches.

I find that people hunger for good preaching because many of us are not as good Bible readers as we should be and we read it and sometimes we don't comprehend it. And sometimes we don't even read it to comprehend it. And one of the strengths I see of our pastor's sermons is that he puts it very straightforward to us to cause us to open up our hearts to what we're hearing to applying the changes that take place in us.

They should tell the people "why" and "how" directly from Scripture so they are convinced the sermon is correct and complete.

We have always prided ourselves in the preaching and teaching we've had. It's always been verse by verse through the Scriptures; not just topical.

They should satisfy the people's need for caution and correctness and thus overcome their temptation not to get involved intellectually or emotionally with the sermon.

What is essentially important is how God feels about it all—not us. He is the one who gets the glory.

Organizer churches like to bring logical order to truth so they can apply it to issues in the church and community.

Our former pastor used to say, "SWWC": "So what, who cares." The presentations always have a practical point of application. We hear the content of the Word but we also need the application to our lives.

These churches create small groups that provide opportunities for processing sermons and teachings.

258

Our pastor's best sermons are ones where I learn something more than I could get on my own. I like how he provides discussion questions. We use those in our family and our small groups and sometimes they are penetrating and help us apply the sermon even better.

However, there is always a minority of people in Organizer churches who feel they don't fit in.

We are so intellectual, we are so scholarly, we are so college educated, that those of us who aren't strong in that area don't fit in. Several years ago someone said to me, "You know, I just don't fit in here. They use all these big words. I don't have a good education. I'm so uncomfortable here. I'm not good enough because I'm too dumb." I'm putting words in her mouth. That's not exactly what she said. But she's not the only one.

The high-relational minority can be very challenging to the Organizer church ways of preaching and doing ministry in general.

We're afraid of our hearts, we're afraid of our feelings . . . "don't go there . . . it might be painful." And it's also . . . on a spiritual level, it's not letting God be God. It's "I am going to stay in control and I'm going to squash something that's a little painful or hard to deal with and I'm going to stay over here where I can analyze it, study it, understand it, and have a sermon with a three-point alliterative . . . ."

However, the Organizer church can "step over the line" from using talent for evaluation and make it an ungodly attack on people.

A number of years ago a young woman shared at the microphone about her abortion and that in part of the healing process God had given her a name for her baby or told her to choose a name. It touched my heart. It was such strong evidence and vulnerable sharing of the Holy Spirit at work in a deep issue that it was tremendous to me. And then afterwards, I heard all this criticism about how bad it was. Okay, maybe she shared too long. I remember thinking she is going on and on . . . okay. But it hurts that we crush our hearts, we crush our emotions.

Organizer churches need sermons and teachings to aid them in understanding the ways of God and how he works in their lives and in the world. They rely on the rationality of the preacher to help them avoid mistakes regarding matters of the faith, so they feel they are standing on solid ground when they apply scriptural principles in their everyday lives.

There is a pattern of preaching that is logical and analytical that is widely appreciated.

Sermons should enable the members to solve moral or ethical problems in a structured manner by concentrating on key details that answer specific questions regarding the primary issues that confront them. Effective sermon or teaching series can direct the learning of the people to reduce erroneous assumptions in their world and life view.

I think it's been good that there are series. I don't know if every church does it that way, but to go through a whole book and not get bogged down with the details but to show how it's one theme, one pattern that it draws on, patterns week to week, those are very good to hear. And in terms of the Word, it shows the depths and the fullness of Scripture.

The members of Organizer churches are uncomfortable giving opinions or making statements about matters of the faith until they have exhausted every trustworthy resource. Consequently, one of the most important services the sermon provides the congregation is guidance in gathering reliable facts and specifics on the key elements of Christianity. Then, with this guidance, they can study more efficiently in forming their belief system.

Surveys indicate that people select a church based on doctrine, fellowship, and the teaching they receive.

260

These churches desire guidance so they can focus on resources that provide answers to the deeper problems of life and understand why God works in the ways he does. Since data collection can mire them down if they follow their inclination to study everything available on a topic, they benefit from sermons that direct them to the most important resources. They need to develop their standards for truth without becoming entangled in insignificant details.

Our pastor's best sermons are aimed at applying Scripture to issues facing people in everyday life.

The Bible on Preaching the Word

Acts 10:42—"And he commanded us to preach to the people and to testify that he is the one appointed by God to be judge of the living and the dead."

1 Corinthians 1:23–25—"We preach Christ crucified, a stumbling block to Jews and folly to Gentiles, but to those who are called, both Jews and Greeks, Christ the power of God and the wisdom of God."

Characteristics of Organizer Church Leaders

Under pressure, Organizer church leaders may tend toward the Aim! Aim! Aim! frame of mind. They are tempted to keep working and planning until they think they will make a faultless presentation. They tend to exhibit a composed, unruffled, dispassionate demeanor that critics may interpret as detachment and coldness. This is because they develop deliberate, cautious methodologies to accomplish their goals.

We are much more comfortable dealing with what the text is saying than we are working through how this is going to form our hearts.

Their natural ability to critique with precision and pragmatic intensity sometimes leads to detachment and overcontrol so that a lack of empathy with people's feelings is communicated.

I don't like personally the feeling that I get that something is wrong with me because I'm older. I don't have really any problem relating to younger people in talking to them. I had young people at my house

261

last night. I can't control how they perceive me but I do sense this attitude in our church somehow that something is wrong with us.

Driven by the Task

Organizer churches establish and manage the procedures necessary for long-term fruitfulness in outreach and assimilation through their skill and efficiency with program planning, strategy, and logistics. However, these preferences can lead to feelings of ambivalence about their task.

> *We are part of the church's ministry where people come to our house for dinner after church and being a structured person I don't just come to church and see who I can invite that day. It doesn't work for me. I have to have my meal prepared and take chairs to the table. But if I look back over that ministry, it's very friendly and hospitable and people love it, but it becomes impersonal because we keep having new people and quit having people who have been around for awhile. And so that's discouraging, and I don't know what to do about that because I keep receiving these lists of people the church wants us to have over. At times I've said, "Don't give me any more people, I'm still trying to . . ." and we don't have time to have over the longer term people . . . like I really want to have . . . , but we already know them and they are not new and so they are not on the list. See the frustration?*

Organizer churches' natural orientation is toward tasks rather than people. From their experience, many people are inconsistent and make things difficult. The more people add their opinions to the mix, the greater the probability of the church becoming unstable and even volatile.

> *We tend to have a cognitive approach to conflict resolution (i.e., follow the right steps and procedure) rather than emphasize (and remain sensitive to) feelings and emotions that arise in the conflict.*

Leaders of Organizer churches usually prefer to serve with people who promote calm and composure. Indeed, when there are arguments in which people become angry and out of control, they want to disappear. Because they desire harmony and serenity, they try to avoid antagonism and belligerence. Over the years, they can insulate themselves emotionally to controversy and strife to the point that they lose touch with people's feelings.

> *Our approach is generally good, but not always the best. It seems that in an organization such as ours, you can't make all of the people happy all of the time. Sometimes people stew about things and we don't know it. Then they blow up and we say, "Where did that come from?"*

Sometimes these churches prefer that their ministries be conducted in a friendly environment among hardworking and conscientious people who do not bring their private problems into the church or expect other people to share their personal feelings.

> *I heard a lay leader say once that this church is friendly on the surface ... it's friendly but people don't make friends. Now, I don't think that's completely true, but that was his impression—that people were very friendly in the sanctuary on Sundays after the worship service but not as much at other times.*

May Not Value Creativity

Organizer churches may doubt the effectiveness of highly creative people, fearing that their judgment may be faulty or that their emotions will influence decisions inappropriately. They especially do not value the creative imaginations of more-innovative people who may be unstructured in their "go with the flow" approach to ministry.

> *I have to work overtime to protect creative people. I can't tell you how many times I've had people come up to me and say, "We are happy to have somebody do something in the church. It's new and it's fun but ... they have to go through proper procedure!" Which effectively means no creativity. Creative people don't plan out their creativity six months in advance and get it to you. And that's been something where just on multiple times I have often had to take people under*

263

my wing and keep them close to me and do some of the communication for them and sometimes just not pay attention to procedure because we have to protect our creative types of artsy people or people who want to do something fun and get something going.

Characteristics of Leaders Who Are Appreciated in This Church

- Focus on accomplishing goals and tasks with excellence, efficiency, and competence.
- Appreciate steadiness and predictability; they prefer an organized, orderly, and scheduled approach to life.
- Understand the need for security and protection of the people from spiritual and physical harm.

When I look at our congregation, here in our community we are a subgroup, but because of the type of church that we are, it draws a certain type of conservative person.

The Bible on Leaders

Matthew 20:26–28—"But whoever would be great among you must be your servant, and whoever would be first among you must be your slave, even as the Son of Man came not to be served but to serve, and to give his life as a ransom for many."

1 Peter 5:2–3—"Shepherd the flock of God that is among you, exercising oversight, not under compulsion, but willingly, as God would have you; not for shameful gain, but eagerly; not domineering over those in your charge, but being examples to the flock."

Worship Style

These churches place a high priority on orderly worship that follows a well-organized and intentional sequence that reflects biblical values and instruction.

Our services are structured—probably goes along with "predictable." You can count on the schedule, the order of worship, the length of sermons, etc.

264

Organizer churches strive to provide a high level of quality and excellence in their music programs, and often have a paid staff member serving as the director of music.

I feel so worshipful when the choir sings, the orchestra plays, the brass ensemble plays, the soloists perform, our organist and pianist. Our Director of Music is incredible as is the entire music program. I can almost see our Lord smiling as the music is offered up to him. The children's music programs have been excellent.

Organizer churches worship the Lord through traditions and rituals. It is important to them that the worship is time-honored, conventional, and orderly. They are generally uncomfortable with frequent change or unfamiliar aspects of the worship. They prefer to follow a coherent structure and order of service. These churches tend to be highly skilled at planning and implementing every aspect of the service. They respect custom and seek to retain what history indicates has aided the people of God in their worship through the ages.

They are not inclined to support change in the worship style in the absence of an obvious problem or "for the sake of change." These churches are so in tune with the time-honored ways of proper behavior within the traditional church that they have a hard time understanding those who might wish to abandon or radically change their customary forms of worship. They like to see things done correctly, and tend to be impatient with those who do not carry out worship forms with sufficient attention to the details prescribed over the centuries.

Characteristics of Organizer Church Worship Services

- Organized, consistent, and sensible, with a minimum of distractions
- Quiet and less engaged, so people may seem impersonal or detached
- Follow procedures and rules that have a logical purpose
- Calm, straightforward, and devoted

- Do not include loose, unstructured forms with unclear outcomes, or high degree of experimentation
- Link what the people are learning to "real-world" issues and avoid too much generalization or ambiguity
- Begin and end on time
- Do not include opportunity for people's expression of emotions and passions

The Bible on Worship

Isaiah 6:1–7—"In the year that King Uzziah died I saw the Lord sitting upon a throne, high and lifted up; and the train of his robe filled the temple. Above him stood the seraphim. Each had six wings: with two he covered his face, and with two he covered his feet, and with two he flew. And one called to another and said: 'Holy, holy, holy is the LORD of hosts; the whole earth is full of his glory!' And the foundations of the thresholds shook at the voice of him who called, and the house was filled with smoke. And I said: 'Woe is me! For I am lost; for I am a man of unclean lips, and I dwell in the midst of a people of unclean lips; for my eyes have seen the King, the LORD of hosts!' Then one of the seraphim flew to me, having in his hand a burning coal that he had taken with tongs from the altar. And he touched my mouth and said: 'Behold, this has touched your lips; your guilt is taken away, and your sin atoned for.'"

Outreach

Affable in a remote way, the Organizer churches connect with people new to the church through ceremonies and rituals. Polite and proper, they are cordial but tend to be reserved. Formal services have great meaning for them, and they appreciate seeing new church members at functions such as holiday services, weddings, and celebration dinners. When they see new people at these gatherings enough times, then they may initiate a relationship. However, because they are usually well spoken and determined, they can intimidate shy people. They prefer to socialize with their own family members and with people who have belonged to the church for a long time. They are quite faithful in their relationships, but new people often have to move toward them to experience their trustworthiness.

Mobilizing our members to do evangelism is a challenge. We'd rather give to outreach efforts than do them ourselves.

Organizer church members can connect with new people through:

- Considering the effect of their thinking and attitude on people's feelings.
- Communicating gratitude to new people for being present.
- Conferring with new people more about events in the church, to prompt in them a sense of involvement.
- Making the effort to nurture new relationships for their own sake.

The Bible on Outreach

Isaiah 54:2–3—"Enlarge the place of your tent, and let the curtains of your habitations be stretched out; do not hold back; lengthen your cords and strengthen your stakes. For you will spread abroad to the right and to the left, and your offspring will possess the nations and will people the desolate cities."

Matthew 28:18–20—"And Jesus came and said to them, 'All authority in heaven and on earth has been given to me. Go therefore and make disciples of all nations, baptizing them in the name of the Father and of the Son and of the Holy Spirit, teaching them to observe all that I have commanded you. And behold, I am with you always, to the end of the age.'"

VOCATIONS OF THOSE TYPICALLY ATTRACTED TO ORGANIZER CHURCHES

Organizer church members are inclined to be employed in the vocations listed below because the requirements, design, and style of these occupations fit them well. Therefore, it follows that the people in the community in these vocations will be more responsive to the ministry style of the Organizer church. The following material is adapted from:

267

- http://www.wsc.edu/advising_services/career_planning/
  exploration/personality_careers
- Allan, Ross. *Connecting Personality Types with Careers and Jobs.*
  Washington, DC: United States Department of the Interior,
  1999.[1]

Sales/Service

- Funeral director
- Government employee
- Insurance agent
- Military officer
- Pharmaceutical sales
- Police/probation/corrections officer
- Sales (tangibles): computers, real estate
- Security guard
- Sports merchandise/equipment sales
- Teacher: trade, industrial, technical
- Telecommunications security

People attracted to Organizer churches enjoy serving in the real world working on tangible projects that require adherence to standard operating procedures. In addition, these churches will attract those who enjoy being in positions of authority and like giving orders. Moreover, Organizer churches resonate with those who sell real things and engage in work that achieves immediate and concrete results.

Technical/Physical

- Accountant
- Auditor
- Clinical technician
- Computer analyst
- Construction worker
- Engineer: mechanical/applied fields
- Farmer

- General contractor
- Health technician
- Paralegal
- Pharmacist
- Technical trainer

These churches are often attractive to those in the technical and mechanical vocations because their work requires them to focus on gathering, organizing, analyzing factual information and engaging in deductive reasoning—all strengths of Organizer churches. Each of these occupations requires a logical and organized work style, which is also appreciated by Organizer church members who prefer a work environment that is orderly and neat as opposed to unruly and inefficient.

Managerial

- Administrator: health services
- Bank manager/loan officer
- Budget analyst
- Chief information officer
- Credit analyst/counselor
- Database manager
- Factory supervisor
- Logistics and supply manager
- Management consultant: business operations
- Office manager
- Purchasing agent
- Regulatory compliance officer

Organizer churches do especially well in creating a wide variety of administrative and supervisory structures for their ministries so they can be efficient in the way they serve. They appreciate those who are competent at making decisions, giving orders and are loyal to established institutions and authority structures. Consequently, those in the managerial fields who direct, monitor and evaluate the work of others will feel at home in the Organizer church.

Professional

- Civil/mechanical/metallurgical engineer
- Corporate lawyer
- Dentist
- Electrical engineer
- Industrial engineer
- Judge
- Pharmacist
- Physician: general medicine
- Stockbroker
- Teacher: technical/trades

The appeal of the professional fields is the ability to work in established, traditional institutions in positions of authority. Dentistry and medicine are technical occupations that generally include hands-on activities—working with real people and tangible objects such as teeth and gums (for dentists) and the human body (for physicians). People in these occupations appreciate the Organizer church members' powers of deductive reasoning and ability to discern cause and effect. They prefer to accomplish tasks by following a clear procedure proven to be effective from their own experience or from that of others whom they respect.

THE CHURCH OF ABRAHAM

Abraham the patriarch was the recipient of the promises of God and father of the Jewish nation as well as the Christian church. Genesis 11–25 describes how he developed into one of history's greatest leaders and was a model of a man of faith—both characteristics of Organizer churches at their best.

Until the age of seventy-five, Abram lived among his relatives in his native land of Chaldea. Then, with his father, family, and household, he left the city of Ur and traveled three hundred miles north to Haran, where he lived fifteen years. The cause of this journey was a call from the Lord (Acts 7:2–3): "The God of glory . . . said to him, 'Go out from your land and from your kindred and go into the land that I will show you.'" Upon the death of his father, Abram received a more definitive call, accompanied by a promise from God (Gen. 12:1–3): "Go from your country and your kindred and your father's house to the land that I will show you. And I will make of you a great nation, and I will bless you and make your name great, so that you will be a blessing. I will bless those who bless you, and him who dishonors you I will curse, and in you all the families of the earth shall be blessed." Soon afterward, Abram left, taking his nephew Lot, "not knowing where he was going" (Heb. 11:8). He trusted the guidance of the One who had called him.

Now, as a leader with a large household of probably a thousand men, women, and children, Abram began a nomadic life, living in tents. At Shechem (Gen. 12:6), he received a promise that included not only temporal but also spiritual blessings: "I will make of you a great nation." (Gen. 12:2; cf. 12:3, 7). This means that he was the chosen ancestor of the Messiah—the great Deliverer whose coming had been long predicted (Gen. 3:15).

When living at Bethel, disputes arose between Lot's shepherds and those of Abram about water and land usage. Abram generously gave Lot his choice of the pasture. Lot chose the well-watered plain on which Sodom was located and moved there. Immediately after this, Abram was encouraged by hearing God repeat the promises he had already made to him (Gen. 13:14-17). Then he moved to Hebron and settled there, pitching his tent by the oaks of Mamre (Gen. 13:18).

Soon after this, Chedorlaomer, king of Elam, brought upon the tribes of the plain his wrath by ravaging the whole country, plundering the towns, and carrying the inhabitants away as slaves. Hearing that his nephew was among those taken, Abram gathered from his own household a band of 318 armed men, and with the chiefs and people of three neighboring tribes, he overtook Chedorlaomer and routed his army. Bringing back all the plunder that had been carried away, Abram returned by way of Salem (Jerusalem) and presented to Melchizedek, king of Salem, a tenth of the spoils, in recognition of Melchizedek's role as a priest of God Most High (Gen. 14:18–20).

After fifteen years' residence at the oaks of Mamre (and a God-given change of name from Abram, "father of nations," to Abraham, "father of multitudes"), Abraham had a son, Isaac, even though Abraham was

271

now one hundred years old. At this point, there is a gap in Abraham's history of perhaps twenty-five years. The next time we see him, his faith is put to a severe test by the command to sacrifice Isaac, the heir of the promises of God, on one of the mountains of Moriah. His faith stood the test (Heb. 11:17–19) as he proceeded in a spirit of unhesitating obedience to carry out the command. When Abraham was about to slay his son, whom he had laid on the altar, the knife in his raised hand was held back by the Angel of the LORD. A ram, provided by God, was entangled in a thicket nearby, and Abraham offered it in Isaac's place. The promises made to Abraham were again confirmed (Gen. 22:15–18).

As a friend of God (James 2:23) and a man who unreservedly trusted the divine promises (Gal. 3:9), Abraham was the recipient of the sixfold covenant (Gen. 12:1–3):

1. "I will make of you a great nation," in natural and spiritual descendants.
2. "I will bless you," temporally and spiritually.
3. "And make your name great"—Abraham is revered among the most prominent men in history.
4. "So that you will be a blessing"—by his example of faith, Abraham has been a worldwide blessing.
5. "I will bless those who bless you, and him who dishonors you I will curse"—nations that have persecuted the Jews and the church have been cursed, and those that have protected them have prospered.
6. "In you all the families of the earth shall be blessed"—this is the great Messianic promise fulfilled in Abraham's descendant, Jesus Christ.

Over the course of his lifetime, the spirituality of Abraham was deepened through four pivotal crises in which his faith was tested. In each case, he was required to relinquish something very dear to him. He was called to:

1. Leave his homeland and relatives and go to a land he knew not (Gen. 12:1).

2. Separate from his nephew, Lot, who was especially close to Abraham because he was a fellow believer and possible heir (Gen. 13:1–18).

3. Surrender his own treasured plans for Ishmael (his son by his wife's maidservant, Hagar, and thus not the true heir of God's promise) and instead focus his hope on the promise of the birth of Isaac (Gen. 17:17–19).

4. Offer up Isaac, his son whom he loved deeply and in whom all his hope depended for the fulfillment of the promises of God (Gen. 22:1–19; Heb. 11:17–19).

Because of Abraham's example as a man of faith and one of history's greatest leaders, he serves as a model for Organizer churches as they serve their communities as leaders faithful to God and his covenant promises.

11

The Adventurous Church

Practical, Problem-Solving, and Change-Oriented
through "Getting Their Hands Dirty" in Community

SUMMARY STATEMENT

For these churches, life is one exciting adventure after another. They are likely to devote considerable energy to solving a problem or completing whatever task is causing stress in the church. However, relational strife can stymie them. Because they are constant observers of what is happening in the community and culture, Adventurous churches prefer working with things that can be seen and examined with their five senses. They are proficient at tactics; i.e., they focus on immediate or short-term aims, more than they concentrate on the broader concerns of logistics; i.e., strategy and diplomacy. Adventurous churches feel debilitated when forced to operate within a set structure that requires conformity to a regulated schedule. For them, change is exciting and challenging because they like putting their practical, problem-solving skills to work. Because their preferred approach to the world is immediate, active, and pragmatic, they display competence especially during events that require rapid response. See Table 10 for a summary of these characteristics.

Table 10: Characteristics of the Adventurous church.

Strong Points	• Handle crisis and problem situations expertly • Are fearless risk takers, filled with optimism
Challenges	• So absorbed in action and the moment, they may lose sight of the long-term strategy • Can be so bored by routine that important day-to-day activities go unattended
Primary Ministries	• The new, the exciting, the adventurous, the risky • Involvement with new opportunities
Ministry Tempo	• Action-oriented, rapid-paced
What Inspires Them	• Spontaneity, autonomy, challenge
What De-motivates Them	• Rules, regulations, structure
Under Stress	• Become excessively pessimistic about the future • Become emotional • Decision-making capabilities erode
Decision-making	• Use logic, analysis, cause-and-effect reasoning
Desires	• A flexible, spontaneous, ever-changing environment
Priority	• Changing things for the good of others
Church Ethos	• Easygoing and cooperative; minimally structured, unregulated
Outward Appearance	• Concentration of attention and resources for quick, powerful impact
Gains Self-Assurance Through	• Connection first with the task
Fears	• Dealing with ambiguity and theory unconnected to reality

MISSION STATEMENT

Adventurous churches are called by God to meet the physical, emotional, and spiritual needs of people in the neighborhoods, schools, and workplaces of their communities through warmhearted words and practical deeds that use the spiritual gifts of mercy, service, and helps to build personal relationships with the expectation that the Holy Spirit will open hearts to the good news of Christ who "came not to be served but to serve, and to give his life as a ransom for many" (Mark 10:45). These offerings of selfless service "with no strings attached" express the compassion of Jesus and act as a humble demonstration of his love that plants a seed of eternity in the hearts of people with the hope that faith in Christ will blossom into salvation.

Theme passage: "In the same way, let your light shine before others, so that they may see your good works and give glory to your Father who is in heaven" (Matt. 5:16).

ADVENTUROUS CHURCH CHARACTERISTICS

Spontaneous

Adventurous churches are comprised of energetic and adaptable realists who like to experience and accept life rather than to judge or organize it. For these churches, life is one action-oriented adventure after another—moving from one exciting event to the next. They have an enthusiastic, uncomplicated approach to life that takes on new projects to learn about why things are the way they are. (Note: quotes in this chapter are from Adventurous or Missional church leaders.)

Church should be like a dance club.—Josh Reich[1]

Friendly, talkative, and outgoing, people in these churches love to laugh, joke, and interact with new people. For these churches, fellowship means finding people to share life's ups, avoid life's downs, and to have fun with. Generally, they are fairly straightforward about the more sensual side of life, regarding the experience of pleasure as part of God's purpose for his people. Autonomy is a basic driving force as they seek to experience and enjoy life to the full. They strive to experience the moment, ride the wave to add excitement to what they care about.

I see this idea of "church as a party" behind much of Missional Church thinking around the world.—Andrew Jones[2]

A combination of finely tuned observational skills, a willingness to respond immediately to what is experienced, and a practical approach to life allows these churches to enjoy events spontaneously as they happen. On the other hand, it's more difficult for Adventurous churches to find value in anything far removed from day-to-day life. They want to be appreciated for their ability to analyze an immediate problem and then solve it. With their ability to respond to the needs of the moment, Adventurous churches are skilled at managing crises and solving real-life challenges.

As the church, we must show God's kindness to everybody. Kindness changes people. Kindness brings people to an understanding of Jesus. Jesus is kind. It's through acts of servanthood that people begin to understand Jesus. Don't just serve the church; serve people. Jesus served people.—Steve Ayers[3]

If and when life becomes too repetitive and routine for Adventurous churches, they find ways to shake things up, either through their own initiative or by responding to the actions or misdeeds of others. They find it stimulating to search out risks in one fashion or another. If these churches are located in the inner city, as many are, they make excellent negotiators and troubleshooters as crises develop. They tend to be logical and analytical in their approach to ministry and have a keen sense of how events and people in the world really work.

Their leadership style focuses on being creative in achieving Adventurous goals within the framework of biblical principles— taking risks, experimenting, dreaming, modifying being the key words. They believe only a radical approach will halt the malaise in church life.—Andy Peck[4]

The ability of Adventurous churches to remain open, flexible, and spontaneous can create problems if they are part of a denomination that calls for more conformity to prescribed expectations. Even then, they demonstrate a flair for drama and style in the ways they interact with the other churches. They're fast-moving, fast-talking people who are good at storytelling and improvising. As a result, they usually are able to argue their way out of trouble.

> *Conservatism is based upon the belief that if you leave things alone you leave them as they are. But you do not. If you leave a thing alone you leave it to a torrent of changes. If you leave a white post alone it will soon be a black post. If you particularly want it to be white you must always be painting it again. . . . Briefly, if you want the old white post you must have a new white post. . . . What people celebrate as "tradition" is usually a thing that has been blackened by time. All things that resist change are changed by that resistance in ways undesired and undesirable. The tradition must be renewed if it is to be worthy of following.—Gary Wills[5]*

The Bible on Enjoyment

Ecclesiastes 2:24–25—"There is nothing better for a person than that he should eat and drink and find enjoyment in his toil. This also, I saw, is from the hand of God, for apart from him who can eat or who can have enjoyment?"

1 Timothy 6:17—"As for the rich in this present age, charge them not to be haughty, nor to set their hopes on the uncertainty of riches, but on God, who richly provides us with everything to enjoy."

Flexible Ministry Style

To be fulfilled and effective in ministry, Adventurous churches develop a lifestyle that offers flexibility and does not impose a rigid structure. They want to do ministry their way, free to respond spontaneously to life's many adventures. Ministry should be fun, not serious and full of rules. Malleable and adaptable, these churches live moment to moment. Rules and regulations are seen as roadblocks, things that can and should be changed as needed.

> We are a nomadic people. A people on a journey. A "pilgrim" people. We are a people "exiled"—a people not at home. Therefore we increasingly need to be a people who resist death (in the sense that Walter Wink and William Stringfellow develop it), who take risks, who resist resting in the familiar and the comfortable.—Paul Fromont[6]

These churches learn from their experiences in a direct way. They often reinvent ways of accomplishing ministries and are adept at trying out new approaches. They like modifying what they already know how to do, and are skilled at creating new solutions to problems. They may even build some excitement into their day by being creative with routine tasks to make them more interesting. This helps them deal with the boredom they experience when dealing with the predictable. Other churches may see this behavior as irresponsible, but the ability of these Adventurous churches to "seize the moment" is a natural gift that makes them effective in chaotic ministry situations in which others languish.

> I belong to what I refer to as a community of "voices"—a "portable (as close to me as an Internet portal)," "self-directed," and "loose network" of wayfarers, priests, prophets, apostles, and friends; a community of "voices" that is both "local" and global simultaneously.—Paul Fromont[7]

Sometimes the church organization will be changed for the sake of change, because the people need the stimulation and excitement of doing something new. However, they tend to become inflexible and rigid when someone threatens their way of doing things. They can respond with a surprising rage that contrasts with their normally laid-back style. At that point, they may go on the attack against structured forms of ministry.

> I'm just not sure that pastors should function like the chief executive officer of a large corporation. In a linear, analytical

world, it's very important to have those kinds of clear leadership lines—to know who's in charge and how decisions get made. If you've hung around the church for any amount of time, you've no doubt seen the business-style hierarchy in action. There may be dozens of committees, a board of elders and a handful of pastoral staff, but someone almost always has the final say. Enter the senior pastor.—Spencer Burke[8]

The Bible on Adaptability

Hebrews 11:13–16—"[They] acknowledged that they were strangers and exiles on the earth. For people who speak thus make it clear that they are seeking a homeland. If they had been thinking of that land from which they had gone out, they would have had opportunity to return. But as it is, they desire a better country, that is, a heavenly one. Therefore God is not ashamed to be called their God, for he has prepared for them a city."

1 Peter 2:10–11—"Once you were not a people, but now you are God's people; once you had not received mercy, but now you have received mercy. Beloved, I urge you as sojourners and exiles to abstain from the passions of the flesh, which wage war against your soul."

Tolerance

Adventurous churches are adept with social relationships. They are energetic and adaptable realists who prefer to accept people rather than to judge or organize them. They are open-minded and demonstrate inexhaustible patience with others' opinions and attitudes because that is how they want to be treated. As a result, they do not mold others in accordance with their beliefs and values or try to influence their decisions in life. They are tolerant of people and accept them as they are. Their natural talents allow them to understand and relate to people in a direct manner.

In the centered set church [defined as our particular values which express God's particular calling to us], community isn't defined by who's in or who's out, or membership, or any other boundaries. And while people certainly gather, the community isn't defined by events that everyone is invited or expected to come to. Rather, we're exploring how the church forms where life happens.—Thomas Knoll[9]

These churches skillfully develop rapport and create a fun, playful atmosphere. Part of the reason that they embrace this ministry style is that Adventurous churches do not function well in relationally stressful environments. They have a low tolerance for anxiety and are apt to leave relationships that are filled with interpersonal tensions. Their high level of tolerance diminishes the possibility of relational stress.

Many of us have misunderstood what tolerance is, and the value of tolerance. You can be tolerant, yet disagree. It's important because none of us have a lock on complete truth.—John Burke[10]

These churches have little tolerance for theory or for that which cannot be proven through direct experience. In regard to doctrine, they are down-to-earth and therefore have little patience with philosophers and traditionalists. They are at ease with their own hunches and free-floating ideas, learning to enjoy them with no need to verify their connection to reality. As a result, they are more willing to make binding commitments to a belief system without feeling controlled by it. Therefore, they are more willing to allow others to do the same.

Spencer Burke intends his Missional Church Web site to be a place where "the various parts of the faith community are like mercury. Try to touch the liquid or constrain it and the substance will resist. Rather than force people to fall into line, an oozy community tolerates differences and treats people who hold an opposing view with great dignity. To me, that's the essence of the Missional church.—Spencer Burke[11]

The Bible on Tolerance
Mark 9:38–40—"John said to him, 'Teacher, we saw someone casting out demons in your name, and we tried to stop him, because

he was not following us.' But Jesus said, 'Do not stop him, for no one who does a mighty work in my name will be able soon afterward to speak evil of me. For the one who is not against us is for us.'"

Romans 14:1–4—"As for the one who is weak in faith, welcome him, but not to quarrel over opinions. One person believes he may eat anything, while the weak person eats only vegetables. Let not the one who eats despise the one who abstains, and let not the one who abstains pass judgment on the one who eats, for God has welcomed him. Who are you to pass judgment on the servant of another? It is before his own master that he stands or falls. And he will be upheld, for the Lord is able to make him stand."

Changing Ministry Environment

Adventurous churches like to be involved in ministry environments that change rapidly, since they are resourceful troubleshooters who jump in and work at down-to-earth problems. Therefore, they are specially suited to act as mission congregations in which the organization is relatively loose and unstructured, with fewer formalities, requirements, or policies in place. They also serve well as established churches in a rapidly changing environment, such as an urban area, because they enjoy a variety of experiences and new people, and dislike being confined by structured or regimented settings. If their environment is not stimulating, they can quickly become bored and lose interest.

> *"Emergent" is a name that is being used at the moment to describe the church's response to the current emerging culture, and the peculiar aggregation of believers being called up out of this culture to follow Jesus back into it.—Andrew Jones[12]*

Observant and five-senses-oriented by nature, these churches notice everything as they continually scan the people and events swirling about them in their church and community. In response, they mold their ministries to what they hear, touch, taste, smell, or see. Because they often have a good memory for detailed events, they can be innovative and polished in their ministry programming.

The greatest challenge the church faces in this day is to impact a society that is moving further and further away from its buildings, its programmes and its preaching. If we are to meet that challenge, I believe we will need to transfer much more of the resources of the body of Christ from the present congregation focused paradigm out into the every day life of the saints. It is out where people live, work and relate that the real battle for the church's future will be won or lost.—James Thwaites[13]

These churches prefer a "do-it-yourself" ministry style, and therefore set up a network of independently operated programs within the church. This approach provides a flexible, spontaneous, and ever-changing ministry environment that fits the people of this Adventurous church. They favor a fast-paced ministry environment with lots of opportunities for creativity that speak to a wide variety of issues. Developing imaginative solutions to everyday problems is energizing for them.

The emerging church must be 100 percent about worshiping God when we gather. No matter what creative form it takes, worship cannot be merely a meeting, a presentation, or a program. We must worship or we cheat God and those who come to our gatherings.—Dan Kimball[14]

People who thrive in a spontaneous environment that allows them to serve autonomously will flourish in these churches. However, there will not likely be much in the way of formal assimilation programs such as membership classes. New people are expected to make the effort to move ahead and learn by doing. In their commitment to flexibility, spontaneity, and a changing environment, these churches have adopted this adaptive style as being the most beneficial for their members.

Operating within a set structure that requires conformity to the programs and schedules set by authority figures will therefore prove debilitating. Such expectations will not hold their attention, and they will quickly be looking for something else to do. They intuitively know that lengthy periods in such a hierarchical setting will lead to inertia, dejection, and eventually depression.

Emergent is in many ways in pursuit of churchless churches: living, self-organizing networked communities of Christ-followers who level traditional hierarchies as they incarnate divine relationality, integrating text, soul and culture in such radically indigenous ways that one church might barely recognize another church.
—Dwight Friesen[15]

The Bible on God-Honoring Change

Matthew 15:1–9—"Then Pharisees and scribes came to Jesus from Jerusalem and said, 'Why do your disciples break the tradition of the elders? For they do not wash their hands when they eat.' He answered them, 'And why do you break the commandment of God for the sake of your tradition? For God commanded, 'Honor your father and your mother,' and, 'Whoever reviles father or mother must surely die.' But you say, 'If anyone tells his father or his mother, What you would have gained from me is given to God, he need not honor his father.' So for the sake of your tradition you have made void the word of God. You hypocrites! Well did Isaiah prophesy of you, when he said: 'This people honors me with their lips, but their heart is far from me; in vain do they worship me, teaching as doctrines the commandments of men.'"

Colossians 2:8—"See to it that no one takes you captive by philosophy and empty deceit, according to human tradition, according to the elemental spirits of the world, and not according to Christ."

Entrepreneurial

Adventurous churches are likely to be entrepreneurial in style. They are resourceful and able to capitalize on events that they did not necessarily foresee, but are able to turn to the good in ways that other types of churches find difficult to do. This ability is characteristic in large part because they do not find satisfaction in developing the formal procedures and policies that are natural barriers to change. Rather, they thrive on their ability to influence the surrounding community in some distinctive way. They are good at this, in part because they instinctively see the unmet needs and problems to be solved in their communities. Adventurous engagement, not ideas, is what counts to them.

284

A Missional church is one whose primary commitment is to the missionary calling of the people of God . . . it is one that aligns itself with God's missionary purposes in the world. . . . The Missional church is a sent church with one of its defining values [as incarnating Jesus' life and values in the culture it is embedded].—Michael Frost and Alan Hirsch[16]

Adventurous churches are the best at quick, pragmatic analyses of ministry opportunities. They don't feel hampered by rules or frightened by any risk they can assess rationally. So they think outwardly while acting as people engaged in an adventure with nothing to lose. This characteristic is especially noticeable in crises or high-risk situations. However, they can grow bored when the mission has been accomplished. Then they may feel lifeless for a while until they can find a new community problem to engage.

We see a new social activism that is both critical and creative: mission is understood to encompass a much wider set of activities than just evangelism.—Andrew Jones[17]

Adventurous churches prefer to focus on the present and forget the past, which is (by their way of thinking) done with, gone, and finished. Nor are they very concerned with planning for the future. For those reasons, they may have trouble sustaining enthusiasm among their people over the long term. They can shift from great success to disaster almost overnight. But their pragmatism keeps them from becoming attached to any one way of doing things, so they can also bounce back from trouble rapidly—often transforming ruin into triumph.

The Missional church is about the Spirit of God producing Adventurous kingdom-minded disciples of Jesus no matter what methodology we use.—Dan Kimball[18]

These churches are resourceful—making good use of what is available while jumping in wherever needed. They are willing to take risks, and want other churches to do the same. They are action-oriented, and sometimes are so inclined to rapid change that they put energy into ideas that are not sufficiently thought through. They may be inconsistent at follow-through, and tend to wing it, wait until the last minute, and put off essential tasks because they are not thought important. Leaders are direct and straightforward in their communication, and value telling it like it is in a frank, brusque manner that sometimes is shocking to the feelings of the more sensitive types among them.

> So I had a shepherd and a sheep on stage, and I brought all the kids down. Then I wanted them to run all over the building, all over the place shouting, "Glory to God in the highest." And at that moment the sheep is pooping on stage. So I'm trying to tell the kids to go, and they're all staring at the sheep. It was a great moment. . . . They were shouting, "Mom, you won't believe what the sheep did. It was awesome!" Not what I expected, but they remember it. Animals, whatever. Whatever it takes. No rules.—Rob Bell[19]

Their impulsive bent discourages doing things in the customary manner. Tradition becomes the foil. In addition, their logic-driven focus on issues immediately before them can lead to relational dynamics being neglected. As a result, the leaders of these churches can foster an abrasive and edgy style that alienates the more sensitive members of the church.

> Two weeks ago I sponsored a "Doubt Night." I said, "I want to talk about my own doubts about God, Jesus, the Bible, salvation, faith. And if you have some, bring them. Write them down and pass them forward, we'll read them and we'll see what happens." We had a huge box—you would not believe—and I just started going through them, reading them and discussing them. It was so awesome.—Rob Bell[20]

Adventurous churches identify themselves as service-driven and not institutionally driven, culturally engaged without being absorbed by the culture, as they plant, grow, and multiply new communities. One of their distinctives is the ability to be responsive to cultural trends. They see themselves as a sent people—expressing Jesus' life and values in the culture in which they are embedded.

We somehow think that the Church is here for us; we forget that we are the Church and we're here for the world.—Erwin McManus[21]

Since Adventurous churches focus on relating to Jesus as they are engaged in mission, doctrinal exactness does not characterize them. Until they can see the mission field and begin serving in it, they feel out of their element. Nonjudgmental and adaptable, these churches work well with many types of people and are able to shift quickly to where the culture is moving. They don't allow themselves to be withdrawn, isolated end users of the gospel. Rather, they believe they have received the gospel to be equipped and sent into the world to love their neighbors and serve "the least of these" as Jesus did.

This has been evangelicalism's model. . . . Fundamentally it's about getting yourself "saved"—in old-style evangelicalism—or improving your life in the new style. Either way, the Christian life is really about you and your needs. Once your needs are met, then we think about how you can serve the church. And then, if there's anything left over, we ask how the church might serve the world. . . . But what if it went the other way? This big circle is the world—the world God loved so much that he sent his Son. Inside that circle is another one, the church, God's people chosen to demonstrate his love to the world. And inside that is a small circle, which is your self. It's not about the church meeting your needs, it's about you joining the mission of God's people to meet the world's needs.—Brian McLaren[22]

The Bible on Mission-Mindedness

Matthew 5:16—"Let your light shine before others, so that they may see your good works and give glory to your Father who is in heaven."

2 Corinthians 5:14–15—"For the love of Christ controls us, because we have concluded this: that one has died for all, therefore all have died; and he died for all, that those who live might no longer live for themselves but for him who for their sake died and was raised."

Communication in the Adventurous Church

The people of Adventurous churches respond to stimulating, first-hand experiences—tending to be less interested in theory than in application of truth to real life. Since their strength is in focusing their five senses on people and things, they have a low tolerance for speculation that is unrelated to their everyday experience. Their philosophy is that learning should be fun; i.e., it should involve role-playing, experimentation, and plenty of stimulation and interaction, as well as enough time to assimilate new ideas. Demonstrations and practical examples are of more use to the growth of these people than sending them off to read or meditate alone.

> *Visual imagery is the primary language of our day and draws together people of all ages, races, genders and classes. People increasingly remember what they see more than what they hear. Church historian Margaret Miles helps make the case for using visual imagery, rather than just words, for sacramental purpose. She details in* Image as Insight *(Beacon, 1985) how during earlier centuries the visual arts made the church more inclusive, but verbal communication made the church more exclusive. Today over 60 percent of our population, under age 60 and raised with television, remembers primarily by what is seen. Only 20 percent of the population, over age 60 and raised with radio, remembers primarily what is heard. (The remaining 20 percent remembers kinesthetically, that is, by doing.) Churches having only verbal worship and preaching may as well use Latin, for the exclusively verbal mode no longer communicates with the vast majority of the population.—Doug Adams[23]*

These are action-oriented churches, and members learn most effectively through personal participation and practical involvement. They are especially unmotivated when worship services are highly structured and unstimulating, with few opportunities to play a part. On the contrary, they tend to plunge into new learning opportunities—discovering as they go. Since variety, sensory stimulation, and active participation maintain their interest, they benefit most from presentations that go to the bottom line with minimal detail, on-the-job learning that has immediate application, and practical, experiential workshops. There should be plenty of opportunities for cooperative interaction, dialogue, and group discussion.

> *I want to rescue preaching. I believe it's an art form and I want to rescue it back from the scientists and the analysts. I want to see the poets and the prophets and the artists grab the microphone and say great things about God and the revolution. I think a whole art form has been lost that needs to be recaptured, a grand ambition for the art of preaching. There's a mystery to a man or a woman in a room, when the text has done something in them and then it's coming out of them—whatever that looks like. It's a parable; it's silence; it's a series of disparate images that don't seem to have any connection, and yet somehow they do.—Rob Bell[24]*

Since these are mercy-ministry-oriented churches, they prefer hands-on training. More than any other type, these Adventurous churches immerse themselves in the immediate challenges of their communities. The people respond to challenges requiring action, flexibility, and interaction with the real world, such as recreational ministries for urban children and health care for the poor.

> *So my understanding in communication is you engage people right where they are; if you don't, they leave. Sometimes I hear people say, "The church isn't here to entertain." To entertain means to hold people's attention, which is clearly something teachers throughout the Scriptures are doing. They engage and capture attention. But we're not here to amuse. To "a-muse" means to "not think." And it's wrong to prevent people from pondering or distract them from thinking. I'm not here to amuse. But of course I want to engage people. I have something to say.—Rob Bell[25]*

Adventurous churches give the people positions of leadership and responsibility to organize team members and coach others. They encourage people to set their own deadlines and targets rather than impose too much structure on them. At the same time, they encourage them to remain spontaneous, flexible, and open to new alternatives that will make the ministry more efficient and effective.

> *Our job is to serve our Creator and Sustainer God by presenting Jesus in containers out of which postmodern people will be clamoring to drink. The mystery of the gospel is this: It is always the same (content) and it is always changing (containers). The old, old story needs to be told in new, new ways. Yes, people's experience of God and of the gospel changes. But no, God and the gospel don't change. Our experience does and it should change through time. But God remains the same. The gospel is timeless. Part of leadership is making sure that the containers don't alter the content.—Len Sweet*[26]

The people of Adventurous churches lose their motivation when the training is essentially passive, i.e., requiring them to work alone, read, write, or reflect by themselves or in a classroom setting, or having them observe others or take notes on how something "should" be done. The leaders make sure there is not too much theory, generalization, or ambiguity. These people learn best through quick, exact, objective training that enables them to minister to the culture around them. If only one adjective would describe the learning style of the people of the Adventurous church, it would be "practical."

> *Within our high-tech society, audiovisuals are the waters in which most people swim. By using what's familiar to the average listener, you increase your effectiveness and can combat the stereotype of an archaic church, too. You'll show how faith can interact in any world, at any time.—Graham Johnston*[27]

Adventurous churches are naturally good at improvising, decision-making, and risk-taking. They don't waste much time on routine events, because people in these churches are quickly bored. They can even become disruptive if their energy and enthusiasm are not properly channeled. So their leaders give them opportunities to plunge into the "actual world" and work with real (as opposed to textbook) problems—using their innate talent instead of what they might be taught theoretically.

We are aware that many will be called to different expressions of Christianity by God and we respect that. At the same time, we know that as some people hear us teach on these values, where we are going and what God has called us to, something deep inside of them will identify fully with this. In that regard, these values are caught not taught!—Association of Vineyard Churches of East Africa[28]

A temptation for Adventurous churches is for people to be like instruments in the hands of leaders who "play" them with impressive ability. If leaders succumb to this temptation, they can handle people with much the same skill as others handle tools, operate machines, or play musical instruments. Because these churches often excel in the roles of entrepreneur, troubleshooter, and negotiator, those in leadership can fall into the trap of being master manipulators of people around them. More than in any other type of church, these leaders possess the innate ability to approach people they know only casually and persuade them to do what the leaders want for the good of the mission. People tend to respond to these requests, even on superficial acquaintance. The pastors can be charming, extremely attentive to others, and smooth in social circles, calling many people by name—somehow knowing how to say just the right things to everyone they meet. These pastors can give the people confidence to go along with what the pastor proposes by maneuvering people in the direction they want them to go. Such tendencies in their ministry style earn these churches a negative reputation from other churches. Leaders of Adventurous churches might be referred to as "schemers" and "operators."

We have a goal. We have a mission. We're going to save the world. We're going to evangelize everybody and we're going to do all this good stuff and fill our churches. This is wonderful. All the goals are right. But this is slow, slow work, this soul work, this bringing people into a life of obedience and love and joy before God. And we get impatient and start taking shortcuts and use any means available. We talk about benefits. We manipulate people.—Eugene Peterson[29]

The Bible on Effective Communication

Matthew 7:28-29—"And when Jesus finished these sayings, the crowds were astonished at his teaching, for he was teaching them as one who had authority, and not as their scribes."

Mark 6:2—"And on the Sabbath he began to teach in the synagogue, and many who heard him were astonished, saying, 'Where did this man get these things? What is the wisdom given to him?'"

Technologically Savvy

Because Adventurous churches find sensory experiences to be the best way for them to learn about the world in which they live, they work hard to perfect their technological presentations. First, they experience the truth relationally and through their five senses, and then they validate what they have learned by teaching from Scripture. Their leaders are strong communicators who engage people at the point where they are, in order to hold their attention in ways teachers did throughout the Scriptures. They engage and capture attention. Through their technology they take an active, realistic, and hands-on approach to communication that causes their people to think and ponder. Only high-quality communication media will meet their requirements to present to the people what they can see, touch, taste, smell, and feel, and connect their senses to the real world.

> *The thing is: we've moved past the MTV generation into the Internet generation and yet many of us are just now responding to the TV generation! Our message must never change, but the way we deliver that message must be constantly updated to reach each new generation. The only way to stay relevant is to anchor your ministry to unchanging truths and eternal purposes but be willing to continually adapt how you communicate those truths and purposes.—Rick Warren[30]*

These churches have mastered highly technical media forms. Much of the communication of this movement is presented online—with the conversation being carried on through blogs, wikis, and other interactive Web sites. Not only is this an effective use of technology, it also demonstrates the non-hierarchical, network-oriented nature of these churches. Often the more complex and demanding the subject matter, the greater they work at presenting it technologically. Their use of technology can involve everything from the use of contemporary music and films to liturgy, for the purpose of making the message more attractive to those outside the church as well as those within. Ideas often are presented imaginatively or in a multi-sensory media form using dramatization or presentations that include music, video, and movement.

> *Multimedia incorporates several elements of communication: text, graphics, animation, sound and video. When properly used, these elements enhance the total worship experience and give new freedom to the worshipper. Thousands of churches are already using multimedia to take worship to new levels. Multimedia in worship is a combination of art, technology and spirit. Every church has a unique personality. Multimedia, when used properly, complements this personality instead of working against it.—Don Wuebben*[31]

The Bible on Dramatic Presentation

Isaiah 20:2–4—"At that time the Lord spoke by Isaiah the son of Amoz, saying, 'Go, and loose the sackcloth from your waist and take off your sandals from your feet,' and he did so, walking naked and barefoot. Then the Lord said, 'As my servant Isaiah has walked naked and barefoot for three years as a sign and a portent against Egypt and Cush, so shall the king of Assyria lead away the Egyptian captives and the Cushite exiles, both the young and the old, naked and barefoot, with buttocks uncovered, the nakedness of Egypt.'"

Acts 21:10–11—"While we were staying for many days, a prophet named Agabus came down from Judea. And coming to us, he took Paul's belt and bound his own feet and hands and said, 'Thus says the Holy Spirit, "This is how the Jews at Jerusalem will bind the man who owns this belt and deliver him into the hands of the Gentiles."'"

Outreach

Adventurous churches are action oriented, and react well to crisis situations by using their communication skills to interact with people in the community to gather whatever information they need to be effective. Opportunities for them to use their ability to act expediently are attractive to them. They can be risk-takers, and sometimes seek ministry situations that are physically challenging and even dangerous. They have to balance their tendency to react impulsively with the need to slow down, evaluate the relevant information, and make good decisions.

> I don't think that the mega-church model is the ideal any longer. I think it has been a suburban aberration that will pass as quickly as it came. It's based on a felt-needs approach that says that the church is about meeting your felt or perceived needs. Instead, we need to take a look at the Adventurous model we see in Acts—and today, internationally—and return to what authors like Lesslie Newbigin have said about engaging culture in an "Adventurous way."—Chris Seay[32]

The ability of these churches to perceive cultural shifts in their communities, and to shape their outreach efforts accordingly, is an essential aspect of their effectiveness. Interacting with the mosaic of their surrounding culture is exciting and challenging to them because they like the opportunity to put their practical, problem-solving abilities to work. These churches are an exciting place because they thrive on difficult challenges, relishing the opportunity to adapt quickly. They generate enthusiasm in the neighborhood because of their abilities, talents, and energy. With their unbending confidence in their ability to respond to the needs of the moment, they are skilled at managing crises and solving real-life neighborhood problems.

> I think outreach will shift from the content to the context. Most evangelism has put a high emphasis on information. But most people come to faith within the context of family and before they have all of the information. This means that churches will need to shape the character of their own faith community, rather than focusing on

content being properly disseminated. Churches will need to tell the Story using a minimum of communication skills and, instead, utilize hospitality and community in a greater way.—Doug Pagitt[33]

The mercy-oriented ministries of these Adventurous churches require the ability to read events and people quickly in order to adapt rapidly to situations and to keep cool under stress. When they see the way to accomplish a task, they do not hesitate to jump in, putting forth the necessary effort to accomplish the mission. However, these churches can be tempted to keep their ties with people in the community on a superficial level because they connect best with others through physical activities rather than through face-to-face dialogue. Their deed-oriented ministries are more enjoyable—and more effective—if they are spontaneous and unplanned, serving no purpose other than the doing of them for the honor of God.

We are still doing this propositional evangelism to an emerging generation that doesn't learn in linear proposition. So we have to change our models drastically; otherwise, we'll continue toward extinction.—Chris Seay[34]

Adventurous churches embody the grit and drive of a take-charge ministry. They know how to use people's abilities and talents to achieve goals. Difficult situations showcase their ability to make decisions and smoothly adapt their responses to fluid events. Because they receive affirmation for their ability to manage differences, they sometimes need a crisis to let them know they are still capable and competent.

Fundamentally, outreach is about relationships, and it will always be that. I don't think we will see any new "tools," although, I'm sure there will always be a place for that. There is not one specific way to reach out, and how we express that depends on how God has wired each of us individually. It should be unique to the individual.—Matt Hammett[35]

Because they enjoy action and willingly take risks, there is an adventurous spirit that pervades Adventurous churches. On the other hand, they can sometimes openly show impatience with people's inabilities and weaknesses. Nevertheless, they communicate kindness with an unpretentious style in ways that make them exceptional at working with people in need, and especially children.

> *I think serving other people is very significant. We earn the right to be heard and gain influence on people's lives when we sincerely care for them, and when we put their needs above our own. When we serve others in a culture that is so self-centered, that service will stand out. It's about intentional acts of kindness toward the people in our lives, saying, "How do I authentically serve you?" as opposed to, "How do I convince you that Christ is the Messiah?" In serving others, I've found that they're not necessarily interested in the faith question right away, but if I serve them and they see that difference in my life, it will lead to dialogue.—Matt Hammett[36]*

Adventurous churches are concrete in their communication and utilitarian in their use of methodologies. Consequently, they are impatient with discussions of complex "what ifs." They are keen observers of their immediate environment and act quickly to deal with day-to-day needs that people have. Skilled at making things work and fixing problems, they use their quickness and flexibility to find the most efficient route to accomplish whatever needs to be done. They will step up, figure out what needs to be done, and then act on their analysis and their instincts to solve the predicament.

> *John Wimber often taught that our values are rather like the sign on the front of the bus that indicates its destination. We welcome anybody getting on the bus provided they are clear as to where we are going and also want to head in the same direction as us! Again, to quote John Wimber, "You don't join the Vineyard, but discover that you are Vineyard!"—Association of Vineyard Churches of East Africa[37]*

For these churches, outreach means finding people in their network of relationships to have fun with so they can draw them into the church to share life's ups and downs in the midst of spiritual community. They establish rapport with people quickly because they are gifted at meeting new people and making them feel comfortable with the church. Fun, excitement, laughter, as well as an element of unpredictability, are characteristic of their relationships.

> *What unites it all is the attempt to bring "Church" into situations where the existing forms of Church fail to reach. (On the other hand) the traditional paradigm of Christian "outreach" suggests a model where the existing Christian community goes out and grabs people from outside to bring them in. Here the Church is seen as akin to a sheepfold or an ark, rescuing those outside of the Church's ambit to bring them to a place of safety and benefit. Most existing parish churches have this paradigm in mind when considering any form of encounter with those beyond their fringe, either in terms of evangelism, publicity or social engagement.—Paul Roberts[38]*

One of the most fun-loving of church types, Adventurous churches often insert practical humor into their outreach efforts. They are usually popular, because they're enthusiastic, fast-paced, friendly, and verbal, and know how to have a good time. Though at times reserved because they do not want to expose themselves fully to others, their warm and sympathetic nature is sensed by people who know them well.

> *A group of people in a Western suburb live together and do outreach work among young people in nearby schools, then share meals and Bible study with them in their home; a group of artists share prayer in the midst of canvas and paint and exhibit works which reflect their religious experience; a couple on the outskirts of Melbourne are building relationships among young people who have experimented with New Age groups and now are seeking a new space to fit; some couples are hoping to occupy apartments in an up-market harbourside development and act as community builders; a suburban church has closed down but a new community is emerging around the childcare centre on their premises.—Bryan Cussen[39]*

Adventurous churches are optimistic about life in general and about the potential of people in particular. They prefer to focus on the positive, uplifting, and harmonious aspects of human relation-ships—paying less attention to negative, pessimistic, limiting, and divisive situations. They are flexible, laid-back, non-controlling people who like to take things as they come. When they interact with others, they operate in the mode of "information gathering," so they tend to ask questions rather than share views. They do not like to sit still, and are often involved in energy-intensive sports and other activities with people. They will offer people the shirts off their backs and give generously of their time and skills to help with building projects, mechanical jobs, house remodeling, car repair, etc.

> *Understanding what it means to reach the next generation comes much more through conversations and through interactions with people. It's still in the "oral tradition," if I can use that historical picture.—Doug Pagitt*[40]

The Bible on Outreach

Romans 12:19–21—"Beloved, never avenge yourselves, but leave it to the wrath of God, for it is written, 'Vengeance is mine, I will repay, says the Lord.' To the contrary, 'if your enemy is hungry, feed him; if he is thirsty, give him something to drink; for by so doing you will heap burning coals on his head.' Do not be overcome by evil, but overcome evil with good."

Colossians 3:12–14—"Put on then, as God's chosen ones, holy and beloved, compassion, kindness, humility, meekness, and patience, bear-ing with one another and, if one has a complaint against another, forgiv-ing each other; as the Lord has forgiven you, so you also must forgive. And above all these put on love, which binds everything together in perfect harmony."

Decision-Making

In whatever ministries Adventurous churches choose to engage, they use their naturally logical approach to analyze each situation in a careful manner. They anticipate immediate, practical needs in situations, and then present a rational, straightforward plan for meeting those needs. In addition to their logical analysis of current problems, their strengths and talents for decision-making include careful attention to detail and their unpretentious communication style. Micromanaging by people in authority does not fit the Adventurous church model.

> *Most people want to wake up in the morning with a general at the foot of their bed saying "Go do this." The problem is there's somebody at the foot of their bed saying, "Once upon a time. . . ."*
> —*N. T. Wright*[41]

Rules and regulations are seen as roadblocks that can and should be changed regularly. Uninhibited by institutional controls, these churches will dive right in, taking whatever approach will solve the problem—today! Tight structures and restrictive time lines are not interesting to them. When plans are rigidly controlled, they grow restless.

> *Emerging church is characteristically postmodern in its suspicion of the controlling structures of religious life and thought: church hierarchy, dominant cultural forms, doctrinal formulations, and so on. So the life and practice of emerging church are marked by a resistance to these structures, but also by a desire to develop positive alternatives.*—*Andrew Jones*[42]

Potential drawbacks for Adventurous churches in decision-making include a tendency to focus only on the immediate present, a break-down in follow-through, and an inability to communicate seriousness and dependability. They have to use their organizational skills to stay on top of projects, make a plan, be on time, remember to follow up with prospective new members, and so forth. As these churches grow spiritually, they also need to learn to evaluate and discern God's will by applying their biblical values to situational needs.

> *The pastor, by his mere presence, causes an unhealthy depen-dence upon himself for ministry, direction, and guidance. Thus, as long as he hangs around delivering sermons, the people in the church to which he belongs will never be fully set free to function*

on their own in a church meeting setting. Further, the pastoral office typically destroys those who populate it. Jesus Christ never intended for anyone to shoulder that kind of enormous responsibility and power.—Frank Viola[43]

The Bible on Decision-Making

1 Kings 18:21—"And Elijah came near to all the people and said, 'How long will you go limping between two different opinions? If the Lord is God, follow him; but if Baal, then follow him.'"

James 1:5–8—"If any of you lacks wisdom, let him ask God, who gives generously to all without reproach, and it will be given him. But let him ask in faith, with no doubting, for the one who doubts is like a wave of the sea that is driven and tossed by the wind. For that person must not suppose that he will receive anything from the Lord; he is a double-minded man, unstable in all his ways."

Risk-Taking

Risk-taking motivates these churches, and is routine for them. Crisis situations produce their finest hour, and therefore their ministry tends to move from one emergency to the next. They aspire to develop the skill necessary to handle any problem, and they are energized by the dramatic and a desire for impact.

> *Many of you are here, but you don't want to be here. You are tired of church but come out of obligation. My suggestion is that you leave and don't come back. But if I can be of any help in what you end up doing for the kingdom, then give me a call.—James Thwaites*[44]

They are prepared to take great risks, but never without good reason. Life on the edge suits them just fine, because during times of emergency they are not hampered by rules or frightened by any risk they can assess rationally. Witty, quick, and enjoyable, they tend to move through life with great fanfare, which makes even everyday events seem special.

We dream of a church where . . . we value innovation and are will-
ing to take risks in order to bring glory to God.—Solomon's Porch,
Minneapolis, Minnesota[45]

These churches delight in the new, the stimulating, the daring, and the uncertain. In times of high anxiety, they concentrate on the needs of the moment by applying their rational abilities to solve problems with dexterity and efficiency. They meet life with a hearty enthusiasm for good things, anticipating the next enjoyable project, always looking for the thrill of inviting the possibility of failure in one way or another. However, if their desire for excitement is not directed constructively, they may channel their energies into challenging tradition for the sake of challenge.

My second beer (creation) is here! Advent Ale is here! It's a refresh-
ing ale, with a touch of Christmas spices. I'd class it as a "dessert
beer." I've never heard this term but it fits. Somehow an ale with
touches of cinnamon and nutmeg doesn't exactly compliment a
hearty, spicy chili. . . . But it's wonderful with oatmeal raisin
cookies!—Marc Pitman, Pastor of Vineyard Church of Water-
ville, Maine[46]

Autonomous, self-sufficient, and confident in their decision-making ability, Adventurous churches are very down-to-earth. If an externally imposed schedule supports their way of accomplishing the task, they consider that a good thing. If it doesn't, then the schedule is ignored. These churches like to be spontaneous, and see little need for rules and supervision. They will not allow regulations to get in the way; they will take whatever path is necessary to accomplish the task. They do not believe in following rules that would prohibit their ability to do it their way. Their dislike of being tightly managed extends to their refusal to control other people. They usually give people a lot of freedom to serve in the unique ways that fit those individuals best.

We need a period of experimentation to discover what forms of
church will connect most effectively with our emerging culture. It's
of the very nature of experimentation that some experiments fail.

This makes the whole attempt risky. But risk is in the lifeblood of mission. The church has seldom advanced without someone taking a risk.—Michael Moynagh[47]

The Bible on Risk-Taking

2 Samuel 22:2–4—"[David] said, 'The LORD is my rock and my fortress and my deliverer, my God, my rock, in whom I take refuge, my shield, and the horn of my salvation, my stronghold and my refuge, my savior; you save me from violence. I call upon the LORD, who is worthy to be praised, and I am saved from my enemies.'"

2 Corinthians 1:10—"He delivered us from such a deadly peril, and he will deliver us. On him we have set our hope that he will deliver us again."

Stress

Persistent stress—especially that which goes along with interpersonal conflict and uncooperative people—causes these churches to lose the joy of being "in the present." Under great tension, they may misinterpret events as being much worse than they are, projecting on them the most negative interpretation possible so that they become pessimistic about the future. They can then become chronically anxious, depressed, uncertain, and sad.

Religious debate can be a lot like pornography, drug abuse, and gambling: stupid yet attractive and potentially addictive, and therefore dangerous spiritually.—Brian McLaren[48]

Although Adventurous churches tend to say that few aspects of ministry are very stressful for them (in comparison with most types of churches), when they do become anxious, they are likely to lose their typical optimistic and their carefree enjoyment of the moment. The combination of the natural upheaval of ministry and the disruption of traumatic experiences can push these churches into serious soul-searching and reconsideration of long-standing purpose and direction. Feeling overwhelmed by mysterious, malevolent forces may lead to a significant change in the laid-back manner in which they usually conduct ministry.

"Jesus Christ is the same yesterday and today and forever" (Heb. 13:8). He is the same Jesus now as He was in the Upper Room and as He appeared to Paul on the road to Damascus. He is the same Jesus as when Martin Luther nailed his ninety-five theses to the door of Castle Church in Wittenberg. He is the same Jesus as when the Enlightenment was in full force. Modern world, postmodern world, post-postmodern world. . . . Jesus never changes. He is the reason for and the focus of all that we do. He is our anchor, no matter which direction the tide may be taking us.—Dan Kimball[49]

The Bible on Risk-Taking

Matthew 6:25–34—"Therefore I tell you, do not be anxious about your life, what you will eat or what you will drink, nor about your body, what you will put on. Is not life more than food, and the body more than clothing? Look at the birds of the air: they neither sow nor reap nor gather into barns, and yet your heavenly Father feeds them. Are you not of more value than they? And which of you by being anxious can add a single hour to his span of life? And why are you anxious about clothing? Consider the lilies of the field, how they grow: they neither toil nor spin, yet I tell you, even Solomon in all his glory was not arrayed like one of these. But if God so clothes the grass of the field, which today is alive and tomorrow is thrown into the oven, will he not much more clothe you, O you of little faith? Therefore do not be anxious, saying, 'What shall we eat?' or 'What shall we drink?' or 'What shall we wear?' For the Gentiles seek after all these things, and your heavenly Father knows that you need them all. But seek first the kingdom of God and his righteousness, and all these things will be added to you. Therefore do not be anxious about tomorrow, for tomorrow will be anxious for itself. Sufficient for the day is its own trouble."

Matthew 28:20—"And behold, I am with you always, to the end of the age."

Primary Temptations

The temptation for Adventurous churches is to overlook the spiritual life because of their focus on real life and the appeal of the material. They can spend too much time on activities and too little time in reflection. In addition, they have a tendency toward self-deception and a reluctance to be transparent before the Lord and people. This temptation is exacerbated when they find it hard to be patient during the inevitable spiritual dry periods. They may at times question the reality of the spiritual and even truths such as eternal life, because it is hard for them to take things on faith.

Another temptation for these churches is in the desire to increase their stature in the eyes of others, especially by flaunting their achievements. Such pride not only fails to recognize dependence on others in the community, but also neglects to credit the Lord as the true provider of all gifts and blessings. This leads to a temptation to crave excitement, stimulation, or entertainment, and to make a god out of their desires and ambitions for power.

> *Consumer Church: Church is seen as a dispenser of religious goods and services. People come to church to be fed, to have their needs met through quality programs, and to have the professionals teach their children about God. Missional Church: Church is seen as a body of people sent on a mission who gather in community for worship, encouragement, and teaching from the Word that supplements what they are feeding themselves throughout the week.*—Dan Kimball[50]

Spiritual Disciplines for Adventurous Church Members

The members of these churches can learn to overcome temptation through a practical regimen of self-discipline and self-sacrifice. They should set aside daily at least a half-hour for formal prayer and Scripture meditation in order to experience the presence, love, and protection of God, to keep themselves on course with firm purpose and deep resolve in the face of changing circumstances. They will do well at engaging in Bible study that focuses on the logical and practical applications of the faith. They need orderly structure to discipline themselves in order to profit most from both public and private prayer. They should feel free to attempt new and varied ways of prayer so they do not become stuck in one form or routine. They will want to read the Scriptures long enough to develop some worthwhile thought on which they can ponder for the next several minutes. This can be followed by prayers of praise, humble confession, thanksgiving, dedication, and petition.

> *Through the discipline of contemplative prayer, Christian leaders have to learn to listen again and again to the voice of love and to find there the wisdom and courage to address whatever issue presents itself to them . . . . For Christian leadership to be truly fruitful in the future, a movement from the moral to the mystical is required.—Henri Nouwen[51]*

During their daily time of prayer, they can think about how their insights from Scripture can be expressed in daily living. Spontaneous prayers of praise and gratitude can be offered throughout the day in order to sustain a close walk with God even in the midst of a busy workday. The more simple the structure of prayer through the day, the more they will find it beneficial.

Because of their orientation to use of their five senses, fresh air and exercise will aid their devotional times. These are the people who at a church retreat are bewildered that so much time is spent indoors in brainwork, practically excluding any time to enjoy the glory of the natural surroundings to which they have retreated. Through the sights and sounds of the outdoors, they will more fully experience the majesty and awe-inspiring power of the Lord. It is helpful for them to be in nature and use those opportunities to ponder the supernatural marvels of God's creation.

> *In this community, there is a deep appreciation for the beauty and sanctity of creation and they have just begun to do nature/prayer walks together. One member is a naturalist and brings interesting interpretations as we walk. We hope someday to create Spiritual Walks with special activities at various points along the trails.—Nashoba Grace Community Church[52]*

Good experiences of community worship are essential to their spiritual growth and are normally found at the Sunday gatherings of these churches, although these experiences can also be found in prayer groups. Structured retreats help them concentrate on their relationship with unseen realities, and maintain faithfulness to their promises and obligations. During these times, the people experience spiritual life as well by appreciating God's gifts through them to help other people, as they learn to trust the sovereign God to take care of things. They need to share their faith experiences with others and have others share their faith with them. This includes talking openly about the difference faith has made in their lives and demonstrating the difference by caring about people during difficult times. Some of their challenges are in learning to live with tension and anxiety by deepening their trust in God's loving care, while being faithful to their commitments and relationships.

> *He [Brian McLaren] cites Dallas Willard and Richard Foster, with their emphasis on spiritual disciplines, as key mentors for the emerging church.—Andy Peck*[53]

The natural generosity and delight of Adventurous church members in coming to the aid of others gives their spiritual expression a down-to-earth quality. If they are not provided such channels for ministry, they tend to feel increasingly distant from God. Work with people—when they know they make a tangible difference in people's lives and are not just part of a crowd—is important to them. They feel most alive in the midst of the action of ministry.

> *We had our first Penny Car Wash today! People came to us, got their car washed, and got a penny with a connect card. Of course, people thought they were going to be giving the penny. Or more. I love creative ways of showing God's love! When asked why we refused to take money, I found myself saying, "God's given us so much already, we just want to give back to the community."—Marc Pitman*[54]

Formalities such as having to dress properly or to sit still through long prayers or lectures detract from their desire to participate. Members of these churches prefer action over prayer, and will need to find ways of prayer that can be used while working. Therefore, these churches do not need as much formal prayer as other types. They truthfully can say that their work is their prayer, provided it is done for the glory of God and the welfare of their neighbor. If their work is to be put in biblical perspective, they need to cultivate a sincere commitment to truth, justice, and selfless giving, and the recognition of the value of others created in the image of God.

> *The fact is that contemplative spirituality will play a huge part in the Church of the future, and candles are just the beginning.*
> *—Duane Cottrell*[55]

The Bible on Adventurous Church Spirituality

Matthew 7:24—"Everyone then who hears these words of mine and does them will be like a wise man who built his house on the rock."

Matthew 25:31–40—"When the Son of Man comes in his glory, and all the angels with him, then he will sit on his glorious throne. Before him will be gathered all the nations, and he will separate people one from another as a shepherd separates the sheep from the goats. And he will place the sheep on his right, but the goats on the left. Then the King will say to those on his right, 'Come, you who are blessed by my Father, inherit the kingdom prepared for you from the foundation of the world. For I was hungry and you gave me food, I was thirsty and you gave me drink, I was a stranger and you welcomed me, I was naked and you clothed me, I was sick and you visited me, I was in prison and you came to me.' Then the righteous will answer him, saying, 'Lord, when did we see you hungry and feed you, or thirsty and give you drink? And when did we see you a stranger and welcome you, or naked and clothe you? And when did we see you sick or in prison and visit you?' And the King will answer them, 'Truly, I say to you, as you did it to one of the least of these my brothers, you did it to me.'"

VOCATIONS OF THOSE TYPICALLY ATTRACTED TO ADVENTUROUS CHURCHES

Adventurous church members are inclined to be employed in the vocations listed below because the requirements, design, and style of

307

these occupations fit them well. Therefore, it follows that the people in the community in these vocations will be more responsive to the ministry style of the Adventurous church. The following material is adapted from:

- http://www.wsc.edu/advising_services/career_planning/ exploration/personality_careers
- Allan, Ross. *Connecting Personality Types with Careers and Jobs.* Washington, DC: United States Department of the Interior, 1999.[56]

Trades and Technical Areas

- Carpenter
- Construction worker
- Electrician
- Laboratory technologist
- Machine operator
- Radiological technician
- Respiratory therapist

Because their members tend to be hands-on and active, Adventurous churches often resonate with those who work in the trades and technical areas—especially if the occupation includes working with equipment outdoors. Many of these vocations also require attention to facts and details, such as making measurements, observing readings and choosing correct parts and components—competencies possessed by people in Adventurous churches.

Emergency Response

- Critical care nurse
- Emergency response worker
- Firefighter
- Lifeguard
- Police officer

Those who serve in emergency response work, which requires observant and quick-acting decision-making in the midst of dealing with crises, will be much appreciated by those in the Adventurous churches. In these types of tasks people find much variety and change as well as opportunities to solve immediate problems. These are talents and abilities valued by Adventurous churches.

Sales, Marketing, Negotiating

- Insurance agent
- Mediator
- Negotiator
- Promoter
- Real estate agent
- Salesperson
- Sports merchandise sales

People in these vocations are good at "reading" others and are often skilled at persuasion and offering immediate solutions to people's needs. Therefore, they will feel at home in Adventurous churches since these are talents and skills found there in abundance.

Research and Analysis

- Auditor
- Consultant
- Financial advisor
- Investigator
- Journalist
- Land developer
- Purchasing agent
- Small-business manager
- Stockbroker

People in these vocations have a mind for details, enjoy digging out facts and conducting research that entails accurate observation and quick analysis. Since these occupations almost always require assessment of opportunities—which is a characteristic of Adventurous churches—the people in these occupations will feel understood and welcomed when they visit.

Business/Finance

- Auditor
- Fund-raiser
- Insurance agent/broker (health or life)
- Investor
- Personal financial planner
- Public relations specialist
- Real estate agent
- Retail merchandiser/planner
- Retail sales/management
- Stockbroker

Adventurous churches do not generally appreciate the world of big business because of the rules, regulations, and bureaucracy such vocations often require. Nevertheless, they do resonate with those in real estate or insurance sales and similar vocations as listed above because these people spend much of their time out of the office, working directly with a diversity of clients, presenting a variety of products. In turn, those in public relations, fundraising, and mediation—vocations in which people use their persuasive talents, often connect well with the abilities of those found in Adventurous churches. The world of finance is often interesting to members of Adventurous churches, especially when it involves rapidly changing situations and contains a certain amount of risk. A love of excitement and taking calculated risks means they often do well investing in the stock market. They are realistic and pragmatic people, enjoying problem solving, even if it means using unconventional approaches. People serving in these areas of finance enjoy interaction with the public and therefore the friendly and easygoing style of Adventurous churches resonates with their talents and values.

Entertainment

- Film producer
- Musician
- Photographer
- Promoter
- Special events coordinator
- Travel agent/tour operator

Adventurous churches enjoy entertaining people in both a formal and informal capacity since they often have a strong sense of aesthetics and a good eye for what is new and attractive. Since their members enjoy travel, these churches interact well with those in the tourist and special events industry who are adept at putting on large events and juggling several projects at once.

THE CHURCH OF DAVID

The Adventurous church most closely fits the leadership and ministry style of David, the shepherd, musician, poet, warrior, and politician who is best known as the king of Israel. His first recorded deeds were his slaying of lions and bears when they attacked his flock. He would beat them to death with his shepherd's club (1 Sam. 17:34–35).

The armies of Israel and the Philistines were set in battle positions against one another sixteen miles southwest of Bethlehem. David, age 20, was sent by his father with supplies for his three brothers, who were fighting on the side of King Saul. When he arrived at the camp, David saw that Goliath, the giant champion of the Philistines, came out to challenge Israel. David strode in to the valley between them, took his sling, and with a perfect aim hurled a stone which struck the forehead of the giant so that he fell senseless to the ground. David then ran up to Goliath and cut off his head with the giant's own sword (1 Sam. 17:51), resulting in a great victory for the Israelites.

David was ideally suited for the role of king that was bestowed on him some ten years later at age thirty. His popular following—his gathering of four hundred "mighty men" and later all twelve tribes of Israel, his victories over the Philistines and other tribes, and his

311

establishment of a powerful kingdom—proved that he was an astute military strategist and exceptional motivator. His uniting of the political factions in Israel and Judah into a single nation that continued in existence for 80 years demonstrated his skills in negotiation. The nation was not oppressed by him as it was by kings who succeeded him, and he lived in harmony with both the priesthood and the prophets. "David administered justice and equity to all his people" (2 Sam. 8:15).

David's talents as a poet, musician, and supporter of music were distinguished as well. His poetry in 2 Samuel and the Psalms demonstrates a lyrical genius. He even played instruments for worship (2 Chron. 29:26). In addition, David displayed—most of the time—a strong spirituality, as demonstrated in the Davidic psalms. Even apart from the Psalms, David's relationship with the Lord, his concern for others' welfare, his immediate repentance when the prophet Nathan confronted him with his sin, and his concern for matters regarding the temple and the faith all indicate great depth in his spiritual life. The indulgence of his sons and his own sins of adultery and murder were forgiven by God, and his gifts, abilities, and accomplishments for the glory of God were remembered. David's achievements were many and varied as a man of action, poet, openhanded leader, astute provider of justice, loyal friend, and devoted follower of the Lord. He is the appropriate model for Adventurous churches and their leaders.

12

The Expressive Church

Energetic, Uplifting, Warm, and Accepting

SUMMARY STATEMENT

Expressive churches are characterized by an exuberant ministry style that is fun-filled, people-focused, and activity-oriented. They have a tremendous love for life, and they know how to connect with people and genuinely care about them. With their zeal for impacting people for good purposes, these churches will reach out to newcomers in an engaging and hospitable manner, always presenting their best public face. They deepen people's interest through a variety of relationally oriented ministries that offer active participation in others' lives in practical ways. Performing or putting on shows of some kind to connect with people comes naturally to these churches. Expressive churches are attractive especially to socially adept people who serve with a realistic but enthusiastic energy. These churches love life and people in an energetic, down-to-earth manner. See Table 11 for a summary of these characteristics.

MISSION STATEMENT

Expressive churches are called by God to be friendly and outgoing in communicating their love for people as a means of motivating them

Table 11: Characteristics of the Expressive church.

Strengths	• Communicative with strong people skills • Take a sympathetic, inclusive approach with new people
Challenges	• Prefer to avoid or deny conflict as long as possible • Will react fiercely if a value has been trampled
Primary Ministries	• Like to be where the people and the action are; right in the middle of things, involved
Ministry Tempo	• Fast-paced action; gregarious and sociable
What Inspires Them	• Spontaneity, excellence, equality, harmony
What De-motivates Them	• Unsettled by conflict among people they care about
Under Stress	• May become uncharacteristically pessimistic, negative, or doubt themselves (though they may not show these reactions overtly)
Decision-making	• Will seek information and advice from all sources • Will consider the human aspect and whether all will benefit
Desire	• To be open about themselves and their concerns (what you see is what you get) and encouraging others to be the same
Priority	• Create an environment where people feel valued and in on things
Church Ethos	• Express concern for people by keeping the focus on the needs of those being served
Outward Appearance	• An exciting, optimistic, and fun atmosphere
Gain Confidence Through	• Being observant, paying attention to what is going on in their community
Fear	• May question their own abilities and fear exposure as incompetent in their most important ministry endeavors

to join in the fellowship. People in these churches like to be at the center of the action as easygoing, optimistic, and considerate people who enjoy talking, laughing, and sharing their lives with newcomers. They build relational bridges by becoming loyal friends and great companions with those new to the church as they express their generosity and eagerness to please through formal and informal entertainment.

Theme Verse: "That which we have seen and heard we proclaim also to you, so that you too may have fellowship with us; and indeed our fellowship is with the Father and with his Son Jesus Christ" (1 John 1:3).

EXPRESSIVE CHURCH CHARACTERISTICS

Joyful

Expressive churches are characterized by an exuberant ministry style that other types of churches may disparage. Optimistic and humorous, their enthusiasm motivates people and makes these congregations enjoyable to be around. Even the older members of these churches continue their fun-filled, people-focused, actively oriented life as they did in their youth. Ministry for them must have some result or application, or else it must be challenging, in order to grab and maintain their interest. (Note: quotes attributed to Young Life were taken from the organization's Web site: http://www.younglife.org.)

> *At camp I met a lot of new Christian friends and had a lot of fun. I overcame my fear of heights by completing the ropes course. Every night I got to learn more about God and the relationship I can have with Him. Camp was a great experience for me and it was definitely the best week of my life.—Young Life*

Animated and playful, members of these churches love to be in the center of the action, surrounded by other easygoing, cheerful, and considerate people, laughing, talking, and sharing common interests and activities. Relying on their strong social skills, they quickly develop rapport with new people and create a pleasurable atmosphere wherever they go. With their passion for performing, they entertain people

315

with a spirit of delight and amusement, always putting their best face forward. These churches are great fun, and the most bighearted of all church types.

> *Many of our kids came face to face with Jesus Christ for the first time [during camp]. Whether they had seen him before or not, they saw that he was real and alive during that week at camp.—Young Life*

Playful and engaging, their interest lies in motivating those around them and awakening their experience with the Lord and the pleasure of being in a relationship with him. They like to win over people to become followers of Christ so that they cast their burdens on him and lighten up. These congregations would love nothing more than for life to be a continual banquet with the Lord, with them in the role of fun-loving servants.

> *Camp made me feel so comfortable and willing to listen because the speakers didn't pretend to be perfect. They made us aware that we don't have to change who we are right away in order to be considered "good" in God's eyes.—Young Life*

These congregations are lively and entertaining and enjoy performing. Naturally happy-go-lucky, they're supportive of others in the church. They try to make sure people are happy and well cared for, and to ensure that their churches are harmonious and attractive places. Their present-moment orientation makes them enjoyable to be around—it is said that the party often follows them. They are not likely to create problems or fuss for people, and are likely to create the most exciting environment possible for ministry.

> *Our approach is relational. We go where kids are in order to build friendships with them and earn the right to make a positive impact on their lives. We want them to know that they are loved and valued.—Young Life*

These ministries have a tremendous love for life and know how to connect with people. They like to bring others along on their fun rides, and are very interesting to be with. They relate to people through quips and witticisms—always seeming to know the latest jokes and stories. For these ministries, nothing is so serious or sacred that it can't be joked about. They love people, excitement, and telling humorous stories.

They bring hope, high energy, faith and love to thousands of needy kids everywhere.—Young Life

Their "go with the flow," fun-loving attitude will extend to their ministry with kids. They are usually remembered fondly by their youth for being upbeat and affectionate, although somewhat absent-minded. They get genuine delight and enjoyment from experiences they encounter in life in Christ, and they love nothing better than to draw a crowd of kids along with them for the sheer joy of it. They seek stimulating experiences and excitement, and will create them if they are not already existent.

What's really neat is when a kid starts to see me as their friend and not someone who is unapproachable.—Young Life

The Bible on Being Joyful

Deuteronomy 16:15—"For seven days you shall keep the feast to the LORD your God at the place that the LORD will choose, because the LORD your God will bless you in all your produce and in all the work of your hands, so that you will be altogether joyful."

Nehemiah 8:10—"Go your way. Eat the fat and drink sweet wine and send portions to anyone who has nothing ready, for this day is holy to our Lord. And do not be grieved, for the joy of the LORD is your strength."

Friendly

Warm, outgoing, and supportive, Expressive churches are usually vivacious and talkative. They are cordial, outgoing, and relational, and people are naturally drawn to them. Generous and eager to help, they are loyal benefactors and emotionally close to people. Their strengths and talents for ministry lie in their easygoing and affectionate nature and their ability to establish rapport easily.

The mission is the "Gospel to every kid." Not just rich kids or poor kids. Not just black kids, brown kids, or white kids. Not just your kids or my kids. Every kid. Not just a lot of kids or even most kids. Every kid. Not just charming kids or beautiful kids. Not just lovable kids or intelligent kids. Every kid.—Young Life

Expressive churches conduct very active ministries because they love socializing and genuinely care about people—especially kids. Their love for people leads them to instigate activities to build rapport with new acquaintances. The members of these churches seem to be in perpetual motion—whether they are just wandering around the building or roaming around the neighborhood chatting with those they happen to see. They are warm and cordial and have the ability to make others feel relaxed and at home in their midst.

Many teenagers today don't have the privilege of learning Christian morals and principles at home. In today's world, many homes are broken into pieces and parents don't have the time, concern or platform to teach their children the values of faith and the need for a Christian foundation. That's just one more reason why our ministry is absolutely necessary.—Young Life

Because these churches are good-natured and caring, they look for practical ways to help people. They radiate warmth and festivity and, whether with their families or engaged in ministry with fellow church members, they lift people's spirits with their contagious good humor and irrepressible joy of living. Their relationships are very important to them, and they are likely to let people know how much they care through small keepsakes, special notes, and cards. They are warmhearted and enthusiastic, even vivacious.

Teenagers are given an example of living a life that is full of promise and fun. Seeds of hope are planted in an otherwise quite apathetic environment. Kids are given opportunity to laugh together in a healthy way, to share their hurts in a safe place, and to expand their dreams of what life might look like. I love seeing

*the "cool" exterior crack and real joy surface in the lives of young
people.—Young Life*

Hospitable and gregarious, inviting, outgoing, and friendly, these
churches are energized by group gatherings and personal interactions.
Decisions are made with sensitivity to the concerns of people and based
on what is best for people in the ministry. These churches take networking very personally, and they enjoy establishing amiable rapport with a
large number of people. Their ministry to children and youth is friendly,
enthusiastic, and active.

> *Our approach is relational. Leaders go wherever kids are to begin
> building significant relationships with them. Leaders go to sports
> practices, high school sporting events, concerts, plays, malls, and
> fast-food restaurants. Leaders are genuinely interested in kids'
> lives and they do what they can to show kids they care about
> them.—Young Life*

The gregarious sociability and adaptability of these churches
make hospitality a major means of reaching out to people in the community. Outgoing and expressive, they are genial and giving, with
simple needs and minimal demands on the people they are reaching.
They are affectionate and expansive in their style of ministry and are
great for giving practical care in the form of ministries of mercy to
people in need.

> *[There are some] who have an actual spiritual gift of hospitality, an
> anointing of the Spirit that causes us to leave their homes refreshed
> spiritually as well as physically. . . . If they exercise hospitality fre-
> quently, they soon have the ministry of hospitality. A ministry may
> or may not be accompanied by formal recognition from church
> leadership. But that is not crucial. Why? Because our focus is on
> service to others.—John Wimber[1]*

These churches are known for having a good time and for genuine
compassion and interest toward people. They have a deep concern for
people, which they show through their demonstrative and pragmatic

319

gestures of helping. They are very observant of people and seem to sense what is wrong with someone before others might, responding cheerfully with a solution to a practical need.

> *Grace breaks down walls. We want to be agents of Christ, ministers to the city, a practical demonstration of the love of Jesus.—Jeff Anderle, Pastor, Vineyard Christian Fellowship of Chattanooga[2]*

These churches develop tenderhearted, generous, loving friendships. They are genuinely, enthusiastically interested in people and like to make visitors feel welcome. They prefer the atmosphere to be light and happy, although their graciousness and affection run deep. They are attentive to people and become more generous and outgoing in the face of encouragement.

> *The fellowship's mission is "real people serving a real God" and its vision is "to love the city into a relationship with Jesus."—Jeff Anderle*

These churches are most likely to find interesting and satisfying those ministries that make use of their breadth of interests, their reliance on facts, their people-centered values and sympathy (i.e., their emphasis on interpersonal issues), and their adaptability. Their personal approach, enthusiasm, attention to detail, and realistic grounding often draw them to ministries that help people in the community in practical ways. There is an affable and personal touch in all that they do.

> *The real emphasis is on being Christ-centered but not being very churchy.—Jeff Anderle*

Because they enjoy getting together and have a large circle of friends both in and outside the church, these congregations tend to conduct activity-oriented ministries. Playful and high-spirited, their primary interest lies in stimulating those around them to deepen their appreciation for relationships within the church and community. In a sense, they charm people to cast off their other concerns and focus on what is really important—their friendships.

Koinonia (i.e., fellowship) took expression in house groups, week-ends away, social events, indeed anything that helped in the sharing of lives.—Anthony O'Sullivan[3]

As Expressive churches, they want and need feedback and appreciation, and they like to give the same to new people. Because they are so outgoing, they can be very entertaining and are often in tune with relational nuances. These churches find it energizing to be out and about talking with people in the community, soliciting their input, developing new ideas, and interacting with one another.

The Church should not only train its people concerning their spiritual duties but also train them to apply biblical truth to all areas of life—including civil government, education, economics, and law.—Anthony O'Sullivan

These churches are comprised of popular, gregarious people who are often busy with each other in a variety of activities. They love people, telling stories, and creating a joyful atmosphere. These are energetic and popular individuals who liven up the community as they keep engaging in new experiences. The busy community orientation and the many active, physical interests of these churches fill every free minute, and they can rush excitedly from one experience to another.

The commitment to fellowship, training, a wholistic gospel, social and political challenge, plurality of leadership, the full role of women, spiritual warfare, and the contemporary reality of healing are all unambiguously present, though subsumed under the Great Commission.—Anthony O'Sullivan

The Bible on Friendships
Proverbs 17:17—"A friend loves at all times, and a brother is born for adversity."
Proverbs 18:24—"A man of many companions may come to ruin, but there is a friend who sticks closer than a brother."

321

Engaging

These churches like to live in the fast lane, and always seem up on the latest fads of dress, food, and drink—the chic new fashion and the hot new musical group—so they can all the more effectively relate to the unchurched people of the community. In the matter of ministry activities, these churches enjoy welcoming people and thus delight in amazing people in ways that will impact them for good.

> *They could hear a pin drop as he opens his Bible and shares with them the fact that God loves them and is interested in a personal relationship with them. We see thoughtful looks on their faces. These are new ideas to consider. Seeds have been planted.—Young Life*

These churches view almost anything they do as a means of valuing people. They easily draw people because visitors sense that their presence is welcomed, and that the people of these churches genuinely enjoy getting together formally and informally.

> *Every day, they'll be surprised at what happens next (at camp). . . . We're talking about the best week of your life!—Young Life*

These churches are bursting with energy and passion for relational outreach. Their spontaneous, impulsive nature is always engaging because they are focused on interacting meaningfully with everyone. With their zeal for making a difference in the lives of people, they will meet the needs of every individual with a spirit of fun and lightheartedness.

> *[We] strive to win the right to be heard, treating each person with care and dignity. This style of relational, incarnational ministry crosses cultures effectively.—Young Life*

These churches find their ability to engage people to be inhibited by rigid, outdated formulas that worked in other times and circumstances, but are not appropriate for them and make them feel constrained in the ways they communicate to newcomers their relationship with the Lord. Because they freely give love and affection to people spontaneously, they will frequently have problems with what they consider too much structure in relationships. They are satisfied with a variety of options that provide them with a range of opportunities to engage people. They do not want programs to be so structured that they cannot stop to smell the roses.

> *God looks us square in the eye, loves us, and personally extends an invitation to follow him into the unknown. There is something about his tone, his calling, his very presence . . . something so enticing, so mysterious that it challenges us at the core. When the disciples heard the call of Jesus, they left everything—EVERYTHING!—and followed him.—Young Life*

The Bible on Being Engaging

Proverbs 27:9—"The sweetness of a friend comes from his earnest counsel."

Proverbs 28:20—"A faithful man will abound with blessings."

Invigorating Worship

Their worship is lively and participatory as people are caught up in the intensity and joyfulness of the celebration. They love the stimulation of worshiping as a large congregation, and encourage a celebratory spirit at every gathering. These churches—comprised of sociable and creative worshipers—make enthusiastic and fully engaged participants, which gives their worship services a good deal of spontaneity.

> *God has provided worship as a means of entry to our rejoicing in the presence of the Ultimate Reality.—Jack Hayford[4]*

It is hard for these congregations to be "down," mainly because of the anticipation of each upcoming worship event. These churches are deepened in their worship by new forms of liturgy and especially original music written by their members. They seek the experience of being in God's presence and will develop worship forms to assist them in extolling his worth.

This is one of those mornings [about every three weeks] when we must learn a new song [often one he has written himself].—Jack Hayford

Worship is conducted imaginatively, often in a multisensory form, by using dramatization or presentations that include music, video, movement, etc. In their worship services, these churches use their eye for beauty and flair for what is vibrant and colorful. They relish worship that draws on their senses and emotions to focus their attention on the Lord.

A worship service is convened (1) to serve God with our praises and (2) to serve people's need with his sufficiency.—Jack Hayford

New worship experiences enliven them and, as a consequence, they tend to plunge into new hymns and songs, learning as they go. In similar ways, their approach to worship is frequently spontaneous and full of exciting and even unexpected experiences. The temperament of these churches makes them very good at adapting to many new practices and enables them to flourish as they create new worship forms to honor the Lord.

I get my ideas [what he does in the worship service and the way he does it] in prayer on Saturday evening.—Jack Hayford

Their worship involvement is deepened by variety, sensory stimulation, and active participation, and they benefit from compelling presentations, adapting as they move through their innovative worship forms. They develop worship services in which they include a lot of variety and range of opportunity to connect to the Lord in fresh ways.

These churches are especially adept at improvising with set liturgy forms that may be normative to their traditional background.

The primary issue is whether we will come—will be led before his Throne and seek him. Because if we do, heaven will break loose on earth.—Jack Hayford

They notice and are stimulated by their immediate environment. Worshiping in a sensually beautiful sanctuary that focuses them on the Lord enhances the quality of their prayer and devotional experience. They live in the here-and-now of worship and relish the pleasant anticipation of connecting to God and the lively enjoyment of his presence.

Worship introduces dimensions of possibility in every life that transcend our sin and our self-imposed limitations as we welcome the Transcendent One.—Jack Hayford

The Bible on Vigorous Worship

Matthew 22:36–37—"'Teacher, which is the great commandment in the Law?' And he said to him, 'You shall love the Lord your God with all your heart and with all your soul and with all your mind.'"

John 4:23–24—"But the hour is coming, and is now here, when the true worshipers will worship the Father in spirit and truth, for the Father is seeking such people to worship him. God is spirit, and those who worship him must worship in spirit and truth."

Merciful

The ability to observe people and events with discernment and then act immediately with practical solutions enables these churches to respond to ministry opportunities as they happen. Because their preferred approach to practical ministry opportunities is focused on what is occurring in the present, these churches are especially capable in situations that require quick reaction. The problems and challenges seem so critical and pressing that they have to exert effort to set goals beyond those they can envision and achieve in the present.

We are committed to serving those afflicted by HIV/AIDS. We feel called to spread the love of Jesus by reaching out to men, women, and children who have HIV/AIDS, ministering to their physical, emotional, and spiritual needs.—Sharon Fryer, Project Compassion, Vineyard Church of Columbus

Expressive churches are drawn to ministries where they can help people in practical ways, since they thrive on seeing the immediate effect of their efforts. Because they like to jump in and help at a moment's notice, they excel at ministries in which people are faced with urgent problems or have to respond to rapidly changing circumstances. Ministry opportunities close at hand in their own neighborhoods are especially invigorating and motivating to them.

> *We ministered to Joe for over four years. He came from a broken home and was exposed to homosexuality when he was a young child, including sexual abuse by adult male members of his family. Joe lived his life as a self described "partyboy" and was an activist in the gay community. Eighteen years ago he was diagnosed with HIV. When he came to us he had just had quadruple bypass heart surgery. His friends had left him.—Sharon Fryer, Project Compassion, Vineyard Church of Columbus[5]*

They have a special knack for deriving enjoyment from their ministry, and live fully in the moment. If these churches find something objectionable, they will strive to change it as soon as possible rather than wait for something to improve in the future. Because they enjoy solving problems and dealing with crises, they are attracted to ministries that move at a rapid pace and involve negotiation, compromise, and persuasion of people.

> *We have gone over to his house to cook and clean for him on numerous occasions. Each time he could see God's love for him, but he was very troubled that all the friends he used to party with didn't come around any more. He couldn't believe that the friends who said that they would be with him forever weren't, and God, whom he had pushed away, was still there.—Sharon Fryer, Project Compassion, Vineyard Church of Columbus*

The Bible on Mercy

Exodus 34:6–7—"The LORD passed before [Moses] and proclaimed, 'The LORD, the LORD, a God merciful and gracious, slow to anger, and abounding in steadfast love and faithfulness, keeping steadfast love for thousands, forgiving iniquity and transgression and sin, but who will by no means clear the guilty, visiting the iniquity of the fathers on the children and the children's children, to the third and the fourth generation.'"

Matthew 5:7—"Blessed are the merciful, for they shall receive mercy."

Helps and Service

Ministries of helps and service attract these churches primarily because of the interpersonal contact involved, and because many in their congregations have a talent for using tools. In addition, their flair for establishing rapport with people facilitates their being able to help people in practical ways.

> *"Jesus Action" is the name of the social action arm by which we serve the community. Just as Jesus said that the works that he did, his Father was doing through him, so we believe Christ's hand is doing in us, doing good works and bringing glory to the Father (Matt. 5:16). These works are very different from humanistic activities and aims. We want to remember to leave Jesus behind when we have finished serving.—Anthony O'Sullivan*

Expressive churches demonstrate their capacity for adapting to new situations and remaining cool in times of stress by "going with the flow" and depending on their ability to adapt in any circumstance presented to them. They are particularly adept at using common sense to adjust to changing events and turn unexpected problems into occasions for the work of God in people's lives.

> *I formed solid friendships with other leaders in the group. These friendships encouraged me and helped to strengthen my relationship with Christ. As a leader, I was able to see God work through the lives of high school students. I saw people's hardened hearts become open to Christ. I was able to watch young people mature in their faith and serve other young people. It is amazing to see God working through these kids and to see answered prayers.—Young Life*

Given an opportunity, these ministries will be creative in developing more edgy ways of doing things in order to connect with people. Since their gift for seizing the moment is an ability that some find difficult to appreciate, other churches may view their behavior as irresponsible. More mature ministries will balance their tendencies to respond quickly to changing events with the foresight to slow down, evaluate information rationally, and then make solid decisions.

> *[Meetings occur] once a week and have been described as an experience in "controlled chaos." Leaders combine songs, humor and group interaction to create an hour of energetic fun where kids can express that teenage tendency to push the limits, but within the controlled context of a safe environment.*
> *—Young Life*

Their capacity to absorb the mannerisms of people contributes to Expressive churches' effectiveness in connecting with new people and establishing rapport. They gather a great deal of information by using their abilities to observe people and get them to talk. It takes them very little time to develop new approaches to ministry that meet the genuine needs of the people to whom they are ministering.

> *Contact work is an integral part of what we are all about. We seek to build contact with young people by placing adult volunteer leaders at schools, sporting activities, shopping centers and anywhere else young people are. All our "programs" are simply tools to help build relationships and connect with young people in their world.—Young Life*

The Bible on Helps and Service

Matthew 20:25–28—"But Jesus called them to him and said, 'You know that the rulers of the Gentiles lord it over them, and their great ones exercise authority over them. It shall not be so among you. But whoever would be great among you must be your servant, and whoever would be first among you must be your slave, even as the Son of Man came not to be served but to serve, and to give his life as a ransom for many.'"

Romans 12:6–7—"Having gifts that differ according to the grace given to us, let us use them: if prophecy, in proportion to our faith; if service, in our serving."

Communication Style

Because Expressive churches are interested in the practical use of new ideas, they gain knowledge best by experiencing and doing. Group sessions that provide interaction with others for reflecting on, summarizing, and integrating what they have been taught allow them to process knowledge and turn abstract information into something more practical and applicable to people. In order to expand their ability to assess issues and events accurately for better decision-making, they need experience applying biblical values to new situational needs.

> *Depending on which camp you go to, you may ride horses, go rock climbing and rappelling, take a dip in a hot springs pool, learn to water ski or parasail or challenge yourself on a ropes course or a thrilling zip line. It is camping to the extreme!—Young Life*

Armed with an awareness of the most effective spiritual development style of their people, leaders of these ministries adapt their communication style to the way their people learn best. Spiritual growth programs then work with their strengths and facilitate a productive experience of development instead of undermining their confidence or frustrating them unintentionally. Those in positions of leadership who disciple the people, organize ministry teams, or demonstrate the means of spiritual growth often present the Scripture imaginatively through multisensory media such as film and drama. The people attracted to these ministries especially desire to strengthen their knowledge of arts and crafts, as well as increase their ability to work well with tools and equipment.

> *When it comes to students, we want to take the time to know their names (and remember them!), to look them in the eye, listen attentively, personally invite them to activities, love them unconditionally, and challenge them to take an honest look at the person of*

*Jesus Christ. And guess what? It's working! We've met tons of new
students this year at various events including: pool parties, paint-
ball, and—my personal favorite—wakeboarding!—Young Life*

Since the traditional classroom setting does not provide as many
opportunities for spiritual growth for these people, they may not enjoy
Sunday school very much. They need information that can be applied
immediately in practical ways, or else be stimulating enough to maintain
their interest. Because they like to learn as they go, they tend to grow
by plunging in to stimulating new experiences.

*In an atmosphere of high adventure, with the backdrop of God's
beautiful creation, kids open up to their leaders, sharing their strug-
gles, fears, and thoughts about God.—Young Life*

Participants in these ministries enjoy interacting with people with
whom they can identify. They especially gain knowledge and perspective
through discussion, sharing experiences, and competition (for instance,
team contests). Because their thinking is clarified through verbalizing
ideas, talking is a vital part of their growth in understanding. They are
sensitive to both positive and negative comments, with the former acting
as a strong motivation to grow and be all they can be.

*I went to the meetings because I liked being around all my friends.
Before long I realized that it is much more than just a good time. I
learned things that were to change my life forever.—Young Life*

Even though they may eventually learn all aspects of a topic, because
of their spontaneity and spur-of-the-moment tendencies, these congregations may jump from one thought to another in rapid fashion, absorbing
random bits and pieces of information. However, as participants in these
ministries mature, they recognize that doing what they want in an unconstrained manner and trying to solve problems outside a biblical perspective
are not the best ways to make important long-term decisions.

*They have the highest regard and respect for a young person's right
to choose where matters of faith are concerned. The leaders' objec-*

tive is to present good information so that their young friends can
make well-informed decisions.—Young Life

Expressive churches like to present knowledge of a subject or
skill through experience-based activities, especially by apprenticing
people with those who are doing what needs to be taught. Otherwise,
the natural tendency of people will be to memorize details rather than
understand the overarching concepts that are keys to problem solving.
By these means, the leaders of these ministries will develop people in
their ability to approach issues and events analytically from a biblical
world and life view.

> *Leaders provide kids with factual information for making good*
> *decisions. They work particularly hard to provide teenagers with*
> *the basic facts concerning Jesus Christ. The information is pre-*
> *sented in a non-threatening manner in terms that kids can under-*
> *stand.—Young Life*

The Bible on Communication

Psalm 25:4–5—"Make me to know your ways, O LORD; teach me
your paths. Lead me in your truth and teach me."

Isaiah 28:10—"For it is precept upon precept, precept upon precept,
line upon line, line upon line, here a little, there a little."

Stress

Overwhelming workload combined with relational conflict is especially difficult for these churches. Not surprisingly, they find structure,
routine, rigid time frames, and inhibiting rules to be draining. When
the relational pressure in the ministry is extreme and persists over time,
these churches tend to weigh the benefits of tolerating the burden against
the daily anxiety they experience. Since they have little tolerance for
interpersonal tension, it is denied as long as possible.

> *As the day progressed, we realized we were to repent and confess*
> *our sin. This was a struggle, but each of us felt we had to try open-*
> *ing our hearts to one another. The effort brought a new reality*

of honesty and earnestness within the group.—Michael Webb,
"Gathering at the Gates of Our City," Equipping the Saints, Vol.
7, No. 4, Fall 1993

Under emotional strain, these churches become increasingly pessimistic as they obsess over negative interpretations of the difficulties
they are experiencing. What they would ordinarily recognize as normal
circumstances and events experienced by most churches, they now are
compelled to see as malevolent forces of evil intent on doing them harm.
When relational tensions persist over long periods, these churches can
respond by developing destructive and even vicious habit patterns in
the treatment of their own members. Not having obtained relief from
their emotional strain through appropriate behavior, these churches feel
driven to behave in ways that can be quite harmful to themselves and
others in the community.

> *Nothing draws people toward a common cause like confronting*
> *"evil." This is especially true in Christian settings when conflict*
> *is at elevated levels. Demonization energizes such high reac-*
> *tivity that rational processes can be more easily subverted and*
> *disregarded.—Thomas Fischer[6]*

Expressive churches become burdened by excessive structure, inflexible people, and too many things to do in short periods of time. In the
midst of interpersonal conflict, deadlines, and having to get everything
organized and structured, they may analyze random cues from a variety
of events and circumstances and then interpret them negatively. When
persistent relational problems cause them to be continually anxious, they
can lose touch with their normally carefree enjoyment of the moment,
and their typical skill at solving immediate problems is diminished. They
become habitually worried, negative, hesitant, and despondent.

> *Organizations are, by nature, anxious. They are composed of anx-*
> *ious individuals. The task of the leader is to provide such emotive*
> *energies which out-weigh the anxiety-level. This is done by incit-*
> *ing "positive" anxieties which help people cope with "negative"*
> *anxieties.—Thomas Fischer[7]*

However, when subjected to extended periods of stress—especially when key leaders are being humiliated—these churches will search for the meaning behind it all in the form of an obsessive interest in the demonic. Since these churches avoid dealing with tension as long as possible (Expressive churches have the lowest tolerance for worry and anxiety in their relationships), problems can build up and blindside them. Under intense pressure, they can become moderately paranoid.

> *When fear and anxiety are incited, all kinds of things start happening. Intimacy patterns are disrupted. Alliances and trusts are doubted. Anxious individuals fearfully run away from what they had perceived to be "safe"—but find "unsafe"—and flee to escape the anxiety by either . . . 1) escaping into isolation, or 2) fusing with other like-anxious types.—Thomas F. Fischer[8]*

Ironically, in comparison with other church types, Expressive churches experience few aspects of their ministry as being very stressful except during the times when relational conflict erupts. Then they are more vulnerable to corporate anxiety than most churches. Some of the resulting symptoms are that they feel overwhelmed internally by pessimism, disturbing images of potential disaster, self-doubt, and loss of connection to what is normal. They become compulsive about being organized—which is contrary to their customary style of ministry. Provoked by the stress of relational difficulties, they can become even more impulsive than ever, which leads to their commitment to more tasks than they can possibly accomplish.

> *Since emotions are closely related to intimacy, the way to incite emotive responses is to threaten core aspects of intimacy. . . . These include trust, familiarity, approval, security, bonding, unconditional love, independence, autonomy, safety, belongingness, etc. Threaten any one or more of the above and watch those emotive responses energize all kinds of responses of the "fear and anxiety" kind.—Thomas F. Fischer[9]*

Expressive churches usually respond to events on a day-to-day basis, and are uncomfortable preparing too much for the future or setting goals far in advance. Since these churches show little interest in looking at the big picture beyond the next month, challenges from the world around them may catch them by surprise. However, when confronted by anxiety-provoking events, these churches get back in control of the situation through their ability to improvise strategies on an emergency basis. They would benefit from understanding that their options are not really restricted if they develop long-range ministry goals, especially if they make use of their relational values as the means of determining what is important to them.

> *Extra-curricular activities beyond clubs and camping can include anything from intramural basketball leagues to simply sitting and having coffee with a leader after school. Young Life leaders are always considering the need of kids to have healthy, creative fun and are consistently making plans to meet that need.—Young Life*

As the challenges increase, such as dealing with interpersonal conflict and uncooperative people, the most effective response for people in these churches is to talk to one another about the issues in order to gain perspective. They typically work on their ministry problems by talking through them with the other people involved. These churches learn to recognize the signs of relational conflict before they fully develop so they can take preemptive steps to keep the situation from becoming destructive.

> *When one individual becomes anxious and/or fearful the greater danger is that this anxiety can set off a chain reaction. Once it starts, the only way to stop it is to try to alleviate anxiety. This can be done by: intervention, allowing time, giving people a voice, publicly dealing with issues, allowing their participation in the solution, giving pastoral support and attention, prayer.—Thomas F. Fischer[10]*

The combination of upheaval that is natural in ministry and with the tension of chronic relational conflicts can push these churches into serious soul-searching and reconsideration of long-standing goals, which lead to significant changes in the spiritual values that drive their ministries. These changes include the experience of spiritual renewal through a reorientation around scriptural authority, prayer, transparency in times of fellowship, a deepened worship experience, and the proclamation of the gospel. As a result, these churches become less apprehensive about the future and more willing to make binding commitments to the Lord and each other.

> *We took a three-day retreat in Estes Park, Colorado, to fast and pray for our town. Fourteen pastors and Christian workers participated, as we focused on the work of concentrated prayer, meeting together, and the joy of worshiping in unity. Worship, praise and adoration set the agenda for the first evening; in fact, we had no agenda for the entire three days. The following day we continued to spend some hours in prayer and worship, each of us being renewed and refreshed by Jesus and his Spirit.*
> *—Michael Webb[11]*

The Bible on Stress

Jeremiah 17:8—"He is like a tree planted by water, that sends out its roots by the stream, and does not fear when heat comes, for its leaves remain green, and is not anxious in the year of drought, for it does not cease to bear fruit."

Philippians 4:6—"Do not be anxious about anything, but in everything by prayer and supplication with thanksgiving let your requests be made known to God."

Serving Responsibly

Concentration on people and their individual needs are such important values for these ministries that their willingness to focus on subjects that are not immediately applicable to their growth and development is limited. Their ministry is characterized by their real-life, hands-on involvement in the genuine needs of people in the present. People's problems in the past and speculations about their future hold little interest for these churches.

> *Rayburn found great success in befriending young people outside the church building on "their turf." He earned the right to be heard by investing time in their lives.[12]*

335

Those in these ministries find it difficult to serve in predictable settings where nothing new and unusual occurs or where they are expected to engage in monotonous and repetitive tasks that have little to do with helping people. If they find themselves going through the motions in completing tedious responsibilities unrelated to interaction with people, they will quickly be looking for something else to do.

> *[These kids] were outside the influence of the Church. They found it stodgy, irrelevant, boring and adult centered. They would not come to church. Jim Rayburn devised a new method for reaching young people that spoke directly to them. Jesus became relevant to their day-to-day lives.*[13]

Expressive church people can resist regulations being imposed on them and can become quite defiant when their sense of freedom is violated. Their disregard for standard procedures will take the form of passive resistance, and they will use their well-honed skills to annoy the people they blame for their loss of liberty. However, their lack of conscientiousness often leads to deterioration in their ability to behave with wisdom in times of crisis, which then makes them feel empty and remorseful.

> *Christian fella, you have a great God-given responsibility toward the ones outside God's family, walk in wisdom towards them—behave wisely—this involves so much—remember they are in the dark—their understanding is nil—their senses are dulled—they cannot receive the things of the Spirit of God. To behave wisely towards them will involve being understanding and friendly, avoiding ugliness or criticism—always being gentle and tactful.—Jim Rayburn, Young Life*

Even though they find structure, planning, and strictly defined duties to be confining, when they take on the challenge of ministering to people they care about deeply then they are willing to push themselves out of their laid-back comfort zone. The experience of ministering to children and youth prompts them to be especially conscientious in doing what is needed even when the task is not very interesting to them.

When the leaders of these ministries succumb to the temptation to avoid or ignore important commitments because they are not enjoyable or stimulating, they will usually be rebuked as unfaithful and unreliable by those more naturally conscientious. These ministries are ambivalent in that they sometimes castigate those who restrict their independence, while at the same time privately respecting the consistency of these same people.

> *Go where they are; seek them. We are God's seekers; people who look for those in hiding. We go to their turf as he came to ours. In Young Life we call this contact work and it is so clearly scriptural, so wonderfully Christlike.—Jim Rayburn, Young Life*

The Bible on Serving Responsibly

2 Corinthians 5:11—"Therefore, knowing the fear of the Lord, we persuade others. But what we are is known to God, and I hope it is known also to your conscience."

Galatians 5:13–14—"For you were called to freedom, brothers. Only do not use your freedom as an opportunity for the flesh, but through love serve one another. For the whole law is fulfilled in one word: 'You shall love your neighbor as yourself.'"

Crisis Management

In difficult predicaments that do not involve relational conflict, these ministries are usually unruffled, resourceful, and highly productive. They are adept at solving problems that deal with uncertain, difficult, or even painful situations. Any situation that requires fast thinking and level-headedness that calms people in the midst of adversity is ideal for these ministries. Their knack for quickly identifying problems and working in the context of rapidly changing events often leads them into urban ministry.

> *Our vision is to develop ministry for young people from diverse ethnic and cultural backgrounds who live in high-density communities, such as the inner city, including those who have a history of being socially or economically disadvantaged.—Young Life*

337

The reason these ministries are so competent in handling emergencies is that those serving in them become immediately energized and totally immersed in helping solve people's problems. They develop effective teaching ministries to people whose lives have fallen apart, a talent that often leads them into ministries in which sensitivity to the pain and suffering of others is needed, particularly children and youth. Their capacity to adapt to rapidly changing events and then help people in the midst of chaotic conditions places them in position to handle emergency situations. Once they have dealt with the immediate problem or crisis, they tend to move on to the next exciting event.

> *Making an impact with teenagers, or anyone in this world, has more to do with love than it does logistics, requires availability more that it does capability, and demands faith rather than fancy formulas.*—Young Life

The Bible on Crisis Management

2 Corinthians 7:4–7—"In all our affliction, I am overflowing with joy. For even when we came into Macedonia, our bodies had no rest, but we were afflicted at every turn—fighting without and fear within. But God, who comforts the downcast, comforted us by the coming of Titus, and not only by his coming but also by the comfort with which he was comforted by you, as he told us of your longing, your mourning, your zeal for me, so that I rejoiced still more."

Outreach

Since these churches are already energized by interaction with people and their challenges, they do not need a program-driven outreach ministry. Rather they prefer to be part of a flexible, spontaneous, and constantly changing effort that focuses on service in the community that is sensitive to the well-being of people.

> *Rayburn saw the high school as a mission field with a foreign population who spoke their own language, had their own customs, rituals, and mores. If an adult could infiltrate this society and gain the trust of young people much could be accomplished for the sake of Christ.*[14]

338

They are sensitive to subtle signals from people and capable of concentrating their attention and resources on those they perceive to be receptive to the gospel. Because they are driven by optimism and have worked hard at being competent and resourceful in order to foster a good image for their ministry in the community, they feel justified in taking risks in their outreach efforts.

> *The core of this approach to youth ministry is called contact. It is often referred to as "creative loafing" in the young people's world. It means hanging out with the young people (primarily in the high schools) where they gather, and talking with them on their turf.*
> *—Churches Youth Ministry Association[15]*

These ministries are characterized by high interactivity with frequent meetings, one-on-one and in groups, for the purpose of deepening relationships. Light and entertaining conversations create harmony while providing warm and friendly support to everyone. For these ministries, outreach is an adventure that focuses on commitment to people which produces transformation of their lives.

> *What's really neat is when a kid starts to see me as their friend and not someone who is unapproachable.—Young Life*

These churches are adept at developing a rapid response to fix problems experienced by people in the neighborhoods surrounding their churches. Therefore, their outreach is action-oriented, hands-on—even frantic at times—and keeps structure, bureaucracy, and politics to a minimum.

> *He was unable to attract them to church, so he began to conduct informal meetings outside of church, in funeral homes or private homes. At these meetings there was laughter, music, and fun, as well as a lively talk about Jesus with personal applications that appealed to kids.[16]*

These churches are willing to change any of their methodologies, including "sacred cow" programs, that do not serve a practical purpose in reaching people effectively. They are motivated to pursue outreach with persistence when the practical benefits to people are evident and they are allowed to be spontaneous in the way they do their ministry. Because they feel they must be independent and unhindered as they do outreach, they appreciate a minimum of structure and organization.

> *The genius of Jim Rayburn is his perception that the emerging teenage identity required segregation from the general population. Jim took what he perceived to be the gospel message and circumvented the unappealing, adult-infested church.*[17]

By connecting easily with people who are different from themselves, they are effective at building relationships. With considerable self-assurance and social ease, they thrive on personal, hands-on involvement with new people. They are stylish, lively, and gregarious, as well as relaxed, attractive, and easygoing as they welcome new people.

> *Description of Young Life Club: "A group gathers in the home of one of the young people for an hour on a school night. An informal atmosphere is developed, singing and crazy skits are characteristic along with some fun event to make the group laugh. This is followed by announcements of a camp or some other activity that is helped to look exciting and good to go to. It ends with some quieter thoughtful music and a personal talk about Jesus and/or some other Christian message."—Churches Youth Ministry Association*

These churches communicate genuine love, care, and concern for people as they build rapport with them. They are fair-minded and communicate respect as they demonstrate patience with people's beliefs and values even in the midst of conflict. They make a good first impression by soliciting opinions from people and then, over time, influence them by facilitating spiritual decisions and behavior.

> *Just as Jesus invaded human history to relate to us as we were, so the adult leader became Jesus to the teenage society, meeting and loving them where they were.*[18]

Expressive churches especially value socially adept people who serve with a realistic point of view that also exhibits enthusiasm and energy. By using their abilities to mediate, they ease the tensions among community people engaged in conflict, and help groups work more cooperatively. Because they encourage their people to serve with creativity and spontaneity, these churches are characterized by a minimum of official procedures, rules, or restrictions. They support their members in handling multiple outreach projects and activities, especially those that utilize their aesthetic taste and sense of design.

> *Mission, that is, evangelism in its local and wider expression, was seen as a calling given to the whole church for the whole year, not something distinct for specially gifted saints to exercise on a two week "revival" outreach. The nature of the Great Commission was interpreted as "incarnational," that is, bringing the whole of Jesus' ministry into people's lives, his works as well as his words.*
> —Anthony O'Sullivan

Rather than isolating their members in programs that are exclusively for the church, these ministries encourage them to be personally involved with people in the community. They want everyone to learn outreach through hands-on involvement in which they are encouraged to use their common sense to gather all the facts as they look for solutions to the problems experienced by people in the community. They want their people to work on outreach projects that are of immediate usefulness and take into account the needs of their friends, relatives, associates, and neighbors.

> *There was an emphasis on joining proclamation with "prophetic" political and social involvement. Jesus did supernatural things, like feeding the five thousand and raising the dead, but he also spent time with the children and washed feet.*—Anthony O'Sullivan

Because they value reaching out to a diverse population, they create an active, social church environment, characterized by variety, fun, and spontaneity. They conduct their outreach efforts in a friendly and relaxed manner and appreciate the hard work and good intentions of their people.

A true reflection of koinonia meant committing ourselves to one another and sharing our lives as fully as we could. In the early days, koinonia took expression in house groups, weekends away, social events, indeed anything that helped in the sharing of lives.— Anthony O'Sullivan

More than other church types, these churches use for the purposes of outreach the bright lights, the party atmosphere, the enthusiasm generated by the celebratory atmosphere of their gatherings. They like to promote change because it is stimulating to these churches that are fueled by new people and new approaches to ministry. These churches create vigorous, if somewhat unpredictable outreach efforts, which may give quieter people within their congregations some anxiety and tension when the church lives habitually on the edge of adventure.

We have found that worship is the pathway and the atmosphere for people—the saved and unsaved alike—to discover their royal calling in Christ, their high destiny in life, their fullest personal worth and their deepest human fulfillment. When worship is warm, it provides the ideal setting for evangelistic results.—Jack Hayford[19]

Expressive churches prefer face-to-face interaction as a means of seeking connection through relational bridge-building and expressing points of agreement. Factual, detailed, and friendly, their presentation of the gospel contains personal examples and centers on people's immediate needs. They think out loud at a rapid pace, with language that is concrete, specific, and even colorful. Their style is to give information about the gospel rather than directives about what is required.

The love of Jesus Christ is communicated in culturally relevant and understandable ways.—Young Life

The Bible on Outreach
Matthew 9:36–38—"When he saw the crowds, he had compassion for them, because they were harassed and helpless, like sheep without

a shepherd. Then he said to his disciples, 'The harvest is plentiful, but the laborers are few; therefore pray earnestly to the Lord of the harvest to send out laborers into his harvest.'"

Luke 9:3–5—"And he said to them, 'Take nothing for your journey, no staff, nor bag, nor bread, nor money; and do not have two tunics. And whatever house you enter, stay there, and from there depart. And wherever they do not receive you, when you leave that town shake off the dust from your feet as a testimony against them.'"

VOCATIONS OF THOSE TYPICALLY ATTRACTED TO EXPRESSIVE CHURCHES

Expressive church members are inclined to be employed in the vocations listed below because the requirements, design, and style of these occupations fit them well. Therefore, it follows that the people in the community in these vocations will be more responsive to the ministry style of the Expressive church. The following material is adapted from:

- http://www.wsc.edu/advising_services/career_planning/ exploration/personality_careers
- Allan, Ross. *Connecting Personality Types with Careers and Jobs*. Washington, DC: United States Department of the Interior, 1999.[20]

Emergency Response

- Critical-care nurse
- Emergency response worker
- Firefighter
- Lifeguard
- Police officer

Those who do emergency response work, which requires observant and quick decision-making in the midst of dealing with crises, will be much appreciated by those in the Expressive churches. In this type of work, people find lots of variety and change as well as opportunities to solve immediate problems—talents and abilities useful in Expressive churches.

Educational/Social Service

- Alcohol and drug addiction counselor
- Child welfare counselor
- Child-care provider
- Early childhood and elementary teacher
- Home health social worker
- Marine biologist
- Special education teacher

The appeal of careers in education, especially those working with elementary and pre-elementary children, is that the work is less formal and structured while offering plenty of opportunities for spontaneous teaching/learning experiences. Since the people in Expressive churches enjoy teaching basic skills and helping children get along with one another—a major emphasis in the early grades—they will resonate with those serving in these fields. These churches appreciate the energy level and activity involved in such careers since they enjoy athletics and athletic coaching. Playing sports, teaching teamwork, and being active outdoors are enjoyable activities for Expressive church members, so they will connect more easily with those who have similar interests and talents.

Health Care

- Dental assistant and hygienist
- Dietitian/nutritionist
- Emergency medical technician (EMT)
- Emergency room nurse
- Exercise physiologist
- Home health aide
- Licensed practical nurse (LPN)
- Medical assistant
- Occupational therapist

- Optician/optometrist
- Pharmacy technician
- Physical therapist
- Primary-care physician
- Radiological technician
- Respiratory therapist
- Veterinarian/veterinary technician

Health-care services provide people in the community with the opportunity to help others through a varied and fast-paced workday. To work in a hospital emergency room requires quick thinking and the ability to calm frightened people during a crisis. These talents fit the skills and temperament of the Expressive churches since their members establish rapport easily with new people and find satisfaction in helping make life easier for others.

Trades and Technical Areas

- Carpenter
- Construction worker
- Electrician
- Farmer
- Laboratory technologist
- Machine operator

Because their members tend to be hands-on and active, Expressive churches resonate with those in the technical areas and trades—especially if the occupation includes working with equipment outdoors. Many of these occupations require attention to facts and details, such as making measurements, observing readings, and choosing correct parts and components—all competencies possessed by many in Expressive churches.

Entertainment

- Film producer
- Musician

- Photographer
- Promoter
- Special events coordinator
- Travel agent/tour operator

Since they often have a strong sense of aesthetics and a good eye for what is new and beautiful, Expressive churches enjoy entertaining people in both a formal and informal capacity. Since their members like to travel, these churches interact well with those in the tourist industry who are adept at juggling several projects at once as they put on large events.

Business/Sales

- Diversity manager: human resources
- Fund-raiser
- Home health care sales
- Insurance agent/broker (health or life)
- Labor relations mediator
- Merchandise planner
- Public relations specialist
- Real estate agent
- Receptionist
- Retail merchandiser/planner
- Retail sales/management
- Sports equipment sales
- Team trainer

Expressive churches do not generally appreciate the world of big business because of the rules, regulations, and bureaucracy such workplaces require. Nevertheless, they do resonate with those in real estate sales and similar vocations in which people spend much of their time out of the office working directly with a diversity of clients and presenting a variety of products. In turn, those in public relations, fund-raising, and mediation—vocations in which people use their persuasive talents—often connect well with the abilities of those found in Expressive churches.

THE CHURCH OF SOLOMON

Solomon loved life and people as the energetic, down-to-earth, entrepreneurial king of Israel. He engaged an exciting world of possibilities and sought to connect with every new experience possible. This confident, poised ruler was hands-on and practical, and sought excitement at every turn.

Solomon's reign was characterized by vigorous activity in international commerce. His empire included trade routes linking Africa, Asia, Arabia, and Asia Minor, thus generating significant income that supported extensive business activities, together with involvement in the horse trade based in Asia Minor. His ships sailed from Ezion-geber on the Gulf of Aqaba to Ophir on the Red Sea (modern-day Yemen).

In his capital city of Jerusalem, Solomon built an intricate palace complex, which took thirteen years to complete, and the temple, which took seven, with the help of King Hiram of Tyre. Solomon's magnificent temple and the royal buildings at Jerusalem were in striking contrast to the rustic architecture of Israel over the preceding centuries. The decorations of the temple, such as palmettos, cherubim, and lilies, were influenced by the Syro-Phoenicians. The cherubim (winged lions with human heads) were inherited from the tabernacle. Solomon's building projects were expensive in both economic and human resources, and his reign marks the peak of Israelite prosperity, both politically and economically. These pursuits brought wealth and a cosmopolitan character to Solomon's kingdom.

He possessed well-developed management skills, as evidenced by his ability to influence people to work together toward the goals he set. He focused on organizing the various sectors of his government by moving everyone along in relative harmony. Solomon divided his kingdom into twelve districts that disregarded old tribal boundaries and became the core of a highly efficient government (1 Kings 4:7–19). As a skillful diplomat, Solomon made friendly ties with the important maritime kingdom of Tyre. Phoenician seamen sailed with Solomon's navy from his port at Ezion-geber (1 Kings 9:26–28). "Once every three years the ships of Tarshish came bringing gold and silver, ivory and apes and peacocks" (1 Kings 10:22). Solomon's extensive commercial dealings by land and sea must have brought him into rivalry with the queen of Sheba. The account of her visit to Jerusalem, as recorded in 1 Kings 10, demonstrates Solomon's wisdom and skills as a diplomat.

As evidenced by his recorded writings in Scripture, Solomon was friendly, outgoing, and fun-loving, and enjoyed telling entertaining stories. He liked to talk to people about people—focusing on relationships and facts concerning people's interactions. Because he possessed remarkable insights about people, social gatherings were stimulating for his guests. He valued accepting and including new people—especially those from cultures that expanded his experiential knowledge and wisdom.

His practical wisdom, especially in relational dynamics, is said to have "surpassed the wisdom of all the people of the east, and all the wisdom of Egypt" (1 Kings 4:30), reflecting the international scope of the influences on Solomon. First Kings demonstrates his ability: to determine which of two prostitutes was the mother of a child in dispute (1 Kings 3:16–28), to answer difficult questions posed by the queen of Sheba (1 Kings 10:1–3), and to speak proverbially and write songs (1 Kings 4:32).

Solomon's extraordinary wisdom also is reflected in the book of Proverbs (see Prov. 1:1; 10:1; 25:1), along with the book of Ecclesiastes (see Eccl. 1:1). In addition, he wrote poetry, as seen in Psalms 72 and 127 and the Song of Solomon. Solomon's sophistication, resulting from his participation in international affairs, created a broadly based and less-stringent attitude in his kingdom. By intermarriage with many foreign women, Solomon succumbed to spiritual decline and crass idolatry. In his later years, he became disillusioned and spiritually numb. The breakup of the monarchy quickly followed his death as a result of the recklessness of his son Rehoboam.

Solomon loved life and people with down-to-earth energy. He strived to engage an exciting world of possibilities, and sought to connect with every new experience possible. This confident, poised, hands-on, practical ruler is an appropriate model for the Expressive church.

Appendix: Church Personality Diagnostic

MY YEARS OF STUDY of the temperaments and personalities of individuals serve as the foundation for classifying churches in a similar manner. This classification loosely parallels the basic personality types as developed by the famous Swiss psychiatrist Carl Jung, and further enhanced by Katharine Cook Briggs and Isabel Briggs Myers. Over several decades, this mother and daughter team expanded and then statistically validated the Myers-Briggs Type Indicator®, or MBTI®, to classify an individual's temperament. The Myers-Briggs work is summarized in Isabel Briggs Myers's *Gifts Differing* (Mountain View, CA: Consulting Psychologists Press, 1980), a modern-day study of psychological type. An independent but related line of work has been carried on by David Keirsey, and his findings are summarized in: *Please Understand Me II: Temperament, Character and Intelligence* (Del Mar, CA: Prometheus Nemesis Book Company, 1998).

THE PASTORAL OR STAFF SEARCH PROCEDURE[1]

Step 1: The search committee or pastor (perhaps along with the governing board and staff) choose thirty men and women in the church who meet the following criteria:

- An opinion leader whose perspectives are valued by the people of the church. In some cases this person might not fit the second through fourth criteria below because of being elderly or disabled, but still be very influential. These thirty may or may not include staff members.
- Active in the ministry of the local church—attendance, giving, etc.
- Involved in a small group—Sunday school class, prayer group, Bible study, support group, etc.
- Involved in a ministry role—Sunday school teacher, board member, small-group leader, prayer ministry, children's ministry, youth ministry, etc.

Note: this should not be an effort to gather a representative sample of the church.

Step 2: By email or letter or in person, invite these thirty key leaders to take the Opinion Leader Inventory below. You can use the explanation given in step 3 to explain the purpose of taking the inventory. You should plan to follow up the invitation with a phone call to confirm their willingness to participate.

Step 3: Brief explanation to the thirty opinion leaders: "As you know, we are committed to find the best person for our church for the position of _____. Therefore, we invite you to participate in a survey that will help us determine our personality or primary ministry style as a church. The results will help us discover practical ways by which we can continue to progress in the fulfillment of our church's calling. These survey results will help us:

- Identify our church's strengths as well as our challenges, and the new pastor/staff person who will fit best with both.
- Minimize our potential problem areas and sources of conflict with a new pastor/staff member.
- Develop a God-honoring plan with specific strategies to increase the new person's ministry fruitfulness."

Each question in the diagnostic contains two opposite ideas that relate to the types of behaviors or traits of church opinion leaders. The questions should be answered according to the opinion leaders' *preference* of interaction and leadership, rather than how they think they should behave as they relate to others in the church.

a. Each numbered box contains two questions that relate to opposite kinds of behaviors or traits. You may want to choose a number under each statement if you believe that both descriptions apply to you, or you may want to choose a number under one side only.

b. The numbers on the scale below each set of questions are your shorthand answers and have the following meanings:

1—Only occasionally true.
2—Sometimes true.
3—True about half the time.
4—True most of the time.
5—Always true for me.

c. Always go with your initial response.

d. Try to respond in terms of how you normally behave, not how you think you should behave. Try to express your own behavior and not mirror what you think others expect of you, or what your family, church, or job situation demands from you. Think especially of how you relate to the Lord and other Christians as you answer.

Information-Gathering	
1. Do I depend on my personal observations in order to gather information about what's occurring around the church? P-5 4 3 2 1	Do I rely more on my intuition and hunches in order to form impressions about what's going on around the church? 1 2 3 4 5-I
2. In church presentations, do I prefer simple ways of speaking and writing—the more specific and down-to-earth, the better? P-5 4 3 2 1	In church presentations, do I like people to use images and concepts to engage my imagination? 1 2 3 4 5-I
3. Am I an observer of tradition in the church, one who does not easily break with custom? P-5 4 3 2 1	Do I break with tradition whenever it seems restrictive for the church and lay aside customs that seem too cumbersome for a new situation? 1 2 3 4 5-I
4. In church meetings, does the here-and-now hold my attention? P-5 4 3 2 1	In church meetings, am I interested in what could be, so that future possibilities occupy my thoughts? 1 2 3 4 5-I
5. In church meetings, do I usually "see the trees before the forest (i.e., details before the big picture)"? P-5 4 3 2 1	In church meetings, do I often "see the forest before I see the trees (i.e., big picture before the details)"? 1 2 3 4 5-I
6. Am I a practical sort of person with a commonsense approach to ministry? P-5 4 3 2 1	Am I more original and inventive with a creative approach to ministry? 1 2 3 4 5-I
7. If someone hangs a new picture or puts a new plant on a table in the church building, will I usually notice it? P-5 4 3 2 1	Am I often unobservant of things in the buildings and objects placed on the grounds of the church? 1 2 3 4 5-I
8. Am I a steady, dependable kind of person who can be counted on to be consistent in my work in the church? P-5 4 3 2 1	Do I tend to work by inspiration regarding my work in the church and find that when my understanding of the purpose for a task fades, so does my interest? 1 2 3 4 5-I

Add the numbers circled in each column:

Practical (P) ____   Innovative (I) ____

Decision-Making

1. Do I generally make my decisions about church matters on the basis of an objective analysis of the issues—weighing the pros and cons of the situation?	Regardless of a pro-and-con analysis, do I base my conclusions on what is important and valuable to the people of the church?
A-5 4 3 2 1	1 2 3 4 5-C
2. Can I usually continue with my work and ministry in the church, regardless of relational harmony?	Do I find that harmonious relationships are essential in order for me to function effectively in church situations?
A-5 4 3 2 1	1 2 3 4 5-C
3. In my church activities, does offering analytical perspective come more naturally for me than speaking a word of approval?	In my church activities, am I more apt to offer an approving word than an analytical perspective?
A-5 4 3 2 1	1 2 3 4 5-C
4. When forced to choose in my church interactions, do I place straight-forwardness above tactfulness?	In my church interactions, do I normally place tactfulness ahead of straightforwardness?
A-5 4 3 2 1	1 2 3 4 5-C
5. Do I find that my contribution to the church's ministry often lies in my ability to help people see impartially?	Do I find my contribution to the church usually flows from my ability to empathize and to help others stay mindful of what's best for people?
A-5 4 3 2 1	1 2 3 4 5-C
6. In conversations at church, am I more concise and to the point than expressive and expansive?	In conversations at church, am I more expressive and expansive than concise and to the point?
A-5 4 3 2 1	1 2 3 4 5-C
7. Regarding church matters, do I believe I am more likely to make the right decision if I go with my rational *head* rather than my empathetic *heart*?	Regarding church matters, do I believe I am more likely to make the right decision if I go with my empathetic *heart* rather than my rational *head*?
A-5 4 3 2 1	1 2 3 4 5-C
8. Am I more task-oriented in my involvement at church, with a greater interest in the job being accomplished?	Am I more personal in my involvement at church, with greater interest in *people* being served?
A-5 4 3 2 1	1 2 3 4 5-C

Add the numbers circled in each column:

Analytical (A) ____   Connectional (C) ____

Lifestyle

1. At church, do I prefer to plan my work and then work my plan? S-5 4 3 2 1	At church, do I tend to be more relaxed in developing and accomplishing plans? 1 2 3 4 5-F
2. Does my service offered to the church usually come from being systematic, orderly, proactive, and decisive? S-5 4 3 2 1	Do I more often exhibit spontaneity, open-mindedness, tolerance, and adaptability in my service to the church? 1 2 3 4 5-F
3. Do I like to bring my church programs and projects to completion and finish the task before starting another? S-5 4 3 2 1	Do I like the feeling of getting new things started at church and having many projects going at the same time? 1 2 3 4 5-F
4. In my work at church, do I like to get the information I need quickly for decisions and bring things to a conclusion in a rapid manner? S-5 4 3 2 1	In my work at church, is it a higher priority for me to wait to be sure I've gathered sufficient information to make the best decision possible? 1 2 3 4 5-F
5. Do I like to set standard operating procedures and routines for accomplishing my tasks at church? S-5 4 3 2 1	Do I prefer to try out new and fresh ways of doing recurring tasks at church so things won't get into a rut? 1 2 3 4 5-F
6. Would the phrase "a place for everything and everything in its place" be descriptive of my approach to church ministry? S-5 4 3 2 1	Do I prefer to leave my schedule open so I can respond to new opportunities and changing events at church? 1 2 3 4 5-F
7. Is it unsettling for me to keep church matters up in the air and undecided? S-5 4 3 2 1	Do I prefer to keep options open at church so we don't rush into a decision and miss what's best? 1 2 3 4 5-F
8. In my church work, do I consider it preferable to be too task-oriented than to be too casual? S-5 4 3 2 1	In my church work, do I consider it preferable to be too casual than to be too task-oriented? 1 2 3 4 5-F

Add the numbers circled in each column:

Structured (S) ____   Flexible (F) ____

Scoring the exercise

a. Place your totals in the appropriate spaces below.

Information-Gathering: Practical (P) ____   Innovative (I) ____

Decision-Making: Analytical (A) ____   Connectional (C) ____

Lifestyle: Structured (S) ____   Flexible (F) ____

b. Go back to "a." and circle the letter in each set that has the higher score. The three letters you circle suggest your ministry style.

Step 4: Give the thirty participants only a few days to take the inventory and send you the three-letter result. For instance, my ministry style is ICS (**I**nnovative, **C**onnectional, **S**tructured), and it is those three letters I would send back to you if I were an opinion leader in your church. Unless your church is small, it is essential that thirty inventories be taken to make the study valid. (See below: "Why do we use thirty inventories?") If your church is under eighty people, then fifteen to twenty opinion leaders are sufficient.

Step 5: When the opinion leaders send back to the search committee or pastor their three-letter descriptions, the results should then be plotted on the wheel in Figure 7 to determine where the thirty opinion leaders cluster among the eight church personalities.

Step 6: After determining where the thirty opinion leaders cluster, go to the corresponding chapter among the eight. Approximately 80 percent or more of the descriptions in that chapter should fit your church. If not, then go to the chapter that corresponds to where the second group of opinion leaders clusters. The following example is a case in which the primary group of opinion leaders (33 percent) clustered as an Organizer church. However, the second-largest group of opinion leaders clusters as the Fellowship

Figure 7: The Church Personality Wheel with personality types.

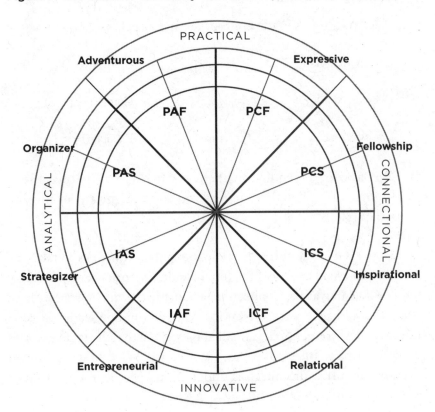

church ministry style with 27 percent of the participants. Therefore, first read through the Organizer church chapter and secondly read through the Fellowship church chapter to determine which ministry style fits better.

Why Do We Use Thirty Inventories to Assess a Church's Personality?

The science of statistics uses a sample of thirty people in surveys of various types because of simulation studies based on the Central Limit Theorem. This theorem and the Law of Large Numbers are the two fundamental theories of probability. To put it roughly, the Central Limit

Figure 8: Example of a filled-out Church Personality Wheel.

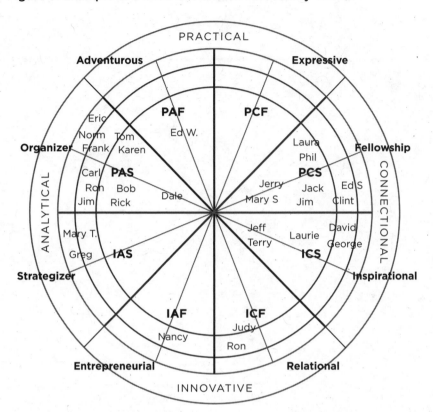

Theorem states that the distribution of the sum of a large number of independent, identically distributed variables will be approximately normal, regardless of the underlying distribution. This is the reason that valid statistical procedures produce accurate results.

For further information on this diagnostic, go to: http://www. douglassandassociates.com. Also, be sure to visit my blog: http://blog. douglassandassociates.com to interact with others using this diagnostic.

Notes

. . . .

Preface

1. Boston: Sloan School of Management, Massachusetts Institute of Technology, 1985.

2. Palo Alto, CA: Consulting Psychologists Press, 1992.

Chapter One: The Value and Importance of Church Personality

1. In some churches' personalities, such vulnerability in a leader is unacceptable and can lead to him being forced out. In other church personalities, if a leader is not vulnerable in his communication, then he is considered too authoritarian.

2. Miriam D. Blum, *The Silent Speech of Politicians* (San Diego: Brenner Information Group, 1988), 6–10.

Chapter Two: Communicating Church Personality

1. My thanks to Rev. Hugh Barlett of Chesterfield Presbyterian Church, Chesterfield, Missouri, for this concept.

2. A profession or testimony of faith should articulate these truths, though not necessarily to an exhaustive or academic level. However, there should be some degree of certainty by the believer that these are true.

3. Thomas Peters, "Kidney Transplant Matching: What It Means," *AAKP RENALIFE 2001 Special Edition*, Vol. 17, No. 2.

Chapter 5: The Fellowship Church

1. Other helpful sites:
   - http://www.teamtechnology.co.uk/careers/careers.html
   - http://www.personalitypage.com/careers.html
   - http://similarminds.com/jung/enfp.html
   - http://www.vocationology.com/Bulletins/VIPRORD2_XL.htm

Chapter Six: The Inspirational Church

1. Other helpful sites:
   - http://www.teamtechnology.co.uk/careers/careers.html
   - http://www.personalitypage.com/careers.html
   - http://similarminds.com/jung/enfp.html
   - http://www.vocationology.com/Bulletins/VIPRORD2_XL.htm

Chapter Seven: The Relational Church

1. Other helpful sites:
   - http://www.teamtechnology.co.uk/careers/careers.html
   - http://www.personalitypage.com/careers.html
   - http://similarminds.com/jung/enfp.html
   - http://www.vocationology.com/Bulletins/VIPRORD2_XL.htm

Chapter Eight: The Entrepreneurial Church

1. See http://www.buffalocreekchurch.com.
2. See http://www.dyingtolive.org.
3. See http://www.thehighlandschurch.net.
4. See http://www.thecrossingchurch.com.
5. See http://www.unityinchrist.com/history/smith.htm.
6. See http://cityviewchurch.net.
7. See http://www.elevationlive.com.
8. See http://www.wayofgracechurch.com.
9. See http://www.marshillchurch.org.
10. See http://www.insideprovidence.com.
11. See http://www.veritaschurch.net.
12. See http://www.lakeridgechurch.net.
13. See http://www.marshillchurch.org/Content/Resurgence.
14. See http://theresurgence.com/tim_smith_2004_missional_worship.
15. See http://www.truenorthchurch.net.
16. Other helpful sites:
    - http://www.teamtechnology.co.uk/careers/careers.html
    - http://www.personalitypage.com/careers.html
    - http://similarminds.com/jung/enfp.html
    - http://www.vocationology.com/Bulletins/VIPRORD2_XL.htm

Chapter Nine: The Strategizer Church

1. See http://www.antiochchurch.com.
2. See http://www.willowcreek.org.
3. See http://www.mcleanbible.org.
4. See http://www.saddleback.com.
5. See http://www.heartmindsoul.com.

6. See http://www.dovefromabove.org.

7. See http://www.oakbridgecc.org.

8. See http://www.pleasantvalley.org.

9. See http://www.universitypraise.org.

10. See http://www.firstfamilychurch.net.

11. See http://www.gracemetroeast.com.

12. See http://www.stm.edu.my.

13. Other helpful sites:
- http://www.teamtechnology.co.uk/careers/careers.html
- http://www.personalitypage.com/careers.html
- http://similarminds.com/jung/enfp.html
- http://www.vocationology.com/Bulletins/VIPRORD2_XL.htm

Chapter Ten: The Organizer Church

1. Other helpful sites:
- http://www.teamtechnology.co.uk/careers/careers.html
- http://www.personalitypage.com/careers.html
- http://similarminds.com/jung/enfp.html
- http://www.vocationology.com/Bulletins/VIPRORD2_XL.htm

Chapter Eleven: The Adventurous Church

1. See http://www.lighthousetrailsresearch.com/emergingchurchquotes.htm.

2. See Andrew Jones, "If Church Was a Party," http://www.tallskinnykiwi.typepad.com/tallskinnykiwi/2003/11/if_church_was_a.html.

3. See http://www.multisensoryworship.com/quotes.htm.

4. Andy Peck, *Christianity* April 2004, http://www.christianitymagazine.co.uk/engine.cfm?i=92&id=62&arch=1.

5. Gary Wills, *Certain Trumpets* (New York: Simon & Schuster, 1995), quoted in www.multisensoryworship.com/quotes.htm.

6. Paul Fromont, "The 'Body Art' of Emerging Church," December 1, 2003, http://www.theooze.com/articles/article.cfm?id=591.

7. Ibid.

8. Spencer Burke, "From the Third Floor to the Garage," www.theooze.com/etrek/spencerburke.cfm.

9. See http://dydimustk.com.

10. John Burke, *No Perfect People Allowed: Creating A Come As You Are Culture in the Church* (Grand Rapids: Zondervan, 2007).

11. See http://www.ooze.com.

12. Andrew Jones, "EmergAnt. 1: Emergent Vocabulary," http://tallskinnykiwi.typepad.com/tallskinnykiwi/2005/03/emergant_1_an_e.html.

13. James Thwaites, quoted in Andy Peck, "Emerging Church—Insights and Concerns, *Christianity* April 2004, http://www.christianitymagazine.co.uk/engine.cfm?i=92&id=62&arch=1.

14. Dan Kimball, *The Emerging Church: Vintage Christianity for New Generations* (Grand Rapids: Zondervan, 2003), 129.

15. Dwight Friesen, "What Is Emergent?" April 18, 2005, http://dwightfriesen.blog.com/174385.

16. Michael Frost and Alan Hirsch, *The Shaping of Things to Come: Innovation and Mission for the 21st-Century Church* (Peabody, MA: Hendrickson, 2003), 229.

17. Andrew Jones, "What is Emerging Church?" http://www.opensourcetheology.net/node/229.

18. Dan Kimball, *The Emerging Church* (Grand Rapids: Zondervan, 2003).

19. Rob Bell, quoted in "The Subversive Art," *Leadership* April 1, 2004, http://www.ctlibrary.com/le/2004/spring/1.24.html.

20. Ibid.

21. Erwin McManus, quoted in http://www.multisensoryworship.com/quotes.htm.

22. Brian McLaren, quoted in Andy Peck, "The Emergent Mystique," *Christianity Today* Nov. 2004, http://www.christianitytoday.com/ct/2004/november/12.36.html.

23. Doug Adams, quoted in http://www.multisensoryworship.com/quotes.htm.

24. Rob Bell, quoted in "The Subversive Art," *Leadership* April 1, 2004, http://www.ctlibrary.com/le/2004/spring/1.24.html.

25. Ibid.

26. Len Sweet, quoted in http://www.multisensoryworship.com/quotes.htm.

27. Graham Johnston, quoted in http://www.multisensoryworship.com/quotes.htm.

28. Association of Vineyard Churches of East Africa, http://www.vineyard-eastafrica.org/join.html.

29. Eugene Peterson, quoted in Mark Galli, "Spirituality for All the Wrong Reasons," *Christianity Today* March 2005, http://www.christianitytoday.com/ct/2005/march/26.42.html.

30. Rick Warren, "Evangelising the 21st Century Culture," *E-life* July/August 2006, http://www.elifeonline.net/elife7-july-august/evangelising.htm.

31. Don Wuebben, quoted in http://www.multisensoryworship.com/quotes.htm.

32. Chris Seay, quoted in Jason Evans, "Voices of the Next Generation," https://www.theooze.com/articles/article.cfm?id=353.

33. Doug Pagitt, quoted in Jason Evans, "Voices of the Next Generation," https://www.theooze.com/articles/article.cfm?id=353.

34. Chris Seay, quoted in Jason Evans, "Voices of the Next Generation," https://www.theooze.com/articles/article.cfm?id=353.

35. Matt Hammett, quoted in Jason Evans, "Voices of the Next Generation," https://www.theooze.com/articles/article.cfm?id=353.

36. Ibid.

37. Association of Vineyard Churches of East Africa, http://www.vineyard-eastafrica.org/join.html.

38. Paul Roberts, "Considering Emerging Church," *Thinking Anglicans* August 28, 2003, http://www.thinkinganglicans.org.uk/archives/000129.html.

39. Bryan Cussen, "Beyond the Fringe—the Church Emerging," http://www.ncls.org.au/default.aspx?docid=3385.

40. Doug Pagitt, quoted in Jason Evans, "Voices of the Next Generation," https://www.theooze.com/articles/article.cfm?id=353.

41. N. T. Wright, quoted in "Story Time," *Marginal Comments* December 6, 2004, http://marginal.typepad.com/marginal/2004/12/story_time.html.

42. Andrew Jones, "What is Emerging Church?" http://www.opensourcetheology.net/node/229.

43. Frank Viola, "Will the Emerging Church *Fully* Emerge?" July 2005, http://www.emergingchurch.info/reflection/frankviola/index.htm.

44. James Thwaites, quoted in Andy Peck, "Emerging Church—Insights and Concerns," *Christianity* April 2004, http://www.christianitymagazine.co.uk/engine.cfm?i=92&id=62&arch=1.

45. See http://www.solomonsporch.com/aboutus_page_group/ourdreams.html.

46. Marc Pitman, "Advent Ale," http://marcpitman.com/2007/11/02/advent-ale-3.

47. Michael Moynagh, quoted in Chris Stoddard, "Emerging or Submerging?" *Christianity* November 2003, http://www.christianitymagazine.co.uk/engine.cfm?i=92&id=185&arch=1.

48. Brian McLaren, "An Open Letter to Chuck Colson," http://www.brianmclaren.net/archives/000018.html.

49. Dan Kimball, quoted in http://www.multisensoryworship.com/quotes.htm.

50. Dan Kimball, *The Emerging Church: Vintage Christianity for New Generations* (Grand Rapids: Zondervan, 2003), 77.

51. Henri Nouwen, *In the Name of Jesus* (New York: Crossroad Pub. Co., 1989), 31.

52. Nashoba Grace Community Church, http://www.aidanandhilda.org.uk/public_html/web/emerging-church_features.php.

53. Andy Peck, "The Emergent Mystique," *Christianity Today* Nov. 2004, http://www.christianitytoday.com/ct/2004/november/12.36.html.

54. Marc Pitman, "Penny Car Wash," http://marcpitman.com/2007/06/09/penny-car-wash.

55. Duane Cottrell, "God Bless the Church," http://homepage.mac.com/duaneco/writing/god_bless.htm.

56. Other helpful sites:
- http://www.teamtechnology.co.uk/careers/careers.html
- http://www.personalitypage.com/careers.html
- http://similarminds.com/jung/enfp.html
- http://www.vocationology.com/Bulletins/VIPRORD2_XL.htm

Chapter Twelve: The Expressive Church

1. John Wimber, "Releasing Gifts in Us," *Equipping the Saints*, vol. 7, no. 4, Fall 1993.

2. Jeff Anderle, quoted in Clint Cooper, "Nontraditional by Choice," *Chattanooga Times Free Press*, March 31, 2001.

3. Anthony O'Sullivan, "Roger Forster and the Ichthus Christian Fellowship: The Development of a Charismatic Missiology," *Pneuma: The Journal of the Society for Pentecostal Studies*, vol. 16, no. 2, Fall 1994, 247–63.

4. Jack Hayford, *Rivers of Revival*, 83, available at http://www.elmertowns.com/books/online/Rivers_of_Revival%5BETowns%5D.pdf.

5. Sharon Fryer, *Signs of the Kingdom* December 2004, http://www.vineyardusa.org/news/testimonies.aspx.

6. Thomas F. Fischer, "Classic Obstructionist Strategies," *Ministry Health* 291, http://ministryhealth.net/mh_articles/291_obstructionist_strategies.html.

7. Ibid.

8. Thomas F. Fischer, "Strategies for Countering Antagonism . . . and the Fear that Drives It," *Ministry Health* 285, http://ministryhealth.net/mh_articles/285_countering_antagonists.html.

9. Ibid.

10. Fischer, "Strategies for Countering Antagonism."

11. Michael Webb, "Gathering at the Gates of Our City," *Equipping the Saints*, Vol. 7, No. 4, Fall 1993.

12. Catholic University Commentary on the papal encyclical "Redemptoris Missia," 10, available online at http://web.archive.org/web/20070102124547/http://www.stfrancisdesales.com/text/Redemptoris_Missia.doc.

13. Ibid., 10–11.

14. Catholic University Commentary on the papal encyclical "Redemptoris Missia," 11, available online at http://web.archive.org/web/20070102124547/http://www.stfrancisdesales.com/text/Redemptoris_Missia.doc.

15. Churches Youth Ministry Association, available at http://www.youthministry.org.nz/?sid=81.

16. Catholic University Commentary on the papal encyclical "Redemptoris Missia," 10, available online at http://web.archive.org/web/20070102124547/http://www.stfrancisdesales.com/text/Redemptoris_Missia.doc.

17. Ibid., 11.

18. Ibid.

19. Jack Hayford, *Worship His Majesty* (Ventura, CA: Regal, 2000).

20. Other helpful sites:
- http://www.teamtechnology.co.uk/careers/careers.html
- http://www.personalitypage.com/careers.html
- http://similarminds.com/jung/enfp.html
- http://www.vocationology.com/Bulletins/VIPRORD2_XL.htm

Appendix: Church Personality Diagnostic

1. This appendix may be reproduced only for non-commercial use (e.g., for use by pastoral search committees).

Philip D. Douglass (B.A., Washington and Lee University; M.Div, Princeton Theological Seminary; Ph.D., St. Louis University) is professor of church planting, growth, and renewal at Covenant Theological Seminary in St. Louis, Missouri. He joined the faculty in 1986 after fourteen years of pastoring in the Washington DC area, where he planted three churches for the Presbyterian Church in America (PCA). Since coming to the seminary, he has started two churches and recently ministered for six years as the weekend pastor of a local church where he mentored students while continuing to teach full-time. He has served twenty-one years on the PCA's Committee on Mission to North America (the church planting agency of the PCA), including five years as chairman, and continues as a member of MNA on the national and presbytery levels. Dr. Douglass is known for taking time to mentor and assist students in clarifying their sense of calling, as well as for encouraging their vision for church planting.